Bernard Shaw's Novels

Portraits of the Author as Man and Superman

Before the Novels: "Man"
Shaw in 1876, age twenty.

After the Novels: "Superman"
Shaw in his Jaeger suit (Ca. 1885)

The above portraits of Shaw are reproduced by courtesy of Mr. Allan Chappelow, M.A., F.R.S.A., from his book *Shaw the Villager and Human Being* (The Macmillan Co.).

Bernard Shaw's Novels

Portraits of the Artist as Man and Superman

Richard Farr Dietrich

University Press of Florida

Gainesville Tallahassee Tampa Boca Raton

Pensacola Orlando Miami Jacksonville

Copyright 1996 by the Board of Regents of the State of Florida
Printed in the United States of America on acid-free paper
All rights reserved

01 00 99 98 97 96   6 5 4 3 2 1

Library of Congress Cataloging-in-Publication Data
Dietrich, Richard F., 1936–
Bernard Shaw's novels: portraits of the artist as man and superman /
Richard Farr Dietrich.
    p. cm.
Includes bibliographical references (p.   ) and index.
ISBN 0-8130-1426-3 (cloth: alk. paper)
1. Shaw, Bernard, 1856–1956—Fictional works. 2. Fiction—Technique.
I. Title.
PR5368.F5D54   1996
823'.912—dc20   95-43722

The University Press of Florida is the scholarly publishing agency for
the State University System of Florida, comprised of Florida A & M
University, Florida Atlantic University, Florida International University,
Florida State University, University of Central Florida, University of
Florida, University of North Florida, University of South Florida, and
University of West Florida.

University Press of Florida
15 Northwest 15th Street
Gainesville, FL 32611

Dedicated to
Lori, Rick, Travis, and Lynn Marie

"No person is real until he has been transmuted into a work of art."

  —Shaw in Winstein's *Days with Bernard Shaw*

"The business of a novelist is largely to provide working models of improved types of humanity."

  —from "Mr. Bernard Shaw's Works of Fiction: Reviewed by Himself"

"Disguises are generally assumed for the purpose of concealing crime."

  —from Shaw's *An Unsocial Socialist*

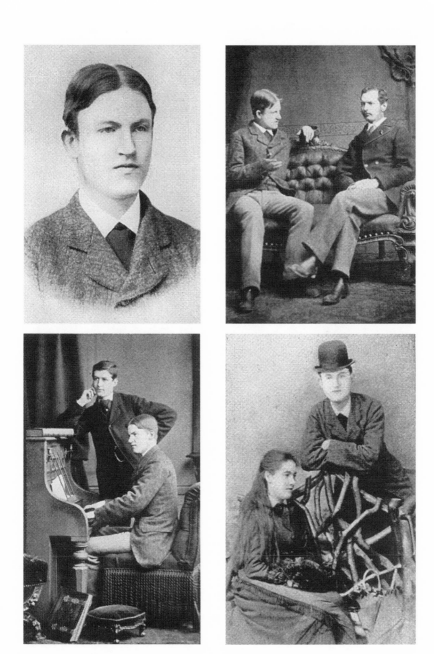

Four photographs of Shaw taken in 1876. Was this Shaw the model for *Immaturity*'s Robert Smith? This page of photographs appears in F. E. Loewenstein's *Bernard Shaw Through the Camera* (1948), photographs by F. Hudson, Lauder Bros., and Barraud. *Upper left:* At Vetnor. *Upper right:* Shaw and Thomas Gibbings. *Lower left:* Robert Moore Fishbourne and Shaw. *Lower right:* Shaw and sister Lucy at Vetnor.

Contents

I never had anything accepted; but if I had never written the five long novels and the bushel of articles that were refused, I should not have been able to do the work that finally offered itself to me. . . . You must keep on knocking your head against the stone wall until it gives way. Only, remember the saying, "Knock, and it shall be opened unto you." There's no use in waiting if you don't knock.

Bernard Shaw, Letter to Florence Farr (1897)

I have a great respect for the priggish conscientiousness of my first efforts. They prove that, like Goethe, I knew all along, and have added more to my power of handling, illustrating, and addressing my material than to the material itself.

Bernard Shaw, Preface to *Immaturity*

Preface

The existence of a discoverable and perfectly definite thesis in a poet's work by no means depends on the completeness of his own intellectual consciousness of it.

1891 Preface to Shaw's *The Quintessence of Ibsenism*

Bernard Shaw once claimed that he must have unconsciously resolved from his cradle to reincarnate Shakespeare, but at first he evidently thought he was reincarnating Henry Fielding or some other novelist. Well before he became a dramatist, Shaw in his mid-twenties made a major effort to launch his literary career by writing five novels in five years, from 1879 to 1883. Those novels attempted to blend avant-garde realism with comic fantasy, social satire of the Dickens or Thackeray sort, parody of the popular novel, and a modernized, antisentimental version of the chivalric romance of Scott. With such a hybrid form—a crazy-quilt of straight, parodistic, and self-deconstructive elements, at once Victorian, modernist, and postmodernist in impulse—Shaw might have altered the direction of the British novel had he found an appropriate and sufficient audience. But in 1883 he stalled as a novelist, ostensibly due to lack of interest from publishers of the paying sort, and an unsuccessful attempt to restart with a sixth novel in 1887 then brought his novelizing to a complete halt. A less determined or less obsessed person would have been stopped much sooner.

With almost nine years passing between the finishing of his last novel in 1883 and the completing of his first play in 1892, the five novels isolated at the beginning of his career make a convenient and tempting unit for critical study of the ur-Shaw, for the novels are to Shaw what the sonnets are to Shakespeare. Thus was inspired the original version of this study—*Portrait of the Artist as a Young Superman: A Study of Shaw's Novels* (1969). The overhaul here of that work is so extensive that, rather than call this a revised edition, it seemed more appropriate to give the study a new title, one that also reflects a modification of the study's thesis.

Other scholars and critics were tempted to take this path before or about the same time I was. Among the dissertations and theses were Alexander Seabrook's "Social Criticism in the Novels of Bernard Shaw" in 1951, Stanley Weintraub's "Bernard Shaw: Novelist" in 1956, and John von Behren Rodenbeck's "Alliance and Misalliance: A Critical Study of Shaw's Novels" in 1964. The book *Shaw the Novelist* (1959), essentially plot and theme summaries, was written by E. Nagaswara Rao. Sections on the novels appeared in books such as S.C. Sen Gupta's *The Art of Bernard Shaw* (1936); in the Henderson, Irvine, and Pearson biographies; and most notably in Homer Woodbridge's *George Bernard Shaw: Creative Artist* (1963). A few articles appeared, the most important being Claude T. Bissell's "The Novels of Bernard Shaw" in 1947, Archibald Henderson's "Bernard Shaw's Novels: And Why They Failed" in 1954–55, and Robert Hogan's "The Novels of Bernard Shaw" in 1965. Of course, as usual, Shaw had beaten everybody to the punch by providing his own treatise, publishing in 1892 the tongue-in-cheek "Mr. Bernard Shaw's Works of Fiction Reviewed by Himself" (*The Novel Review*, 236–43).

But the approaches taken in these works were very different from mine. Although I found the novels interesting enough as narrative art, as genre studies, as cultural artifacts, as adumbrations of the plays, as evidence of intertextual play, and as fictionalized accounts of raw experience, I was more interested in the possibility that the need to resolve a major psychic crisis was principally responsible for driving Shaw through the writing of five seemingly unpublishable novels in five years. What else could have so possessed him? No doubt other motives figured in, such as the sheer drive to practice his art or to get noticed and earn money, but my suspicion was that at a deeper level the shy, uncertain, immature Shaw had employed the novels to escape an ineffective personality and to pursue the possibility of becoming "G.B.S."— the mature, serenely self-confident, swashbuckling "Superman." It was in 1880 as he was finishing his second novel, in fact, that Shaw signed a letter "G.B.S." for the first time, and in 1881, for the first time, he grew the devilish beard and banked up his hair at the front corners for satanic effect, clearly indicating that *as he was writing the novels* he was attempting transformation, basically from introvert to extrovert, but more subtly from earnest and priggish "good boy" to ironic "bad boy."[1] He was *writing* his way through a psychic birth process, to be "reborn the child of his own writings" (Holroyd 14), in what we now call "Joycean fashion" but should perhaps consider renaming "Shavian fashion." The photographs opposite the title page show the physical evidence of a remarkable transformation that was more than just the usual physical maturing or cosmetic change, and the epigraphs to the Introduction (p. 1) suggest that Shaw's transformation was deliberately effected by imaginative means. If I was correct in my theory that Shaw had employed the novels for personal transmutation, then the novels had an importance out of all proportion to their importance as art (or anything else) because they revealed the imaginative, experimental piecing together of the unique Shavian persona—perhaps the most famous literary persona of that time, and certainly one of the most intriguing of all time—in answer to deep psychological needs.

As my approach to Shaw's novels has often been mistakenly termed "biographical," I want to make clear this time that my approach is actually psychological. A biographical approach would be content to show, for example, how Shaw converted his taking of boxing lessons in 1882 into the materials of his boxing novel, *Cashel Byron's Profession*; my approach, on the other hand, emphasizes the way such fictionalizing of experience served Shaw in his psychological transmutation into a more aggressive personality. I am much more concerned with, say, how characters act as symbols of a private imagination than with how they are literally connected to particular models in the external world.

Please note, however, that my treating of Shaw's characters as symbols of the author's psychological conflict is not at all supportive of the agenda represented by the critic Vaughan in Shaw's *Fanny's First Play*. To denigrate Shaw's powers of character differentiation, Vaughan asserts that "all Shaw's characters are himself: mere puppets stuck up to spout Shaw" (*Collected Plays with Prefaces* 4, 438). While it is always problematic, when an author draws characters based on objective models, as to what extent the models were chosen because they served the author's need to project some aspect of himself ("I have no clue to any . . . personage save that part of him which is also myself," said Shaw [*Major Critical Essays* 284–85]), in Shaw's case such use of models nevertheless resulted in an astonishingly varied gallery of vividly individualized characters, testimony to the variety of personality within Shaw that he was able to see in others as well.

The original version of this study was written in 1964 as a dissertation and revised for publication in 1969. Interested in doing a second edition, Walda Metcalf of the University Press of Florida asked me if there was any point in doing a revision. As I have been aching to straighten out the kinks in the work of my younger self, even as Shaw was in revising his novels, I leaped at the opportunity. But of course, once one does the research and then turns the demon word-processor on such a project these days, more than youthful kinks get attended to, so this turned out to be more than a simple revision. Hardly a page here has escaped revision, and much new material has been added, about 50 percent of the book being new wording, and that 50 percent obviously affecting the other half. The new wording includes an index one can hardly believe was overlooked originally. The bibliography has been updated and considerably expanded, and some important reorganization and highlighting of organization has occurred, resulting in a more useful book.

In terms of content, I have made my thesis and its psychological import clearer while altering my thesis to include Shaw's portrayal of himself as a young man within the general portrait of himself as a young "Superman," an alteration that is reflected in my new title. My thesis now is that Shaw's employment of his five novels to draw a self-portrait began as a critical, self-mocking portrait of the artist as a young man (that is, of Shaw as he had recently been) but by the second novel became a portrait of the artist as a young Superman (that is, of Shaw as he envisioned he might be)—so as to facilitate a psychic transformation in the author from ineffective intellectual to effective statesman-poet. By "psychic" I mean that the transformation was not just a matter of appearances, as Shaw later sometimes tried to make it seem, but was deeply embedded in his personality and wired into his brain. Note that he later dramatized such character transmutations as incomplete if the inner person was not changed along with the outer, an important qualification of his role as socialist reformer (see *Pygmalion*).

In pursuing this psychological import, I have placed greater emphasis on the novels as proving ground for that quintessence of Shavian psychology known as *The Quintessence of Ibsenism*. And, by looking at works written both prior to and after the novels, I have provided more context for my thesis in the form of a "frame" for Shaw's self-portrait. Finally, I have been much more explicit in connecting this study of self-portraiture to Joyce's *A Portrait of the Artist as a Young Man*, both the parallels and the differences being instructive. In suggesting a connection between Shaw and Joyce, I find that I anticipated such works as Stanley Weintraub's "A Respectful Distance: James Joyce and His Dublin Townsman Bernard Shaw" (1986), and Martha Fodaski Black's *Shaw and Joyce: "The Last Word in Stolentelling"* (1995), and I am delighted to find such overwhelming corroboration in their works. It seems Shaw's use of the *Künstlerroman* to "parent" himself preceded Joyce's similar strategy in *Portrait*, and Joyce's suppression of Shaw's "fathering" of him was for the sake of preserving that cherished illusion of "self-parenting."

Most of these changes reflect my greater awareness of both the general critical climate and the state of Shaw studies. As to the former, today's concern with critical theory has caused me to think more about "problematics." As to the latter, one particular recent study (Grene) of Shaw's first novel, for instance, so threw into question some basic assumptions of my original chapter "The Art of the Novels" that my need to answer the question almost alone justifies this revision. And, in general, thirty years of thinking and writing about Shaw have made it possible to see things more clearly, not to mention how clarifying the history of the last thirty years has been.

I contemplated an even more extensive revision, one that looked at Shaw's novels with poststructuralist eyes, but that would have involved, not just a revision, but the writing of an entirely different book. My original study of course was, from today's perspective, naively pre-poststructuralist. The present version is still pre-poststructuralist in much of its terminology, but I now invite readers to put all such terms "under erasure," if they like. I deliberately chose to make little use of current jargon because it seemed to me sufficient, for the purposes here, to just open up the old bottles to new wine. If, for example, you prefer to think of "the self" as the locus of intersecting physical, psychological, and cultural forces, impulses, or rhythms, or as a "subject-in-process," as opposed to the notion of the self as a fixed, autonomous, centered subject, there's no reason that such theoretical substitution can't be made. It makes no practical difference. The fixed "self" may be a fiction, as Shaw the evolutionist very well knew, but it's a convenient and perhaps inevitable one *in practice*. Poststructuralist theory may have effected a revolution in metaphysics, but I have yet to see any effect of this revolution on human behavior; everyone *behaves* as though he or she had a fixed "self" because it's impossible to do otherwise (just as it is impossible in practice to treat language as anything but referential). Shaw himself was well aware that his "self" was actually a plurality of selves, a constant work-in-progress, and that the selves were to a degree externally imposed "masks" of personality—this book, in fact, shows Shaw in the process of trying on certain masks. His awareness of plurality, however, did not prevent him from performing *as though* he had a definite, inner self in any given situation, for he realized such is the only way "to be." *Not* playing the role is "not to be," a lesson today's academic Hamlets will have to relearn.

A strictly poststructuralist treatment of Shaw's novels would be valuable, no doubt, but it seemed more important for me to get this approach to Shaw's novels into the best shape possible for the benefit of subsequent scholarship and criticism. In the meantime, anyone interested in a view of Shaw as proto-postmodernist might start with my tentative article, "Deconstruction as Devil's Advocacy: A Shavian Alternative," in *Modern Drama* (September 1986), and Eileen Sypher's "Fabian Anti-Novel: Shaw's *An Unsocial Socialist*," in *Literature and History* (Autumn 1988).

In short, though this revision is not as radical as it could be, it is quite substantial. It has resulted in a significantly different and, one hopes, improved book.

My thanks to Walda Metcalf for starting the demon computer, and to the many editors and craftsmen at the UPF, especially Alexandra Leader and Judy Goffman, for their transmuting of manuscript into book. Thanks too to those whose writings on Shaw have inspired me over the years, with particular thanks to Eric Bentley, Martin Meisel, Stanley Weintraub, and Dan H. Laurence, and with special thanks to the last for his meticulous reviewing of this manuscript. I owe special thanks too to Nicholas Grene for straightening me out on *Immaturity*. And I want to make up for the egregious oversight of not mentioning book dealer M. H. Mushlin in the original edition; he helped considerably with manuscripts. Also helpful with manuscripts were the Irish National Library and the British Library. My son, Rick, is to be thanked for his typing and my wife, Lori, for her ready reader's response.

$\mathcal{P}art$ 1

Introduction to the Novels

The truth is that all men are in a false position in society until they have
realized their possibilities and imposed them on their neighbors. They are
tormented by a continual shortcoming in themselves; yet they irritate others
by a continual overweening. This discord can be resolved by acknowledged
success or failure only; everyone is ill at ease until he has found his natural
place whether it be above or below his birthplace. . . . This finding of one's
place may be made very puzzling by the fact that there is no place in ordinary
society for extraordinary individuals.

The mere rawness which so soon rubs off was complicated by a deeper
strangeness which has made me all my life a sojourner on this planet rather
than a native of it. Whether it be that I was born mad or a little too sane, my
kingdom was not of this world: I was at home only in the realm of my
imagination, and at my ease only with the mighty dead. Therefore I had to
become an actor, and create for myself a fantastic personality, fit and apt for
dealing with men. . . . At the time of which I am writing, however, I had not yet
learnt to act, nor come to understand that my natural character was impossible
on the great stage of London.
—Bernard Shaw, Preface to *Immaturity*

The preliminaries of this study of Shaw's novels include looking at their historical and biographical contexts, providing a rationale for the particular psychological approach taken here, and noting special facets of the methodology.
I begin with the historical-biographical context.

A History of the Novels

The story of Shaw's novels begins with Shaw's pre-Joycean exodus from a
despised Dublin in 1876, at the age of twenty, to take up residence in great
London. He went there, he said, primarily because London was the literary
capital of the English language, which was to be his principal "weapon" in an
Irish counterattack on Ireland's morally perverse conqueror, England in all
its innocence having immorally conquered half the world in the name of virtue, truth, and goodness. Dublin had made it clear that a literary destiny of

global import was not to be had there, at least not yet. Leaving behind a rather broken, alcoholic, and impecunious father, abandoned earlier by wife and daughters, and quitting his unfulfilling job as a clerk in a prominent firm of Dublin realtors, a job at which he was all too good and rising fast, Shaw went to London to live with his mother. Mrs. Shaw (Bessie) had separated from her husband and her son in 1873 to pursue a career in teaching voice and, possibly, to follow her lover, music impresario George Vandeleur Lee, though that affair, if such it was, seems not to have lasted long once it was transferred from Dublin to London, as London seemed to bring out the worst in Lee. Mrs. Shaw allowed her son to room with her for the next twenty-two years, first in South Kensington (where he wrote his first novel) but mainly in upper Bloomsbury, until his marriage in 1898. His mother's care of him, and his of her, was hardly exemplary, relations between them being rather cool. Shaw's latest biographer, Michael Holroyd, specializes in finding that Shaw's adult actions can be attributed to the deprivations of love in this mother-son relationship, the need to redress childhood's traumas yielding not one inch to genius in Holroyd's book. I argue that Shaw's genius budged that need a good deal more than an inch.

Jobs were hard to come by for an Irish immigrant of "shabby gentility," and Shaw compounded the difficulty by applying for jobs in a way that subverted his own efforts. He later joked about his horror of earning his living by honest labor, but that joke covered the discomfiture of a young man who didn't want to waste his time on improper work. Thus for years Shaw was unemployed except for a few assignments ghosting articles on music for Lee in 1876–77, a short stretch as a clerk for a telephone company in 1879–80, and some freelancing as writer/editor here and there. He got most jobs through friends or family, including some miscellaneous assignments from Lee (probably disguised charity) until Lee's death in 1886. Some work, such as assisting Lee at rehearsals (paybacks for charity?), was apparently unpaid. Shaw's share of the modest room and board was afforded mainly by a small stipend from his estranged father, until his death in 1885. Fortunately, about that time, at the instigation of friend and critic William Archer, Shaw was hired as an art and music critic and book reviewer for such various publications as the *Dramatic Review*, the *Magazine of Music*, the *Pall Mall Gazette*, and the *World*, launching him on a distinguished journalistic career. But those previous years of chronic unemployment, particularly in light of the severe economic depression that seized London in those years, must have been demoralizing for Shaw were they not redeemed by the young man's habit of keeping himself busy, getting himself educated in life and art, in preparation for his proper vocation.

Certainly his leisure was not wasted. "My office training," he wrote, "had left me with a habit of doing something regularly every day as a fundamental condition of industry as distinguished from idleness" (*Immaturity* xxxvii). For example, in addition to all the writing he was doing, he spent many hours in the Reading Room of the British Museum acquiring a comprehensive if unsystematic education. This effort occasionally resulted in some intellectual dyspepsia, but Shaw claimed he felt at home "only with the mighty dead" (*Immaturity* xliii). Of greatest relevance was his wide reading in the English novel, the Victorian success of which as the dominant genre in literature—drama having almost ceased being a form of literature—undoubtedly made the novel seem the obvious form for the young tyro seeking literary fame.

In 1879, at the age of twenty-two, after trying other literary forms with scant publishing success, he began writing novels with incredible persistence. For five years, he said, he religiously wrote five pages a day, inspired or not. This argues both an unusual industry and a compelling obsession. But the little brown packages he sent to publishers kept returning, sometimes with encouraging if somewhat confusing letters from the baffled reviewers, always without remuneration.

Shaw's novels were hopelessly misunderstood by conventionally minded reviewers and critics. The novels were criticized for being "disagreeable" or "without plot or issue" or "too devoid of any sort of emotion." They were "disagreeable" because they attacked or subverted perverse Victorian standards, they were thought "plotless" because their plot structure was unconventionally open, organic, and problematic, and they were thought lacking in emotion because they were deliberately antisentimental. And so the rejections piled up. Shaw complained to a publisher in 1885 that there "must be a few thousand who would keep me in bread and cheese for the sake of my storytelling, if you would only let me get at them." But, as Weintraub notes, "It was mistakenly clear to [publishers] that the English public would not purchase books which ridiculed its most cherished ideals, traditions, and institutions" (*An Unfinished Novel* 13). The publishers judged "mistakenly" because there were, in fact, many Victorians experiencing the stirrings of anti-Victorian feelings who would have welcomed novels that so wittily embodied that.

The novels in general are about a new spirit rising out of the Victorian ethos, gradually becoming aware of its own mutant character, and finding itself in rebellion against the standards of the day. It is a sign of the complacent times that Victorian reviewers regarded the most significant issue of the late nineteenth century—namely, the clash between the "Victorian" and the "modern"—as no issue at all, thinking that these works so pregnant in meaning were sterile.

The novels did not experience publication until Shaw's new socialist friends came to his rescue with serializations in their monthly magazines. In 1884, shortly after thinking himself finished with novel writing, the last novel, *An Unsocial Socialist* (begun July 9, 1883, as *The Heartless Man* and finished November 1, 1883), served as padding in a little monthly socialist magazine, *To-Day*, serialized between March and December. In 1887 the novel was put out under one cover by Swan Sonnenschein & Co., followed by a cheap edition in 1888 that added an epistolary appendix supposedly written by the novel's hero to the author, an appendix that now has a postmodern look to it. An American edition by Brentano's appeared in 1900 and in 1914 an edition by Constable.[1] The current foreword was not added until 1930. The 1884 serialization paid Shaw nothing, but it did get him started. Thereafter the other novels, with one exception in England, were published in the inverse order of their creation.

Cashel Byron's Profession, novel number four (begun April 12, 1882, and completed in early February 1883), was serialized second in *To-Day*, between April 1885 and March 1886. Its relative popularity prompted the publication of a book edition, also in 1886, by the Modern Press (which also published *To-Day*), the first of Shaw's novels published in book form. G. Munro's Seaside Library published the first American edition in 1886, followed by a Harper's Handy Series edition later that year. Walter Scott published a revised edition in 1889. A further revised 1901 edition by Grant Richards (and Stone & Co. in Chicago) includes *The Admirable Bashville*, Shaw's blank verse adaptation of the novel for the stage (done hastily to establish American copyright in the face of an attempt at piracy). The current preface is from the 1901 edition, as well as the postscript, "Note on Modern Prizefighting."

In Annie Besant's *Our Corner* appeared *The Irrational Knot*, novel number two (begun in June and finished in December 1880), from April 1885 to February 1887, and *Love Among the Artists,* novel number three (begun in May and finished in December 1881), from November 1887 to December 1888.

Brentano's published the first book edition of *The Irrational Knot* in 1905, apparently in a form actually revised in 1892, and with its current preface, and Constable followed in the same year. *Love Among the Artists* was published in book edition in 1900 by Stone & Co., Chicago, and by Constable in 1914. These two editions contained a prefatory letter, "The Author to the Reader," that was deleted in the Collected Edition (1930) and the Standard Edition (1931).

Only *Immaturity* (begun in March and completed in September 1879), first to be created and last to be published, avoided serialization. It was brought out in a book edition in 1930 as part of the author's *Collected Edition* and in 1931 as part of the *Standard Edition*, both with preface (drafted in 1921) added.

Shaw insisted that in revising the novels for publication he made few changes, humanizing here and there and, in the case of the last two, either painting out or better harmonizing with the rest bits of socialism daubed in for the edification of the leftist readers of *To-Day*.[2] In fact, however, in keeping with his "silent textual toying" with his works in general (Weintraub, Intro. to *Cashel Byron's Profession* xv), he made considerable revisions in at least two of his novels, cutting out two whole chapters from the *Our Corner* version of *The Irrational Knot* and liberally revising throughout (mostly in 1892), and, in addition to cutting out two mice-damaged chapters from *Immaturity*, subjecting it to a stem-to-stern overhauling after he exhumed it in 1921 (Grene 225–38). (The effect of revision on *Immaturity* will be addressed later in "The Art of the Novels, Or, The Maturity of *Immaturity*.") In the other three novels the revisions were not as great—if not stylistic or to cut verbiage, consisting mainly of typographical changes, changes of names and terms where their topicality made them unintelligible to the modern reader, changes of detail in keeping with his better understanding of aristocratic manners, and additions of historical and geographical addenda wherever such would clarify a point for the modern reader.

Because his revisions, mostly stylistic in any case, do not significantly alter my reading of the novels or my particular slant on them, and in fact only reveal a Shaw more aware of what he had done in the novels, I have chosen to quote from the only widely available editions, those in the Standard Edition, although for the record and for their useful prefaces and notes I cite other recent editions in the bibliography. My intention is to present the novels *as they are* as I speculate on how they served Shaw when they were written. With the exception of *Immaturity*, I will not indicate revisions unless they consist of entirely new wording or, in the case of rewordings, seem significantly to alter meaning.

Perhaps encouraged by the book publications of *Cashel Byron's Profession* in 1886 and of *An Unsocial Socialist* in 1887, and despite aggravating negotiations with the publisher on the latter, Shaw tried his hand at a sixth novel in 1887 but left it unfinished, possibly because its autobiographical content, focused on a developing ménage à trois similar to one he was involved in at the time, would have been embarrassing to its models, Edith Nesbit and Hubert Bland. His secretary dug it up late in his life, confronted him with the evidence of his own handwriting, and forced him to concede that he must have written it, although he had no memory of it. The fragment was published posthumously (Weintraub, *An Unfinished Novel*). The raw manuscript reveals a perfunctory effort, with no gain in narrative skill. In 1890 Shaw contributed a few pages to another novel, *The Salt of the Earth*, written in collaboration for serialization in *The World*, but he repudiated the results (Crawford 39–78). *The Adventures of the Black Girl in Her Search for God*, published in 1932, is the longest narrative Shaw wrote after his five novels, but it is probably not to be considered a novel; its value here is that it presents the possibility that when Shaw wrote fiction as he pleased, he wrote naked fables, without any "realistic" camouflage. Shaw also wrote nine or ten short stories, some of which will be touched on later.

Typically turning negatives into positives, Shaw claimed he gave up novel writing not so much because he was discouraged by lack of publication (indeed, he thought the novels did a respectable business after he ceased to care about them) but because he was busy with something new. His witnessing of a lecture by Henry George in 1881 and his reading of Karl Marx in 1882, which led to his becoming a Fabian Socialist in 1884, revealed to him the extent of his ignorance of the economic motives of society. This was brought home to him, he said, very misleadingly, when the attempt to write an immense Marxist study of capitalist society in fictional terms broke down in "sheer ignorance," leaving us with only the first two chapters, which we now treat as the complete novel *An Unsocial Socialist*. At this point Shaw left the society of his novels for the society of friends and Fabians, spending the next decade establishing himself as a very social socialist before taking up playwriting with anything like serious intent.

It might be salutary to close this brief history of Shaw's novels with an anecdote. When the novels were brought out in American book editions around 1900, the publisher unwittingly confounded reviewers by inverting the order of their creation, publishing the fifth novel first and the fourth second. The reviewers, "unaware that the publisher was working backwards through the list, pointed out the marked advance in my style, the surer grip, the clearer form, the finer art, the maturer view of the world, and so forth" (Preface to *Cashel Byron's Profession* x). The moral is plain if painful to the trusting critic, and I shall try to keep it before me in the pages that follow.

The Novels as Self-Portraiture

Shaw's fame as a voluminous dramatist and preface writer, not to mention as a critic, raconteur, debater and orator, gadfly, and outrageous public figure, has served to obscure the novels to the point where they are seldom read and even more seldom criticized. The novels do not deserve such obscurity—they make good reading for anyone acclimated to the Victorian novel, and they are superior in many respects to most of their contemporaries—but Shaw himself is partly to blame. He would occasionally say of his novels something characteristically intemperate like "I am ashamed of the whole boodle of them" (*Collected Letters* 179), or, in revising them, compare himself to a dog returning to its "vomit" (Grene 227). Such denigrations may have expressed an apprehension about how publication of the novels would affect his reputation, or, as Holroyd speculates, Shaw's professed hatred of his novels may have been a redirecting of an intense hatred for the memory of his early, rather bleak life in London, those long years of unremitting failure.

Whatever the case, there are many indications that Shaw secretly thought highly of his early works and wished them well. As Archibald Henderson infers, Shaw "publicly pretended to hate his novels, but in private he entertained for them a sneaking sort of affection" (*Man of the Century* 120). Weintraub further notices that "although he publicly denigrated the nearly stillborn novels of his nonage, he carefully preserved the mice-chewed manuscripts for decades, and belabored publishers about them even after he had loudly declared them dead" (Intro. to *An Unfinished Novel* 4). He once confided to a publisher, "my works are magnificent," and then excused them on the grounds that "they are not business" (*Collected Letters* 178), but my theory is that Shaw's secret valuing of his novels had less to do with his estimation of their literary worth or superiority to commercial concerns than with their importance as a record of his personal transmutation. As he put it in the "Epistle Dedicatory" to *Man and Superman*, "Every man who records his illusions is providing data for the genuinely scientific psychology which the world still waits for" (*Plays with Prefaces* 2:517), and the novels, I believe, make a mighty contribution to that field.

The fact that the novels are undervalued and relatively unread obliges me to spend some time summarizing plots and demonstrating the novels' art. But I try to do so in a way that provides context for the principal thrust of this study—the examination novel by novel of the young Shaw's trying on in the privacy of his art of the various masks of personality that he thought might be authentic to his being. His characters provided symbols for a private psychomachia; they are social equivalents of an inner struggle. Disliking the introspection that he had been prey to as a youth, because he sensed it led to Prufrockian paralysis or, worse, maiming of the psyche, Shaw typically projected psychic dissonances into the materials of his art, where he could deal with them as external objects.

"All my happenings have taken the form of books and plays," he admitted (*Sixteen Self Sketches* 6). "My imagination has always rearranged facts into stories" (Henderson 946). And "the best autobiographies are confessions; but if a man is a deep writer all his works are confessions" (*Sixteen Self Sketches* 6). Further, "I have no clue to any historical or other personage save that part of him which is also myself. . . . The man who writes about himself and his own time is the only man who writes about all people and about all time" (*Major Critical Essays* 284–85). Given such indications, it does not seem outlandish to argue that Shaw used the art of the novel to pursue the art of being Bernard Shaw. As he sent characters into action, he was testing elements of his own personality for the sake of achieving a more authentic and connected and thus more effective being. That more effective being, connected to the universe by "the Life Force," he later called "the Superman." (More about the Superman and attendant ironies follows in "God Being Dead, The Proper Study of Mankind Is Superman.")

As for the poststructuralist notion that all selfhood is culturally/linguistically constructed, Shaw would perhaps say that this invasion of the person from outside is that of the Life Force, and what matters is not the unavoidable invasion (though it *is* life-giving) but how artistically one shapes it and centers it in one's being. One may not start out as a centered, autonomous self, but one can become more so. Life is given, but then life is an art, or can be. And, said Shaw, "no person is real until he has been transmuted into a work of art" (Winsten 187). That quotation would more likely be expected from such high priests of modernism as Yeats and Joyce, except that Shaw was referring less to the transmutation of the artist's self into the materials of his art than to the use of such materials to transumute himself into a more effective being.

Shaw's first novel constitutes a "Joycean" portrait of the artist to the extent that it pictures a discarded self, but his last four novels differ in their greater emphasis upon the artist's remaking of himself—indeed, *becoming* himself—as he draws his own portrait. In the cases of both Shaw's first novel and Joyce's *Portrait,* the artist becomes himself by separating his younger, more immature self from his present, more mature self, such distancing devices as satire and irony allowing him to treat his former self as an object of sympathetic ridicule, even as that self serves as the protoplasm from which the new self mutates. But that remaking of the self is much more emphasized in Shaw's case and becomes the principal action of his subsequent novels.

In Shaw's case, then, the "portrait of the artist as a young man" transmuted into a portrait of the artist *as a young Superman.* Unlike Joyce, Shaw was ultimately less interested in portraying the self he was escaping from than in portraying the self he could imagine becoming, the better self. Though obviously there's an element of wishful thinking in any projection of a superior self, Shaw must have asked himself, after his first novel in which "in Joycean fashion" he portrays an immature self he's escaping from, why wallow in a miserable past if you can create a better future? Joyce's Dedalus ends *A Portrait of the Artist as a Young Man* by heroically proclaiming his intention to create such a future ("Welcome, O Life! I go to encounter for the millionth time the reality of experience and to forge in the smithy of my soul the uncreated conscience of my race"), but some critics detect mockery in Joyce's tone here, and in any case *Portrait* is mostly about the suffering and thinking that led to the proclamation; Shaw's last four novels, on the other hand, embody the experimental attempt to realize that proclamation, as he sought "to forge in the smithy of [his] soul the uncreated conscience of [his] race." He would create that conscience, not just by providing a nicely polished looking glass for the Yahoos to see themselves in, but more by projecting into his heroes and heroines the "moral originality" he felt in himself and that he hoped through art would permeate his "immoral" culture. There may be Shavian overstatement in the following: "The business of a novelist is largely to provide working models of improved types of humanity" ("Mr. Bernard Shaw's Works of Fiction. Reviewed by Himself," in Lawrence, 311), but his novels seem to follow through in artfully creating a "new man" for life to imitate.

Of course Dr. Frankenstein had similar hopes for his project, and therein lies a major problematic. "In trying to be more than man," said William Blake, "we become less." The danger in trying to create a "new man" is that the attempt may produce monsters instead, and the heroes of Shaw's novels do indeed have something of the monster about them as they embody overdoses of certain "virtues." Of course another argument is that Shaw's heroes are merely *ironic* "monsters," monsters only from the point of view of the "less evolved." In any event, my chapter titles in Part III refer to this possibility of monstrosity.

Another major problematic arose from Shaw's decision to present his mutant self in the less threatening guise of joker. Frankenstein's monster might indeed have fared better if he had been possessed of a sense of humor (without, that is, going to the lengths of television's Herman Munster). Still, joking is figurative and is thus a form of disguise; the joker is not what he seems and does not say what he means. This ambiguity creates questions in the minds of the "less evolved" or the literal-minded about the joker's true identity. "Disguises are generally assumed for the purpose of concealing crime," concedes the hero of Shaw's last novel (*An Unsocial Socialist* 100), Sidney Trefusis being the first Shaw hero to see the need for a "saviour of mankind" (104) to "clown up" a bit his denunciation of the scribes and Pharisees so as to avoid the fate of the more solemn Christ: being criminalized. This "G.B.S." the young Shaw was creating would be a "Christ" who would tell jokes at his trial, so to speak, in order to deflect the scapegoating emotion of his judges and jurors. Even so, some of them would not be amused.

Thematically, as Shaw explores such problematics, the novels proceed in a dialectic. *Immaturity* presents us with the proto-Shavian, its hero, Robert Smith, being a rather undefined and essentially parentless and vocationless young man who is certain of only one thing—Victorian society is a moral horror. Smith has the soul of a "smithy" who would forge a new, more moral world, but he has no idea of how to begin. He engages society in a rather priggish and vague rebellion, tempered by an inordinate desire to be found acceptable as a gentleman, which makes him rather a monster of propriety as he can find no way of expressing his "moral originality" except through an excessive and comic probity. The hero of *The Irrational Knot*, Edward Conolly, a superefficient and superrationalistic inventor of an electric motor, is no longer vague about the need for rebellion and is no longer insecure about himself. Victorian society, he discovers, like the institution of romantically conceived marriage upon which it is based, is totally irrational. It will take a man of "inhumanly" cool and superior moral intellect to reform it—a monster of reason, in fact. *Love Among the Artists,* however, suggests just the opposite. Shaw had gone overboard in his enthusiasm for the powers of rationality; in his third novel he corrects this by going overboard in his enthusiasm for the instinctive powers of creative genius. Its highly emotional hero, Owen Jack, a composer of passionate, avant-garde music, is a highly inefficient but nevertheless effective smasher of the fragile teacups of Victorian society. Shaw's first real diabolonian, Owen Jack reacts spontaneously to the call of his moral passion and pronounces himself ready to take on the Victorian God Himself. Shaw calms down a bit in his fourth novel, *Cashel Byron's Profession,* as he arranges a theoretical compromise between the rational and the intuitive powers. The hero, an instinctive boxer who's mostly brawn, marries the heroine, a rich rationalist who's mostly brain, and their marriage symbolizes to Shaw the need for fusing one's intellectual and creative powers. *An Unsocial Socialist,* his fifth novel, begins with this very important issue all worked out, in theory, and that is why its hero, a wealthy Marxist with a sense of humor named Sidney Trefusis, seems to be a relatively complete human being, ready to put theory into practice.

Shaw has, in a sense, put himself together out of the bits of identity that presented themselves to him one at a time. Most important, in Sidney Trefusis he has finally projected a character who can laugh at himself (thus serving as an objectification of Shaw's ability to laugh at his own Frankenstein inclinations). Trefusis even takes delight in ironic, comic impersonation, making it central in fact to his strategy of reform. Trefusis is a man relatively in control of his essential self, who knows that he must take action in order to realize that self. He is, for the first time in Shaw's novels, a hero with a conscious religious purpose, happily supplied to him by the very blessed St. Karl Marx, whose economic diatribes primarily provided Shaw with a certain evangelistic attitude toward the reforming of society. As Trefusis says, "With my egotism, my charlatanry, my tongue, and my habit of having my own way, I am fit for no calling but that of the saviour of mankind" (104). As his way of saving the world is neither as a scapegoat-redeemer nor as a moral scourge, the usual sorts of saviors, but is accomplished through working his reformist wiles as an ironic devil's disciple and clown-prophet, we see a familiar Shavian strategy emerging, designed to right a perverse world.

This study is essentially an essay in the psychology of the creative mind, the chief obstacle being its subject, who, as said, intensely disliked self-analysis of the modern "depth psychology" sort and who always strove to externalize things, to project psychological issues as cultural issues—social, political, religious, or whatever (and anyone who insists that all of these are at bottom language issues would get no argument from Shaw, except to point out that that fact makes no practical difference). This externalization was not intended to disguise psychic problems but to expose their communal manifestation and their life in action, since no man is an island, and an individual's psychic dilemmas matter to others only insofar as they are acted out in communal life.

Despite Shaw's resistance, he attracts me as a figure for psychological investigation because he illustrates so well the possibility that the mechanistic view of things taken by much modern psychology is not a complete view. He exemplifies, I believe, the artist who may escape psychological systems and categories by virtue of the relative strength of his "figural will to power" (Norris 106), who surmounts to a degree the victimization of childhood trauma by making the mechanism of compensatory fantasy his own. All the reductive studies of this artist and the other along Freudian/Lacanian lines seem to accomplish their goal only by leaving out what made the artist an artist, namely the creative play with a certain medium—language, in Shaw's case— in the interests of remaking the self. Such play allows the artist to escape temporarily such formal systems of definition and analysis as the psychologist invents to constrain the psyche. In the midst of the creative act at least, the artist plays imaginatively with the psyche, shifting its elements and forces to meet the needs of the creative act, thereby making it possible to avoid the textbook boxes of identity. "We are not here . . . to fit ourselves into puzzles," says Prola in Shaw's *The Simpleton of the Unexpected Isles,* "but to wrestle with life as it comes" (*Collected Plays with Their Prefaces* 6:839), and that pertains to Freudian puzzles as well. No doubt the artist dips into the common stock of psychological ideas and imagery, as witness all the father figures that Victorian/Edwardian writers slew, Shaw included, but the artist makes the psychological sign his or her own by fashioning a particularity of experience for it, unique to its time and place, and by engaging it in a figurative play that allows an unusual, though temporary, freedom to experiment with identity. Whatever postmodernist debunking we wish to subject writers to, it remains the case that out of the smithy of their souls artists are unusually adept at forging new selves from givens, at least in the midst of the creative act. Outside that act, of course, they're likely to get just as stuck as everyone else.

This study, then, assumes that the psychology of the creative mind, *when it is being creative,* differs from others to the degree that it is rather more "invented" and less "given" or "imposed." William Blake's "I must create a system or be enslaved by another man's" probably speaks for most artists. For the critic, that statement means having to choose between trying to impose a ready-made psychological language, such as the Freudian, Jungian, or Lacanian, or, more empathetically and perhaps more fruitfully, working inductively from the unique psychological language the artist has invented to explain himself to himself. In Shaw's case, for instance, I've chosen, for the most part, to use the language of that primer of Shavian psychology known as *The Quintessence of Ibsenism,* even though that approach often results in using what is ordinarily thought nonpsychological language. But ready-made psychological languages are so reductive of the creative mind that all art seems but expressive of ordinariness. As ready-made psychology, like ready-made morality, imposes its grid of behavior upon the individual, something may be revealed about the artist's ordinary humanity but usually at the cost of failing to learn anything about what made the artist extraordinary. Freudian or Lacanian readings, especially, are like Lilliputians tying down Gulliver; they bring the giant down to earth all right but do not explain his size.

Many have thought that the mighty G.B.S. sprang spontaneously into existence at the writing of his first play, at the rather advanced age of thirty-six, much as the people in the last part of his *Back to Methuselah* emerge fully grown from eggs. But Shaw's novels reveal that there was long preparation for this emergence as a "Superman," and the psychological acrobatics of the ur-Shaw *ab ovo* are fascinating to behold. He sensed that in order to become more capable of dealing with a world so morally perverse that evil was often proclaimed good and good, evil, he had to be born again "upsidedown" (from the world's perverse point of view) and wearing the mask of a jester, what Eric Bentley called "the Fool in Christ" (183); only in so doing could he call attention to this mad moral reversal in a way that would effect peaceful change. His was the mask of a man born to set things right but hoping to jolly or ridicule the world into changing, having concluded that coercion by the Superman is "morally suicidal" (*Collected Plays with Prefaces* 2:753) and that accepting crucifixion/ostracism only leads to "Crosstianity" (see the prefaces to *Androcles and the Lion* and *Major Barbara*). Other than through coercive dictatorship, the only alternative to being "the fool in Christ" was to offer oneself up for another "crucifixion," scapegoating for the would-be savior being the world's preferred way of dealing with its guilt at not living up to its own moral ideals. The replacing of the potential, solemn-minded dictator or scapegoat by a diabolically joking, paradox-minded Superman/scapegrace is what Shaw's novels principally display. They show Shaw consciously declining martyrdom and dictatorship, the two alternate careers he was most suited for and attracted to.

Arguably, these weren't real choices for Shaw, for no one offered him either Caesar's throne or a crown of thorns, but neither were they "offered" to those historical figures who did take them. The question is whether Shaw could have undergone sufficient transmutation of character to "take" either fate. In the first case, lesser men with lesser gifts of persuasion have found themselves in the role of dictator, and there are photographs of Shaw haranguing throngs of workers in the East End that remind us that he had the opportunity for an attempt at dictatorship, had he cared to trim his rhetoric and had he been able to reshape his personality to that end. As for crucifixion, he came close enough on several occasions, most notably when *Common Sense About the War* brought him betrayal, extreme opprobrium, and a very real ostracism. And of course there were always people who thought he *deserved* crucifixion, some of whom would have enacted it if they could have. In any case, it's what a writer imagines to be true about his potential that serves him as symbols of self, and Shaw's sensing of alternative personalities and paths for himself must be credited as valid literary symbols for himself at least and for others as well insofar as they resonate as universals. His Napoleon, Caesar, Andrew Undershaft, Captain Shotover (with his death ray), and King Magnus are symbols of the self that desired power, and his Dick Dudgeon, Caesar (as he returns to Rome to be assassinated), Barbara Undershaft, Lavinia, and St. Joan are symbols of the self that anticipated, with some ambivalence, "crucifixion." Shaw's comic undermining of their self-sacrificing poses is symbol of his triumph over alternative possibilities of personality development.

The Frame of the Portrait

Though the five novels constituted Shaw's main effort to launch a literary career prior to his taking up playwriting for good in 1892, the years before and after his writing of the novels found him attempting other works. These works are worth considering in that they provide a frame for the novels' portrait of the artist as a young man and Superman.

In the pre-novels period, after the ghosting of music articles for Lee in 1876–77, Shaw experimented in 1878–79 with a variety of forms—among them, reviews, philosophical essays, learned treatises, short fiction, heroic drama—and though they met almost entirely with rejection, some of them contain major previsions of Shavian archetypes. Chief among such works were *My Dear Dorothea*, completed in 1878 but unpublished until 1956, and *Passion Play*, a fragment from 1878 unpublished until 1971 and then in 1974 included in the *Collected Plays with Their Prefaces*, vol. 7.

A send-up of books of advice to the young, *My Dear Dorothea*, originally entitled *A Practical System of Moral Education for Females*, is a treatise in an entertaining epistolary form that gives ironic "bad advice" to a fictional five-year-old named Dorothea: "Be as selfish as you can"; "get into mischief as often as you can"; "never listen to religious instruction" (25, 51). The work establishes the pattern of Shaw's lifelong habit, indeed pursued more in letter form than in dramatic form, of playing Pygmalion to younger females, as Shaw tried to persuade females to live up to the liberated girl of his and their dreams. From the first, even before Ibsen's *A Doll House*, Shaw sensed the need of Victorian females, particularly the younger ones, to find moral precepts that would allow them more scope and freedom. That is, at the very beginning Shaw instinctively seized on the potentially rebellious young Victorian female as the principal agent of his projected revolution in manners and morals; she was, as he said later, both closer to the Life Force than the male and more influential in social arrangement. Indeed, a Dorothea who took Shaw's advice here might very well end up as a Vivie Warren, a Mrs. Clandon, a Cleopatra, a Lady Cicely Waynflete, a Lina Szczepanowska, a Lavinia, or a St. Joan (to name just a few of Shaw's "liberated" heroines from the plays).

But it's noteworthy how often in *Dorothea* Shaw balances out a promotion of liberated "selfish" individualism with cautionary words, foreshadowings of the later socialist, about the need to "get along" and act for the welfare of the group. *True* selfishness, "selfishness in the proper way" (35), was somehow socially beneficial. True selfishness meant natural self-control, not self-indulgence. *Dorothea* is the first sounding of the familiar Shavian paradox of selfless egotism, the selfishness that looks and acts like selflessness because the individual is so connected to the universe that doing what he or she wants accomplishes the will of the universe. Shaw would have understood the charity of a Mother Teresa as essentially selfish because she's doing what she needs to do to fulfill herself, and he would not have been the least alarmed by the assertions of recent studies such as Robert Wright's *The Moral Animal* (Pantheon 1994) that morality and altruism are adaptations designed to maximize genetic self-interest.

Though focused on the dialectic between self and society, this little "Quintessence of Shaw" that *Dorothea* is sounds all the major Shavian themes in a surprisingly mature ironic voice; it does not sound like the voice of a twenty-one-year-old. Shaw's immaturity in 1878 was relative only to his own, later, hard-won maturity; his 1878 voice seems mature enough relative to his culture. And that voice prepares us for the shock of Shaw's first novel, begun by a twenty-two-year-old, in which a surprisingly mature narrator, somewhat reminiscent of the slyly mocking narrator of Joyce's *Portrait*, satirizes an entire society for its immaturity, including its ineptly rebellious hero.

However, Shaw's growing maturity as a moral thinker was still compromised in 1878 by a certain artistic greenness, which especially revealed itself in his next work, the unfinished *Passion Play*. It is hard to believe that in 1878 Shaw was capable of the classic error of trying to write "high drama" by the method of imitating the Shakespearean five-act, blank-verse, heroic tragedy, the very error that he would later so strenuously castigate as a drama critic and proponent of the New Drama. But even the "father of modern drama," Henrik Ibsen, was in 1878 just beginning to find his way out of the nineteenth-century aesthetic morass of conventional forms to discover modern dramatic form, so it's not surprising that the much younger, unpublished Shaw, who had then not yet heard of Ibsen, was not ready to become modern in his forms. Hardly anybody was. But the novels gave Shaw a vehicle for approaching modernity, as he experimented with the creating of genre antitypes and the mixing of genres for ironic effect.

In its less than two acts, *Passion Play* (originally entitled *Household of Joseph*) dramatizes the early home life of Jesus of Nazareth and his tempting away by a visitor named Judas Iscariot, who sets him on the road to Jerusalem. The humanizing of history that Shaw later became known for, as in *The Man of Destiny* and *Caesar and Cleopatra*, is here initiated in the characterization of Mary as a pious but shrewish housewife, Joseph as a drunken, henpecked, priest-baiting husband, Jesus as an illegitimate son and bohemian idle dreamer, and Judas as a rich nobleman of rational probity. Judas's entry into the picture sets up a familiar Shavian dialectic between compelling forces contending in Shaw: Jesus represents the fervent idealist and poetic dreamer whose vision of a better world is so radical that it can be reached only by escaping this world, and Judas represents the analytical skeptic whose outraged moral sense can find vent only in personal probity, iconoclastic criticism, and, inevitably, compromising political activism, all religions having been exploded for him. At the end of Act 1, Judas the humanist-atheist acts as synthesizer by acknowledging that Jesus' dreams of a life after death in a heaven of brotherly love are a poetic displacement of his own aspirations for creating a sane, just, and equitable society on earth, and so he offers friendship to Jesus and common cause.[3] The balancing of such opposites will become a favorite device in the novels.

In an article entitled "Shaw and the Uncrucifying of Christ," I explored the possibility that *Passion Play* was Shavian ur-work in the sense that, like *Dorothea*, it established another major pattern in Shaw's life and career. Shaw's uncharacteristically leaving *Passion Play* unfinished, I theorized, was due less to his stated reason, that Jesus' refusal to defend himself at his trial rendered him undramatic, than to his unwillingness to follow the career of Jesus to its New Testament conclusion in the crucifixion, which he thought an emblem of death worship and moral evasion ("Crosstianity," he called it). I then demonstrated how in his later career as a dramatist, though he continued to use the pattern of a hero or heroine forced into circumstances that threatened or brought martyrdom, Shaw found many different aesthetic solutions to the problem that had stopped him in *Passion Play,* ways to undermine or to undo crucifixion scenes so that the final emphasis was always on the triumph of Life over Death. (It is in this way, for example, that the comic epilogue of *Saint Joan,* serving as satyr play, counters the tragedy of Joan's martyrdom at the end of scene 4.) As this compulsion to set up and then evade "crucifixion" finds its initial expression in Shaw's novels, it was obviously a problem central to his being. Again, with a reformist agenda as extreme as his and the talent and temperament to attempt executing it, his alternatives were to try to force the world to change, as a moral dictator, or let it "crucify" him in rejection, or joke it into change. Stephen Winsten's calling Shaw "the Jesting Apostle"[4] indicates the choice made: he combined the joker with an apostolic persona. The church where you must not laugh, said Shaw, is giving way to "the Church where the oftener you laugh the better, because by laughter only can you destroy evil without malice, and affirm good fellowship without mawkishness"

(*Our Theatres in the Nineties* 1:vi). Given the failure of *the* Crucifixion to reform the world and that of numerous moral dictators to coerce reform, Shaw's choice was at least worth trying. And it better suited who he was.

Other work worth noting in the pre-novels stage includes some attempts at fiction. In a planned novel called *The Legg Papers* (1878), perhaps not carried much beyond the outline stage, and in three completed short stories—"The Miraculous Revenge" (1878), "The Brand of Cain" (1878; lost), and "The St. James's Hall Mystery" (1879), Shaw employed a supernatural background and/or the theme of privileged lunacy to establish two dominant Shavian ideas. The first of these would mature through the novels and plays into, as Bringle says, "a reformative philosophy of mind conquering matter," and the second would be further developed by the "temperamental renegades" of the novels (Bringle 289). In particular, the use of a resuscitated Mozart in "The St. James's Hall Mystery" to criticize the present is a harbinger of many Mozartian and anachronistic moments to come in Shaw's career. And "The Miraculous Revenge" is noteworthy for expressing Shaw's exasperation at finding how determined society was to criminalize him. It tells the story of an iconoclast who can't find community even in death, as an entire graveyard of the respectable mysteriously transports itself elsewhere when his corpse is buried in their midst.

These works combine with *Dorothea* and *Passion Play* to make a very instructive pre-novels "Quintessence of Shaw" in literary form, whose themes are reinforced and explained in the principal work Shaw wrote after the five novels and just before his first completed play—*The Quintessence of Ibsenism* (1891). Many critics have insisted this might more accurately have been called *The Quintessence of Shaw*, but that's an overstatement. What Shaw did in *The Quintessence* was abstract from Ibsen's plays a certain pattern of meaning that really was there but that was by no means the whole of Ibsen's meaning, a pattern that happened to coincide with a pattern Shaw had developed independently in his own novels and would develop further in his plays.

Shaw's novels were the proving grounds for the theory of character types he announced in *The Quintessence*—the realist, the idealist, and the Philistine being recurring types in the novels. The novels also illustrate in another way Shaw's habitual externalizing of the psychological, for what he presented in *The Quintessence* as the *sociological* types of realist, idealist, and Philistine he employed in the novels (as later in the plays) as *psychological* forces at work in inner conflict as well.[5] That is, realist, idealist, and Philistine principles operated like, say, id, ego, and superego within the individual psyche. But just as individuals can be typed in the Freudian system according to the principle that dominates the psyche, so too in Shaw's system individuals could be sociologically typed because in moments of crisis the individual psyche tends to be dominated by one of the psychic principles. An idealist, sociologically speaking, was one whose idealist psychic force dominated his Philistine and realist psychic principles.

Of course the object of this sociopsychological system was to show that evolutionary forces were at work pushing the realist element or type as the most desirable, the most highly evolved, the door to the future. It was Shaw's none-too-modest way of explaining to himself his difference and alienation from others—he was estranged because more highly evolved, not less moral than society but more so, and more trustworthy because most of his moral control was genetically powered from within rather than, as with most, being imposed against the grain by laws and enforcers. The Shavian realist with his built-in "moral passion" was an earlier term for what Shaw later called "the Superman." The novels show clearly how Shaw differentiated realism as a character trait (that characterization, by the way, being perhaps the most revolutionary technical achievement of Shaw as novelist), which prepared the way for the writing of *The Quintessence of Ibsenism*.

The post-novels part of the frame of the novels has other elements that contain occasional bits of self-revelation readable as echoes or permutations of the self-portraiture of the novels. On the post-novels side of the frame are the criticism and reviews Shaw wrote between 1885 and 1892, the diaries begun in 1885, the unfinished novel of 1887–88, and a few short stories written before 1892, all revealing the further development of the G.B.S./realist/ Superman persona. This frame having been established, a detailed consideration of the novels is in order, after a note on methodology.

A Note on Methodology

For handy reference, I summarize here two of the more important distinctions this book makes as a part of its methodology—distinctions between different editions of Shaw's novels and different kinds of realism.

As indicated before, quotations from Shaw's novels come from the *Standard Edition of the Works of Bernard Shaw*, the principal exception being in the case of *Immaturity*, where distinctions are made typographically between the 1930 text of the *Standard Edition* and the 1879–81 text of the original, unpublished version so as to highlight revisions that affect my discussion of the novel's art. For *Immaturity* only, brackets {**and boldface**} indicate words in the original text that were deleted from the published version. Brackets {with no boldface} indicate words inserted in the 1930 published version. When the revision is too lengthy or too different to fit in, brackets enclose, first, the revision, followed by the phrase *Original Wording:* and **the original in bold**. For the other four novels, I summarize or indicate revisions (in the Notes, for the most part) only if they consist of entirely new wording or, in the case of rewordings, seem to significantly alter meaning in a way that would affect my theses.

It would also be helpful to remember that the word *realism* is used in many different ways in this book, symptomatic of its being one of the most semantically troubled words in our lexicon and of Shaw's deliberate playing on that. Shaw knew what he was doing when in *The Quintessence of Ibsenism* he allied Ibsen with Plato and Shelley as examples of Shavian realists; this was a deliberate attempt to rescue the word "realism" from its use by cynics, scientific materialists, and literary realists, to make it serve, as it had once served, to denote the sort of vision that sees behind appearances to the deepest truths, available to intuition but scientifically unverifiable. But Ibsen's reputation as a *literary* realist (an imitator of surface reality) as well as his being designated a *Shavian* realist (a visionary who sees past the surface) confused the issue. Shaw meant that it was possible to be both kinds of realist but that, among literary realists, only the great ones like Ibsen, who used the surface to evoke the depths, possessed the vision he called realistic. To indicate Shaw's sense that there was something shallow or bogus about literary realism in the hands of lesser writers, I normally put "realism" of the literary sort in quotation marks. Realism without quotation marks usually refers to Shavian, visionary realism—the genuine article. It would also be useful to have a typographical way of distinguishing Shavian realism from the "realism" of the cynic or the scientific materialist, but nothing of that sort has been attempted here.

While Shaw would agree with the problematizing of "reality" current among poststructuralists, having fully grasped the relativity and plurality of reality long before most, he would insist that that problematics should not paralyze anyone or serve to excuse any behavior. Shaw thought one had to *choose* among realities, and, in terms of their harm or benefit to the person, the group, the planet, and the universe, he saw some choices as morally superior. Unlike many poststructuralists, he believed that the great artists had special abilities to perceive and display the choices, and that great literature had special powers to remake the world.

$\mathcal{P}art$ 2

The Art of the Novels, Or,
The Maturity of *Immaturity*

As to the literary execution of the books, I suppose it will not now be questioned
that I am no mere man of genius, but a conscientious workman as well.
"Mr. Bernard Shaw's Works of Fiction. Reviewed by Himself" (1892)

[*Immaturity* is] a very remarkable work, I assure you, but hardly one
which I should be well advised in letting loose whilst my livelihood depends
on my credit as a literary workman.
"The Author to the Reader," *Our Corner* (November 1887)
(Also appears in prefaces to 1900 and 1914 editions of *Love Among the Artists*)

This section of the book might be viewed as a digression from the main thesis in that it focuses on the art of the novels rather than on the novels as self-
portraiture, but it discusses the art of the novels in a way that sets the stage
for the treatment of Shaw's novels as self-portraiture.

Before demonstrating how Shaw's novels constitute self-portraiture, I was
concerned originally to show first that Shaw's self-portrait *was* of an artist and
specifically that the *novels* were written by an artist. There were some doubts
about Shaw's being an artist because he had so often declared that he wasn't.
Of course he had also declared that he was one, but all too many made no attempt to see the contradiction as a resolvable paradox. It is now well understood in Shaw studies, if nowhere else, that Shaw's insistence on being a propagandist and didact was typical overstatement, uttered whenever he wanted
to agitate the art-for-art's-sake crowd or reassert his credentials as a practical
reformer. No one who really knows Shaw takes such assertions straight any-
more. But, alas, there are still many scholars and critics around, particularly
those with modernist axes to grind, who haven't gotten the word. One still
finds among Yeatsians, Joyceans, Poundians, and others a prejudice either that
Shaw was "no artist" or that because his sentences were intelligible his art
was of an inferior rationalist or journalistic sort.[1] Given such attitudes, a demonstration of Shaw's artistry is not wasted even today.

Portrait of the Artist as an Old Reviser

In my original study I assumed that if I could show, through a careful "close reading," that Shaw's first and surely least skillful novel, *Immaturity*, was artful work, then that point would be made for all five novels, and I could get on with my self-portraiture thesis. I tried to discuss the art of *Immaturity* in a way that would set the stage for that thesis. But the task of proving Shaw an artist by way of a careful reading of *Immaturity* is greater than I knew at the time. Trips to foreign libraries in those days being beyond my means, and access to manuscripts of Shaw's novels not being available by any other means, I took Shaw at his word that he had left the original *Immaturity* largely untouched in readying it for his *Collected Edition*. In his 1921 preface, Shaw proposed "to make no attempt to correct the work of the apprentice with the hand of the master: that such as it is it must remain" (xxxviii). I often wondered afterward if I had been right to trust this statement, particularly as evidence accumulated that Shaw could not be trusted in such matters (Shaw being both a scholar's exasperation and employment), but my wondering ceased when I read Nicholas Grene's "The Maturing of *Immaturity*" (1990). After checking the manuscript at the National Library of Ireland against the published version, Grene found that Shaw had revised the novel "quite thoroughly" and apparently had written the 1921 preface, in which he guaranteed no revision, *before* he reread the novel, supposedly in late 1922, and concluded it needed some "correction" if it was not to embarrass him. The final version, prepared as he was working on *Saint Joan*, was finished on July 30, 1923, and published in 1930. As Grene's article made plain that the original *Immaturity* was rougher work than I had thought, and proving artistry by New Critical methods being out of fashion anyway, I considered eliminating this chapter altogether.[2]

But after checking the handwritten 1879 manuscript against the typescript of it that Shaw's secretary typed in 1921 and/or 1922, I found that my appreciation of the artfulness of *Immaturity* needed adjustment but not cancellation.[3] It was a matter of degree, and not of large degree. Shaw at twenty-three was somewhat less mature as a writer and person than I had thought, but he was still considerably more mature than the Robert Smith he had satirized and certainly more mature, at least in terms of moral intellect, than his culture. So on that score, I saw no reason to drop the chapter.

A more serious problem follows from the disrepute, justified or not, into which New Criticism has fallen at the hands of poststructuralists. Although my work was not at all concerned with critical theory, I am of course haunted by my assumption that one proved artistry by methods sanctioned by New Criticism. "Close reading" revealed a novel's careful art—the foreshadowing, the echoing of imagery, the interweaving of motifs, the building of character, the patterning of character relationships, the structuring of plot, the manipulating of point of view. It was thought that the skillful handling of such elements of fiction led to the creation of an autonomous and unified artifact, the meaning of which was there for the intelligent reader's discovery upon use of the proper critical tools. Such critical labor was important because true artists did not make direct statements of meaning; they *implied* meaning. In the days of New Criticism, you could distinguish writers from critics because critics understood that their job was to convert the writer's artistic implications into critical statements of overt meaning, while apologizing for the relative poverty of critical prose and the prosaic age that required it.

In these days of interactive reading, with writers and critics supposedly collaborative, we've heard much about the shortcomings of New Criticism and have learned to make no pretension that works of literature are autonomous, self-contained, undeconstructionable wholes, the expressions of centered subjects who are rational, willing agents. Our language apparently writes us more than we write it. But the discrediting of New Critical theory did not discredit its chief method, probably because "close reading," in and by itself, serves everybody's purpose, as evidenced by the fact that few poststructuralists can do without it. At any rate, as long as I make no claim that Shaw's art is undeconstructionable or that I have made the one true interpretation, I see no objection to employing "close reading" in the following exegesis. Much good can come of noticing that Shaw from the beginning was, by the lights of his time, a careful craftsman who knew how to shape a novel and who was not as often distracted from storytelling by didactic urges as sometimes thought, and that even in such cases he knew how to subordinate the message to the medium and to "show" rather than "tell."

So I have retained the chapter, with its close-reading method, but I bow to the possibility that the unity of the work demonstrated is problematical. And I have lowered my estimation of this particular novel in its original form, though not of the novels *as they are* in their final state. It is further worth repeating that most of the major revision, stylistic in any case, occurred in only the first two novels.[4]

The handwritten 1879 manuscript of *Immaturity* (see pages following) reveals that Shaw from the beginning knew how to revise, the many deletions and insertions indicating how rapidly he was progressing in his art. The improvements are often clearly visible, with many deleted words not obscured by his cross-outs. He understood that verbosity was his special failing, for there are thousands more words deleted than added, mainly in the exposition. Huge chunks of character analysis and plot reflection were excised, leaving a much more dramatic narrative. Many chapter endings, of a summary nature, were cut, letting the action speak for itself. Dialogue and action were seldom deleted. One may speculate, as Grene does, that Shaw's excisions were motivated more by a desire to cover up self-revelatory "brooding introspections" (231), but Shaw had solid artistic reasons for his cuts as well: "I . . . excise[d] every word that betrayed the least consciousness on my part of my own design. I also cut out pages of analysis of character, because I think the dramatic method of *exhibiting* character the true one" (*Collected Letters* 27). This was similar to explicit advice he gave to a would-be woman novelist in 1882 (*Collected Letters* 52).

Of course this all assumes that the handwritten deletions and insertions on this manuscript were made in two early revisions, first in 1879 before Shaw sent it out for the first time and then by January 3, 1881, in response to the early rejections. The very messy manuscript that resulted, by the way, might alone account for many of the rejections; it would take a very patient reader to follow it, which is why Shaw had it typed up for his own convenience in 1921–22. This typescript appears to be a faithful copy of the 1879–81 manuscript, sans deletions, and it was either on this typescript or on galley proofs that Shaw in 1922–23 made his revisions for the final version. Grene cites a letter dated December 26, 1922, that refers to Shaw's reading of the novel as evidence that his rereading, at least with any thoroughness, did not occur until the typescript had been finished, but the typescript's elimination of chapters 11 and 12 of book 2 (which though mice-chewed at top and bottom of a few pages could have been reconstructed)[5] and its omission of the first two pages of the epilogue suggest that Shaw had reread the novel in serious editorial mode *before* the typescript was made. Can we therefore be certain that none of the handwritten insertions and deletions on the 1879–81 manuscript date from the 1920s, some perhaps even made prior to having the manuscript typed? Apparently we can't, but experts such as Dan Laurence, Stanley Weintraub, and Nicholas Grene take the view that nothing was added to the manuscript in the 1920s.

Whatever the case, in my quoting from *Immaturity*, I have tried to give some idea of the nature and extent of Shaw's revisions by indicating variations between the 1879–81 manuscript and the work published in 1930. Brackets {**and boldface**} indicate words in the original text that were deleted from the published version. Brackets {with no boldface} indicate words inserted for the 1930 published version. When the revisions are too lengthy or too different to fit in, brackets enclose, first, the revision, followed by the phrase *Original Wording:* and **the original words in bold**.

However, I was surprised to discover how little Shaw's extensive revisions of 1923 changed substance, at least as far as *my* thesis was concerned, and how wrong Shaw was in 1887 to declare *Immaturity* unfit for serialization in the shape it was (see the second epigraph of Part 2). A messy manuscript certainly needed to be recopied, but the 1881 *Immaturity* is not significantly inferior to the four novels that were serialized, and in some respects its gentle, pre-Thurberesque satire of the would-be hero as a sympathetic boob trapped in an idiotic world gives it a peculiar charm that some would find more attractive than the harsher satirical atmosphere and would-be Supermen of the other novels. *Immaturity* is a more "human" book than the others. It is more like Joyce's *Portrait* than the subsequent novels in that it tells a wry tale of the touchingly vulnerable, severely tested humanity of a self the author had recently outgrown rather than, as the other novels do, of the author's experimenting with possible new and improved selves.

Grene's article notes about a dozen ways, major and minor, that Shaw's revisions altered the novel, both in the original revisions and in the 1923 revision. As an example of a minor 1923 revision, Shaw altered back into literal fact what he had originally fictionalized, the fictional name of the Alhambra dancer that Smith was infatuated with being changed to the historical name of a dancer the young Shaw had admired, which no longer needed to be disguised. More significantly, Shaw's nailing down of the time of the novel's initial action as 1878, rather than leaving the date unspecified as he originally did, transforms what appeared to be an up-to-the-minute novel into a historical period piece and creates an awkward improbability in the time sequencing: as Grene says, "given that the novel covers a period of some years, [identifying the time of the initial action as 1878] projects the action into a future beyond the time of composition" (228).

Grene as Irishman scrutinizing an Irish emigrant's manuscript is most concerned, however, with the way Shaw de-Hibernicized himself in this novel,

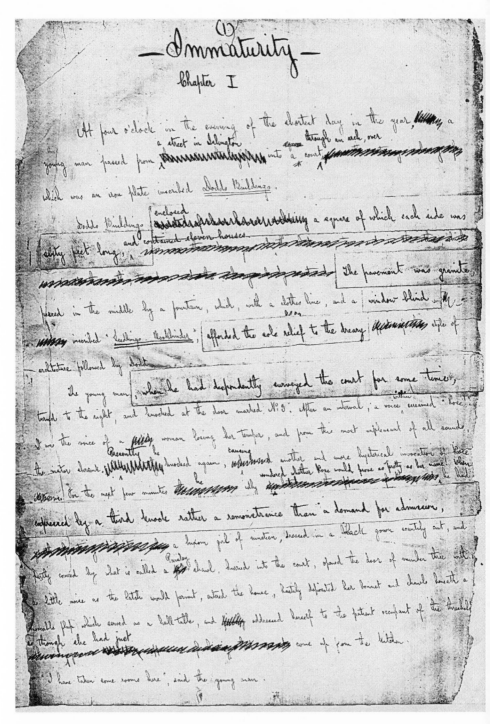

The opening page of the original 1879–81 manuscript of Shaw's *Immaturity*, as preserved at the National Library of Ireland. Reprinted here with the permission of the National Library of Ireland and the Society of Authors and the Shaw Estate.

C H A P T E R I.

At four o'clock in the evening of the shortest day in
the year, a young man passed from a street in Islington
into a court through an arch, over which was an iron plate
inscribed Dodds Buildings.

Dodds Buildings enclosed a square of which each side
was sixty feet long, and contained eleven houses. The pavement was granite, pierced in the middle by a fountain, which,
with a clothes line, and a window blind inscribed "Seedlings,
Bookbinder", afforded the sole relief to the dreary style of
architecture followed by Dodd.

The young man, when he had despondently surveyed the
court for some time, turned to the right, and knocked at the
door marked No.3. After an interval, a voice within scream-
ed "Rose!" It was the voice of a woman losing her temper,
and from this most unpleasant of all sounds the visitor
shrank. Presently he knocked again, causing another and mor
hysterical invocation of Rose.

For the next few minutes he idly wondered whether Rose

particularly in the original revisions, by distancing himself from what he was ashamed of or disliked in his own Irish nationality (as, for example, by eliminating Smith's Irish grandmother). But Grene doesn't mention Shaw's 1923 changing of the hero from a tenor to a baritone, a move that draws the hero closer to Shaw biographically yet contributes to the author's Anglicizing by avoiding a possible hidden connection between "Irish" and "tenor." As Grene explains the general strategy, "Shaw creates in Smith an imagined English alter ego, partly wish-fulfillment model allowing him to escape from his provincial status as Irishman, partly caricature of the uptight Anglicized prig he aspired to become" (233). (Perhaps it would be more accurate to say "*feared* he might become.") Grene sums up Shaw's revisions thus: "The manuscript enables us to see what relatively ordinary adolescent impulses lay behind that extraordinary persona GBS, the tendency towards introspective self-analysis, towards fantasy wish-fulfillment, albeit only moderately fantastic, the self-justifying defence of what felt like failure as the potential for success to come. The author of *Immaturity*, as detected in the writing and re-writing of the novel, stands revealed as a more human, a more vulnerable person than the relentlessly confident public performer that was to be Bernard Shaw" (238). But on the whole Shaw's 1923 revisions, while many, were mostly of the harmless, tinkering sort that affected style more than substance. Even at that, the majority of the manuscript was untouched. Of the ninety-five quotations my original study took from the published *Immaturity*, seventy-six (80 percent) were unchanged from the 1879–81 manuscript to the 1930 book, and only eight (8.5 percent) consisted of entirely new wording, which even so did not violate context or make significant alterations, except in the case of the epilogue. Most revisions involved the cutting of verbiage or the adding of a few words to lend color, wit, or precision. A number of quotations that I would have bet were added in the 1920s were found to be original phrasing, giving support to Shaw's contention that the novels show that over the years he added more to his style of presentation than to the content.

Portrait of the Artist as an Old Critic

If Shaw couldn't be trusted about the truth of his revisions of the novels, he also couldn't be trusted in his critical statements about them. And even less to be trusted were the critics because so much of what they said was what Shaw had put into their heads to say. Stanley Weintraub's 1956 dissertation turned a skeptical eye on some of this misconceiving and misconstruing, but the major breakthrough, as far as published criticism was concerned, came with Robert Hogan's 1965 article "The Novels of Bernard Shaw."

Hogan explains why Shaw's novels had met with very cavalier treatment, first from Shaw himself. Shaw's actual fondness for the novels, says Hogan, "was tempered by an uneasy suspicion that others might think them unworthy of a pre-eminent dramatist—mere apprentice work, in fact" (63). Further, because "his later work was so consistently and universally successful . . . even the mature aplomb of a Shaw might have felt uneasy about the consistent and universal failure of his first work" (64). As a result, Hogan believes, Shaw set up "a smokescreen of bantering insouciance" to disguise his diffident conviction that the novels were far from being inferior (64).

The critics, largely biographers who give the impression of having merely skimmed through the novels, took Shaw's strategic comments as straightforward critical commentary. If the author was flippantly contemptuous of his early works, so too were the critics. If the author was facetious and superficial in his explanation of the novels' origins and intentions, the critics followed suit. In Hogan's words, "Shavian criticism has tended to accept Shaw's own simplified estimate of his work for the full and sober statement, just as people have tended to accept the Shavian mask for the real face. Behind Shaw's harlequin mask, however, was the face of a man of genius, compassion, and, surprisingly, diffidence. Indeed, even in the apparently unbridled egotism of the self-advertisements, that curious diffidence kept rising to the surface."[6]

That curious diffidence misled his biographers, busy chronicling other parts of his long and eventful life, into hasty readings of the novels and incautious acceptance of the critical clichés coined by Shaw himself. Archibald Henderson summarizes friendly critical opinion (prior to Hogan) when he writes that "Shaw's novels survive as a thin tail to his soaring dramatic kite; they are chiefly memorable as prentice tentatives, in an ill-chosen field, for works of genius in his true literary metier of the drama" (*Man of the Century* 8). The metaphor of the kite might do if its object were to emphasize that the kite cannot fly without the tail, but Henderson instead means to glorify Shaw's dramatic talents at the expense of his novels, the familiar pattern in Shaw criticism. Even more explicitly Henderson wrote: "Is Shaw a great novelist? Answer: a resounding No. His novels are amusing, eccentric, stilted, jejune, and filled with acute but inexpertly expressed observations on life and art and music and pugilism and marriage and society and Socialism. . . . Shaw was inexperienced and immature; and he lacked inside knowledge of, behind-the-scenes acquaintance with, the society and the individual social types of the period. Of his novels, he once remarked to me, with pawky humor: 'The best I can say of them is that neither Dickens nor Trollope could have written them'" ("Where Shaw Stands Today" 4). To this Hogan cogently replies, "Mr. Henderson apparently did not realize that, despite the tone of rueful deprecation, the best Shaw could say of the novels was that they were beyond the capabilities of two pre-eminent masters of English fiction" (64).

Hogan sums up his introductory point by declaring the many condemnations "highly inaccurate—as if the critics had swallowed *in toto* Shaw's tongue-in-cheek deprecation of the novels, without having closely scrutinized the books themselves." There is some excuse for their not having penetrated Shaw's "smokescreen," however, for it was a masterful disguise: "In later years, through his prefaces, Shaw perfected the pose of literary master of ceremonies who introduced and interpreted his own work. This practice was not so unfortunate when the work was a play which had finally to stand alone for judgment on the stage, but novels have no such separate life, and the diffident Shaw succeeded only too well in his diffident depreciations. When diffidence is cloaked in tones of fluently witty assurance, it is not too curious for that diffidence to be taken as aversion" (64).

The various charges against Shaw's novels, unified by their questioning of the novels' "realism," take six main forms—that they are unreal in their portrayal of life, stilted and unnatural in their language, plotless and disorganized (the assumption then being that "realistic" novels had plots), inconsistent in their characterization, propagandistic and "talky" in subordinating action to a discussion of ideas, and often irrelevant in their detail. I will conjecture later that these charges could be thrown out, for the most part, simply on the grounds that the critics were mistaken in treating the novels as strict, pious attempts at literary realism. But it is possible to defend the novels as examples of "realism," a job that Robert Hogan began in his 1965 article. Though he agrees with some of the six charges, Hogan has expertly refuted the first two.

According to Hogan, "the most damaging accusation leveled at Shaw's novels is probably Archibald Henderson's assertion that Shaw did not know what he was writing about" (106). Each of Shaw's novels is essentially a study of manners, and Henderson argued that Shaw's knowledge of the society he was writing about was too limited to enable him to create a convincing verisimilitude. As usual, Henderson got this argument from Shaw himself. In the preface to *The Irrational Knot* Shaw confessed that his novel was indeed marred by a special ignorance of life. Upon exporting himself from Dublin to London he was "in a condition of extreme rawness and inexperience concerning the specifically English side of the life with which the book pretends to deal" (v). What he lacked, he said, was "the touch of the literary diner-out" (viii). Shaw seems to be damning himself here, but further investigation of the same preface reveals an equally spirited defense of the reality his novel creates. For one thing, he had a sort of "backstairs knowledge" of high society gained in his previous position "in the office of an Irish gentleman who acted as land agent and private banker for many persons of distinction," and, furthermore, "it is possible for a London author to dine out in the highest circles for twenty years without learning as much about the human frailties of his hosts as the family solicitor or (in Ireland) the family land agent learns in twenty days; and some of this knowledge inevitably reaches his clerks, especially the clerk who keeps the cash, which was my particular department" (ix). Thus if the novels err in their portrayal of aristocratic life, the error is not the very crucial one of idealizing that life, but merely of missing its economic basis. As Shaw says, "If, as I suspect, I failed to create a convincingly verisimilar atmosphere of aristocracy, it was not because I had any illusions or ignorances as to the common humanity of the peerage, and not because I gave literary style to its conversation, but because, as I had no money, I had to blind myself to its enormous importance, with the result that I missed the point of view, and with it the whole moral basis, of the class which rightly values money, and plenty of it, as the first condition of a bearable life" (x). But if Shaw's portrayal of aristocratic life is incomplete because of his ignorance of its moral basis in economics, the same is true of the portrayals of Fielding, Austen, Dickens, and every other English author who wrote without knowledge of Marxism. On that point, they all stand or fall together, and all are today grist for the mill of a universal deconstruction.

Actually, Shaw's novels are rather remarkably less flawed in their portrayal of aristocracy than were most of his predecessors' and contemporaries'. As Hogan says, "the chief pitfall for the portrayer of high society is attributing to it an intelligence, a charm and a wit never seen on land or sea. This specious glamor pervades even the fumbling, if commercially successful, attempts of writers like Michael Arlen and Noel Coward. Shaw, even in his teens, was too perceptive to be so easily taken in, and he saw 'that the aristocratic profession has as few geniuses as any other profession'" (107). A further point is that portrayal of aristocratic life is not primarily Shaw's subject, proved not only by the existence of many characters and settings that are middle or lower class or Bohemian, but also by his focus on the way that the developing "supermanship" of his heroes is superior to aristocratic ways.

To conclude Hogan's argument on this point: "For our purposes, it is significant that Shaw did not finally attribute any lack of verisimilitude in the novels to either social ignorance or lack of artistry. The partial failure of the world he describes in the novels is, according to his view and mine, more philosophic or sociologic than it is artistic. Most of the masterworks of the world have taken, however, a similarly limited view. A work of art is a selection, a focusing upon a certain aspect of a subject" (107–8). In the sense that in his novels Shaw has created "one unified world, impelled by the same single view, discussed in the same single language," "a world that is inimitable, full and convincing" (108), then, Hogan believes, the world of his novels is as real as anything in fiction.

The second of the charges, that Shaw's language was stilted and unnatural, cannot be refuted for every page, but Hogan has summoned more than enough evidence to prove that the charge is exaggerated, and one can argue the stilted language serves satiric purposes insofar as it is reserved for the characters of whom it is ridiculously characteristic, such as Smith in *Immaturity* when he is being pedantic or trying too hard to be properly English. Once again, the source of the charge is Shaw himself. "I can guarantee the propriety of my early style," said Shaw. "It was the last thing in correctness. . . . I resolved that I would write nothing that should not be intelligible to a foreigner with a dictionary, like the French of Voltaire; and I therefore avoided idiom" (*Immaturity* xxxix). Furthermore, "I had . . . the classical tradition which makes all the persons in a novel, except the comically vernacular ones, or the speakers of phonetically spelt dialect, utter themselves in the formal phrases and studied syntax of eighteenth century rhetoric. In short, I wrote in the style of Scott and Dickens; and as fashionable society then spoke and behaved, as it still does, in no style at all, my transcriptions of Oxford and Mayfair may nowadays suggest an unaccountable and ludicrous ignorance of a very superficial and accessible code of manners" (*The Irrational Knot* viii–ix). Shaw could be excused, then, in that the meticulous, pedantic style he generally used for aristocratic speech was the literary fashion of the day. In fiction, persons of quality were expected to speak a noble, decorous language that befitted their rank; the lower classes were expected to reveal their depravity by a corrupt use of the language. Further, if the narrator himself presumed to be noble, his exposition and narrative line were also expected to walk on stilts.

In view of the powerful hold that this vogue of artificial language had upon a long line of eminent English writers, the wonder is not that Shaw partially succumbed to it but that he so often escaped it. True enough, *Immaturity* is often rather stiffly worded, even in some exposition and in some of the dialogues of nonaristocratic characters, but there are also many instances of a distinctly modern style emerging even here, and by Shaw's second novel his language was increasingly vitalized by idiom, and his sentence structure was considerably more direct and forceful (see Hogan 65, 73–76). By the time of Shaw's fourth and fifth novels, his language has lost a good deal of its formality and seems by comparison with his contemporaries' astonishingly modern. Try comparing the style of even *Immaturity* with that of Henry James's *The Madonna of the Future,* Thomas Hardy's *The Return of the Native,* and George Meredith's *The Egoist,*[7] all written about the same time, and it will be clear that not a single contemporary novelist of the years 1879–83 had so successfully escaped the formal demands of the day's rather starchy rhetorical patterns. Shaw's novels are so shot through with such living language as idioms, colloquialisms, jargon, argot, and slang that the inability of Shaw's perceptive critics to see this is, as Hogan says, "high testimony to the hypnotic persuasiveness of Shaw, the creator of critical clichés" (65).

Of course this discussion of style assumes that Victorian novels are to be judged by the standards of literary realism, and their modernity by the degree to which they have sloughed off Victorian rhetoric. But that view of things is now well past, and perhaps it is time to appreciate Shaw for the fabulist and fantasist he essentially was and to delight in Shavian rhetoric as one delights in Shakespearean blank verse. In 1965 Hogan still struggled with the assumption that the apologist for Shaw's novels had to defend their *literary* "realism," as Shaw himself generally did, and they played that game well, but there seems to be less point to that in these days, when such "realism" has been found to be an illusion, and "rhetoric" is no longer considered a vice. As a playwright, Shaw himself quit pretending he was a "realist" early in his career, finding "stage realism" a contradiction in terms. Even earlier, in *The Quintessence of Ibsenism* he attempted to shift the meaning of *realism* to connote *visionary perception* rather than scientific observation or literal-minded photography. Perhaps it is now time to recognize that, in novel writing as well,

Shaw was more among the modernist rebels against "realism" of the literary sort than not, though for a while he kept up appearances for strategic reasons. His keeping company with the likes of the Fabians and the Ibsenite William Archer, who demanded "realism" in literature, encouraged this strategy; Shaw needed to be thought avant-garde and hardheadedly "objective" to get a hearing from them and from a segment of the public he wanted to influence. But the veneer of literary "realism" he gave his novels covered up such Shavian predilections as those for dialogue more articulate than natural, for symbolic action and character, and for the mixing and subverting of genres for parodistic effect, all of which served the projection of an essentially subjective reality of fantastic and fabulous aspect. As with many of his early plays, the result of the tension between apparently objective and secretly subjective modes of expression was a series of novels that can be viewed as either sui generis or as genre antitypes.[8] "Magical realism" might be an appropriate term for the novels if the term had not already been appropriated by novelists who make the subjective, fantasy element in their works more evident than Shaw did. On the other hand, as John Updike recently put it, "everything that happens in a book is magic" (*New York Times Book Review,* February 6, 1994, 27).

At any rate, the other charges—that the novels are plotless, talky, propagandistic, often irrelevant in their detail, and inconsistent in their characterization—are serious even if they are not leveled against the novels' "realism." But dealing with such criticisms convincingly requires a more thorough method, and it is to be hoped that someday a substantial book will accomplish that for all of the novels.[9] Here I will attempt to explore such charges only through a detailed account of the art of Shaw's first novel, *Immaturity,* for what is true for it is more or less true for the others. This representative but least polished of Shaw's novels displays sufficient art to prove that the novels in general, taken as "realistic" or not, are largely innocent of the charges against them or that the charges are exaggerated or misconceived.

As for the possibility that defending the 1930 version of *Immaturity* is not the same as defending the original, I repeat that Shaw's 1923 revisions were mostly stylistic and did not significantly alter either narrative structure (even in dropping two chapters) or, with few exceptions, characterization, the two most important components of novelistic art. Point of view—third person omniscient—*was* affected by the revisions to the degree that Shaw's cuts made his narrative more dramatic and his insertions perhaps added to the mocking nature of the narrative voice. At any event, I quote in what follows from both versions, leaving the reader to make the decision.

A Relatively Mature Portrait of a Decidedly Immature Artist

Shaw's "figural will to power" was strong from the outset. If he could not overpower the conventional world with the imaginative world he created in this initial novel, he at least, if published, would have strongly challenged it with the telling of an unusual tale. Contrary to what many critics have said or implied, Shaw was an excellent storyteller if judged by his ability to entice the reader into riding along on his narrative vehicle, for even those readers of his other novels who complained that they wanted to get off, didn't. His storytelling ability contributed mightily in fact to his later success as a dramatist. But of course his unusual stories weren't told in the usual way, and his heroes and heroines were not the usual ones. Worse, all this unusualness referred to the usual in a "disagreeable," satiric, spoofing way that gave conventional Victorian readers a hard time.

A bare summary of *Immaturity*'s main plot gives little clue to the novel's charm but clearly indicates why a Victorian reader would be frustrated by it. Rather than being the story of a dashing, aristocratic hero, *Immaturity* is the story of plain Robert Smith, who exists on the heroic plane only in his imagination. Working for a carpet wholesaler named Figgis & Weaver, Smith is a proud young clerk, opinionated but inhibited, good at his work but despising it because possessed of a largely unrealized artistic sensibility. He is seeking roots and identity, this unstated search being the primary action.

The published version is divided into four books.[10] The first book, entitled "Islington" (a middle-class section of London just northeast of that Bloomsbury where Shaw would soon live with his landlady-mother), deals with Robert Smith's "adventures" in a suburban lodging house. Here Smith encounters Harriet Russell, the expected romantic interest, a dressmaker and orphaned Scotswoman befriended by Smith's landlady, Mrs. Froster. Harriet's practicality, common sense, and rationalistic skepticism are important to Smith's appreciation of those virtues, as they help him differentiate similar yet different features in his own personality, but the book ends with Smith's rather inept and ambivalent flirtation being disrupted by Harriet's removal to another residence, caused partly by the sale and impending demolition of

Mrs. Froster's house. The course of true love ne'er runs smooth, fortunately for the reader, but since here the ineptitude of the lover is to blame more than circumstances, the Victorian reader would be feeling uneasy by this point.

The second book, entitled "Aesthetics," takes place mostly in two settings, one being Perspective Park in Richmond (in southwest London, a fashionable area Shaw did not know well then), the estate of a wealthy would-be patron of the arts, Halket Grosvenor (whose name probably echoes that of the then-new Grosvenor Gallery, financed by dilettantes). He conducts a semibohemian open house for poets, painters, and musicians (a set the young Shaw felt both attracted to and repelled by), who also congregate at Lady Geraldine's Wilton Place, the other main setting. Harriet's aunt being an employee at Perspective, Harriet sets up shop nearby. Soon a promising young painter, Cyril Scott, makes Harriet's acquaintance and becomes infatuated with her, thus satisfying the romantic hero's need for a rival. Meanwhile Smith has moved to a corner of Chelsea more artistically associated and, through a sort of luck unknown to his creator, has changed jobs for the better, becoming secretary for an Irish member of Parliament, Mr. Woodward. Scenes dealing with the life of Smith alternate with scenes at Perspective. The connection is made by Mr. Woodward's daughter, Isabella, a practiced flirt who maneuvers for the attentions of Cyril Scott, a satisfying complication for the hero's rival. The Victorian reader would be somewhat encouraged that this situation seemed to be heading after all to a satisfying conclusion in which Smith, after a battle, would get the girl—Harriet.

Alarms go off, however, when the third book is surprisingly given a title that would be expected of the final book: "Courtship and Marriage." Our Victorian reader would then be revolted to see that the courtship and marriage turn out to be that of Harriet Russell and Cyril Scott, for Smith was expected to show his romantic mettle by besting his rival. Smith compounds his romantic failure by serving as witness to the wedding and otherwise assisting the couple in an all-too-civilized manner. Smith is invited along with the wedding party to the house of Lady Geraldine, where he attends a recital by the poet Hawkshaw, friend of Cyril Scott. Here the novel makes clear not only that Smith is nature's nobleman, protecting Harriet from a rude former suitor, but that, even more revolting, the point of it all has been not to get Smith happily married but to show his natural superiority to the assorted frauds of the art world.[11] The horrified Victorian reader discovers that the marriage scene that was supposed to end the novel is subordinated to and rendered anticlimactic by Smith's and the novel's questioning of conventional artistry, which turns out to have been more important to Smith all along.

The fourth book also has a surprising title—"Flirtation." Flirtation is supposed to come early in a novel when boy meets girl, or in the middle for complication. Things are out of order here. Perhaps there would be some consolation for the conventional reader in the novel's at least being back on the romantic track were it not for the way the hero invariably gets off the track when his search for an authentic self takes precedence over romantic interest. Though Smith becomes involved in a triangle with Isabella Woodward and Hawkshaw, he confounds Hawkshaw with his probity and disillusions Isabella by his honorable intentions, on the one hand, and by his rationalistic criticism of her cherished Catholicism on the other. Whatever hopes the Victorian reader would hold for things turning out all right after all are dashed again by Smith's deliberately inept romancing of the rather frightening Belle Woodward. After the triangle breaks up, the book ends with Smith's decision to go into the civil service for lack of anything better to do and, some unspecified time later, in a much-revised epilogue, with a diagnosis of Smith's immaturity by a now matronly Harriet.

The original epilogue found the 1879 Shaw daydreaming for two pages (subsequently cut) that Smith after five years' civil service employment in South Kensington has triumphantly overcome most of his emotional and psychological disabilities and is now possessed of a serene philosophy. After he woke up, the 1879 Shaw canceled that serene Smith out by returning his hero to an essentially negative position, not much further along. The original has more tying up of loose ends than the final version, but even it lacks the sense of resolution the Victorian reader would expect, for Smith ends up in a very unsettled condition, no "happily ever after" anywhere in sight.

Shaw's alternate title for this novel was *A Quadrille,* a title he could have given to many of his works that express his sense of the dating game as a chancy dance. Smith enjoys the exchange of partners in the dance of life he rather bumblingly takes part in but, perhaps cleverly, escapes them all, for he has a higher destiny than domesticity if only he can wait for it. But the reviewers were right that a Victorian audience would have found this inconclusiveness "unattractive." It's not so much that the young Shaw lacked a sense of an audience when writing these novels, as some critics have charged, but that the audience he envisioned was either one he wished to attack (he had an all-too-vivid sense of *that* audience) or one he had to create, something like that "pit of philosophers" he later envisioned for *Man and Superman*. But writers can't create audiences unless publishers cooperate.

Shaw joked that even the mice hadn't been able to finish the manuscript of his first novel, referring to the universal dyspepsia of the reviewers whose cultivated Victorian tastes prevented them from adequately digesting it (*Cashel Byron's Profession* ix). Hear the reader for Macmillan:

> I have given more than usual attention to this M.S., for it has a certain quality to it—not exactly of an attractive kind, but still not common. It is the work of a humourist and a realist, crossed, however, by veins of merely literary discussion. There is a piquant oddity about the situation now and then: and the characters are certainly not drawn after the conventional patterns of fiction. It is dry and ironic in flavor. . . . Recognizing all these things, I ask myself what it is all about; what is the key, the purpose, the meaning of a long work of this kind *without plot or issue*. . . . It is undoubtedly clever, but most readers would find it dry, unattractive, and *too devoid of any sort of emotion*. And then it is very long." (Morgan, *House of Macmillan* 119; italics added)

It is not surprising that the Victorian reader missed the point of the novel, for its point was inimical to the Victorian. The book is about a new, mutant spirit rising out of the Victorian ethos, seeing itself in rebellion against the standards of the day and seeking an effective identity to help it engage the Victorian world in a way that would force cultural growth. With Robert Smith the modern world arrives, whether Smith knew it or not, and it is a sign of the age's complacency that the educated Victorian reader did not see the point.

As for the reader's finding the novel dry and without emotion, that criticism would plague Shaw for the rest of his life, as he sought to open new channels for emotion and close the old gushers down. Used to wallowing in the salt sea of Victorian sentimentalism, many Victorians found normal emotion "dry." But now that the classical spirit has reemerged in modern literature, after the melancholy, long, withdrawing roar of the Victorian sea of sentimentalism, it is possible to return to Shaw's novels with the understanding that emotion does not have to drip or gush from the page if it is to be called emotion. "Dryness," we have relearned, is itself a way of expressing emotion. Shaw was using the "objective correlative" long before that term appeared in criticism.

The following scene, appearing at the end of book 1, perfectly illustrates the young author's control over the emotional charge inherent in his material. Robert Smith has taken Harriet Russell to the railway station for her removal to Richmond from the lodging house in Islington where they have both been living and romancing. He "was surprised to find tears in his eyes" at their parting, and once again sees all the "occult charm" in her bearing that he had come to regard as romantic delusion. After leaving her seated in the train, "he strolled away, noticing the grime of the station, and wondering how long it would take *a single man* to clean it. He endeavored to dismiss this impertinent idea, partly because he wanted to think about the dressmaker, and partly lest it should recur to him in a nightmare. But it would not be dismissed; for he thought of nothing else than of giddily swinging on a ladder among the sooty girders, trying to clean them with a towel and a small basin of water" (97; italics added). As his only real friend abandons him, young Smith can think of nothing but the prodigious and giddy task of cleaning up the grime of the world in solitary effort, the nightmare of a lonely reformer. The presence of such objectification of emotion should have informed the Macmillan reader that Shaw's art was far from being emotionless.

The Macmillan reader was equally obtuse in his notion that the novel was without plot, by which of course he meant the sort of mechanical contraption many writers used to tease their readers into reading further and to give them the outcomes that satisfied sentimental expectations. From the start, Shaw could not fulfill such expectations, as he explained, for all his works, in the following ironic disavowal of plot: "I can guarantee you against any plot. You will be candidly dealt with. None of the characters will turn out to be somebody else in the last chapter: no violent accidents or strokes of pure luck will divert events from their normal course: forger, long lost heir, detective, nor any commonplace of the police court or of the realm of romance shall insult your understanding, or tempt you to read on when you might better be in bed or attending to your business" ("The Author to the Reader," *Our Corner* 265). One of the anomalies of the nineteenth-century "realistic" movement was that it continued to use the old plot structures without considering the fact that, life itself being generally plotless, an art that presumed to photograph or copy it ought also to be plotless. In making his novels "plotless" in the sense meant by the nineteenth-century reviewers, Shaw was ironically being more faithful to the aims of literary "realism" than other novelists who had great reputations as "realists" but who sacrificed verisimilitude to for-

mulaic plotting. Attempting to see life freshly, as a poet sees it, Shaw let character be generative of action rather than impose the same old plot grids upon
character. He understood plot as the organic development of character.[12] In
that sense his novels do have plots, a plot being a structure of significant action that leads from point to point in a way that reveals human character and
develops a theme (the theme of universal immaturity, in this case), leading to
an open-ended conclusion that mirrors life's problematics. Where and with
what sort of woman can the incipient Shavian realist and artist-philosopher
feel at home? That is the question *Immaturity* poses and deliberately does not
answer in its plot, for there was no answer at the time, the New Man's New
Woman not yet being extant, at least not in young Shaw's limited circle.

Shaw's immediate model for plotting was the very popular bildungsroman
of Dickens. As in *David Copperfield* or Joyce's *Portrait,* the bildungsroman is
a "long, developmental novel, in which a young man serves his apprenticeship to life with its attendant failures and successes, to end up a wiser man."
It is "necessarily episodic—the structure of the novel follows a long development from childhood through success or failure, scene following scene in
chronological order" (Karl 16). A bildungsroman that focuses on the life of
an artist is called a *Künstlerroman. Immaturity* does not follow the life of its
hero from wretched childhood to successful adulthood, part of Shaw's aim
being to undermine such automatic conclusions, yet it does portray the more
modest progression of a significant part of that life in chronological order in
the bildungsroman manner. The possibility that Shaw had his eye on the
bildungsroman pattern when writing *Immaturity* is strong, but of course he
always saw things differently, so it's not surprising that his use of a convention turned out dissimilarly, so different in this case that perhaps it presaged
radical changes to come, such as a sense of plot that was ironically more "realistic" than that of the day's "realists."

Robert Hogan defends Shaw against the charge of being disorganized in
his plotting by arguing that Shaw did not intend to write a bildungsroman
"depicting one major character" (66) but was attempting a new sort of plot, a
sort that when later called "Chekhovian" was praised for being more organic,
more naturalistic than the old style of plot. The Chekhovian plot employed
ironic counterpointing of various tales, Hogan says, to effect "a comprehensive satire upon the totality of a society. . . . In the really accomplished uses
of this structure, the various tales are intertwined with much dexterity and

subtlety of effect. An author like Chekhov . . . will move rapidly and bewilderingly back and forth among the various strands of his plot, ever twisting them into a more cohesive unity by ironic juxtapositions and parallels. The final effect is rather like a half-dozen vari-colored strands being so delicately meshed together that the ultimate rope appears an integral one-colored unity of rare excellence" (67). Never mind what a deconstructionist would do to that "one-colored unity," the illusion of unity is what counts. Hogan believes, however, that Shaw's use of the Chekhovian pattern was not entirely successful: "Shaw's 'rope' appears, by contrast, formed by cutting the individual strands into long lengths and knotting one strand to another almost at random. This handling of the structure seems arbitrarily episodic rather than coherently meaningful, and this inchoate impression is further confused by several purely illustrative incidents intruded throughout the books, as well as by a number of ensemble scenes which predictably lack the cumulative irony of such scenes in a Chekhov play" (67).[13]

Of course in 1879 Chekhov himself had not yet written the works that would earn the epithet "Chekhovian," so it's hard to fault Shaw for not being ahead of his time. Beyond that cavil, is it possible to see *Immaturity's* plot as less "arbitrarily episodic" and "more coherently meaningful" than Hogan sees it? Can we show Shaw working more purposefully and artfully to achieve certain narrative aims that end in as much unity as a novel ever achieves, regardless of whether we see the outcome as Dickensian or Chekhovian, "realistic" or not, or as some hybrid? Perhaps we can see a more subtle art working than has so far been noted.

The problem is Robert Smith's absence from so much of the novel. Grene finds that Shaw's original deletions "pared back Smith into his final attenuated form," a "passive, hardly characterized observer of . . . others," thus producing "a novel without a hero" (231). For Hogan's part, although he sees thematic unity in *Immaturity*, his belief that "Robert Smith is not the book's dominating character" (66) precludes unity of character or action. But such a judgment depends partly upon the meaning of "dominating." Smith in fact "dominates," not by always being present on the page, nor by being the instigator of action, nor by using the force of his personality (as Oscar Wilde did in dominating drawing rooms). Smith is dominant in that the point of *all* the action is to help the reader, and Smith, understand who Smith is. It's a mystery novel, the "mystery" being that of grace. Smith has been touched with a special grace, but how and why and to what end he knows not. We are made to see Smith's specialness through a technique of contrast with other characters. Hogan is correct that Smith is too often missing from the narrative to make the novel a fully traditional bildungsroman, yet this argument evades the possibility that the scenes from which Smith is absent are told principally for the sake of further characterizing him by way of ironic contrast, a technique appropriate to both the bildungsroman and the Chekhovian pattern.

A possible misunderstanding of Shaw's technique is pointed out in the following insightful comment of William Irvine on the genesis of *Immaturity:* "Shaw was probably worried about London, too. Like most puritans, he was acutely conscious of the integrity and importance of his own individual soul. In the midst of so much indifferent humanity, of so much irrelevant striving and working and succeeding and failing, the clear, sharp contours of the mind and personality of Bernard Shaw grew a little vague, even a little insignificant. Surely a 350-page definition of that fanatically honest and independent individual would be extremely valuable. To write a novel was obviously a duty of spiritual clarification. This book was finished in 1879" (*The Universe of G.B.S.* 21). Despite his sarcasm and the tendency to forget Shaw's ironic handling of Smith, Irvine was acute enough to see that the novel was an attempt at self-definition; unfortunately, the rest of Irvine's comments on the novel reveal that he is generally oblivious to Shaw's technique of defining himself partly in contrast to his immature hero and partly in terms of his hero *in relation to others.* When the novel's hero is off the page, Irvine is unable to see the relevance of the novel. But everything that happens in *Immaturity* happens primarily because it contributes to the identification of Robert Smith, a "gracehopper" of Joycean proportions if there ever was one.

The novel is most vulnerable to the criticism of relevance in the Aldous Huxley–like orchestration of the Perspective and Perspective-related scenes, from all but the last of which Smith is absent (the original version recounts a Smith visit to Perspective near the end of book 2, but the final version merely alludes to that visit). Do the many discussions of art and life in this section of the novel take place merely because the twenty-three-year old author felt like voicing his current opinions on such subjects, or because they are an integral part of the novel's art? Irvine complains of these scenes that "the characters utter rationalistic opinions on philosophy, ethics, religion, literature, music, painting, and take a weighty interest in nearly everything except in getting on with the story" (23). Assuming that Irvine is *not* arguing that intellectuals or would-be intellectuals have no right to exist in novels or to behave like intellectuals if they do exist, his argument is that Shaw was abandoning the novel for the sake of reviewing his own weighty opinions on art and life, using the Perspective characters as mouthpieces.

But Irvine, indulging in a familiar vice of Shaw critics, does not consider, first, the fact that the opinions uttered by the characters are generally in keeping with their very different natures and that they function to develop the characterizations. More important, Irvine does not seem to notice that the reader is considerably clearer about the artistic temperament of Smith because it has been put into ironic juxtaposition with the temperaments to be found at Perspective. That was Shaw's intent in using the pattern of alternating scenes, a scene dealing with Perspective characters followed by a scene dealing with Smith. This approach is not just a way of keeping up with two different stories that will eventually intersect; rather a great irony accumulates as each scene dealing with the separate life of Smith reflects upon the group scenes among the Perspective types, as the life of a true, emerging artist reflects upon the lives of false but established artists. The two alternating themes are brought into rather discordant conjunction at the aesthetically right moment, near the end of the third book, just before Smith meets Perspective society at Lady Geraldine's Wilton Place, when Smith witnesses the marriage of Harriet Russell and Cyril Scott, the marriage of sense and sensibility. This marriage, struggling for realization within the psyche of Robert Smith as well, makes Mr. and Mrs. Scott feel foreign to Perspective society, just as Smith feels foreign to it. Perspective and Wilton Place are no more the proper lodging houses for the true artist than Islington is for the true man, nor are Grosvenor and Lady Geraldine as patrons an improvement over Mrs. Froster as landlady. A plague on both their houses, that of bohemia and that of middleclass respectability, the novel seems to say.

The Perspective scenes are, Hogan notes, relevant to the novel's central theme—the theme of immaturity. As Hogan says, *Immaturity* presents "a comprehensive gallery of immaturities. . . . Shaw is quite as concerned with the immaturity of Cyril Scott the painter, or Hawkshaw the poet, or Fenwick the wastrel, or Davis the brooding preacher, or Isabella Woodward the flirt, or mousey Fanny Watkins the shopkeeper's daughter, as he is with that of Smith" (66). One should add that Shaw is interested in the immaturities of the others principally because they help to define the immaturity of Smith. Smith's immaturity is not of the usual sort, Shaw is saying. To continue with Hogan's point:

> Actually, Shaw devotes much space and "plot" to his minor adult characters, and he apparently is showing that these characters are quite as immature as the young principals. Woodward, the Irish peer, possesses a clear practicality about some personal matters, but is hopelessly muddled in business and uninformed about Irish politics. Halket Grosvenor, the "munificent patron and hospitable entertainer of artists of all denominations," is almost totally lacking in taste and perception, and art is to him a toy valued primarily for its social prestige. Even Lady Geraldine Porter, one of the more perceptive older people, fribbles her life away by visiting her friends and by arranging artistic afternoons of an inanely frivolous character. Mrs. Froster, Smith's quondam landlady, in one scene throws a tantrum which reduces her to tears. In another scene, Smith intervenes to save another landlady whom her husband is smashing over the head with an iron skillet. That lady immediately turns on Smith, and, in petulant outrage, denounces him for interfering. Mrs. Watkins, Fanny's mother, is a foolish and irritable domestic tyrant who must be coddled out of the sulks by her husband and daughter. Indeed there are so many minor as well as major instances of immaturity—in art, in politics, in religion, in domestic life—that Shaw's purpose seems quite emphatically the revelation that society, in all levels and classes, is hopelessly, helplessly and irretrievably immature. (66–67)

To this one should be added that none of the immaturities cited are committed by Robert Smith, for *his* immaturity is of a special sort—a stubborn, priggish negativism, perhaps best understood as an inadequate reaction against all the other immaturities.

Rodenbeck has noticed too that *Immaturity* exemplifies the "posture of opposition" Richard Ohmann finds fundamental to Shavian heroes: "*Immaturity* supplies us with a kind of fundamental Shaw, a Shaw without the 'ideas' that so many critics find either confusing or annoying, a Shaw in which we can see the posture of opposition operating as a motiveless attitude."[14] This novel, says Rodenbeck, proves that the code of beliefs critics have come to associate with Shaw (Creative Evolution and socialism) were preceded by an almost pure negativism. Smith discovers himself in an environment that he does not like but immaturely can think of nothing better to do than priggishly oppose its values. Not until the last novel, *An Unsocial Socialist,* will the hero possess anything like a positive program.

A perfect example of a character who exists principally to define the immaturity of Smith as a reaction against the immaturities of Victorian society is St. John Davis, a tubercular evangelist who is ruined by his obsession for Harriet Russell. Woodbridge is typical of critics in finding "no real function" for Davis (7). But obviously there is a reason why Smith keeps bumping into Davis. Consider their original meeting. One Christmas day Smith ventures into one of Davis's revival meetings, where Smith is handed some tracts that "he found neither credible, {Christian}, nor interesting" (19). As he is musically inclined, he cannot resist joining in the hymn singing ("We will all be happy over there"), but he is vastly amused by a young man, "earnest and proud of his oratory, who offered up a long prayer, in the course of which he suggested such modifications of the laws of nature as would bring the arrangement of the universe into conformity with his own tenets" (20). Finally, when Davis gives a very affective peroration on his nearness to death and his trust in the Greater Physician to reward him with celestial good health for his perseverance in his evangelistic duties, there is much weeping and wringing of hands, but Smith, "proud of his cynicism," "looked as scornful as he could" (20).

What is Davis's function? Obviously, for one thing, Davis serves to distinguish Smith's superiority to the sort of immaturity that romanticizes existence for egotistical reasons. As Hogan points out, Davis "reduces everything, even religion, to a supporting role in a drama starring himself" (71). On the other hand, Davis also serves to further the characterization of Smith as sophomoric scoffer. The tone of Shaw's narration makes it quite plain that while he considers this example of Victorian religion to be extremely foolish and immature, it is no more so than the priggish young hero who scorns it. Smith, like so many young people who are repelled by the falsity of social and religious convention, confuses being rational with being wise. Seemingly a reaction against a hypocritically pious upbringing, Smith's rationalism combatively declares its agnosticism and insists that churches are abodes of barbarous superstition.

That this immaturity does not much improve in the course of the novel is proved by Smith's reaction in the fourth book to the Catholicism of Isabella. He dismisses her church as an "ecstasy shop," and after a lively debate with her on the subject of religion, he "strode home, excited by his hatred of religion, {puffed up by the success of his legitimate priggishness}, and amusing himself with visions of destroyed Churches and confuted priests" (376). But the Shaw who knew that Davis's condemnation of society was essentially correct, who would eventually add similar tones of prophetic denunciation to his repertoire of voices, and who would someday found his own religion, also knew that the agnostic Smith had gone overboard in his skepticism.

The typical path of Smith's sort of immaturity is from disgust with the real to infatuation with the ideal. After extensive reading in the works of such lofty souls as Ruskin, Mill, and Shelley, Smith "became intolerant of everything that fell short of his highest ideal of beauty and power. . . . He planned an austere religion for the worship of Truth; and made an attempt to become a vegetarian, which was frustrated in three days by the inability of Rose to vary a regimen of boiled cabbage. He was credulous when a reformer pointed out abuses, and skeptical when a conservative defended institutions" (54–55). In short, the young Shaw writes, in merciless summation of his previous immaturity, Smith was in that phase of development "in which acute perception, hatred of falsehood, love of liberty, pregnant truths, and scrupulous purity, are complicated with mental color blindness, unconscious sophistry, intolerance, platitudes, and subtle epicureanism. Being through the defective induction of inexperience unable to discriminate accurately the natural from the accidental, he acquired that fine instinct for the prettiest half of the truth which makes young men thorough in partisanship only" (55).

If Smith is immature in the manner of his rebellion against society, nevertheless the principal blame for his alienation lies upon society itself. Shaw makes this point in many ways, but especially effective is his use of setting. The novel begins with Smith's search for lodgings in Islington, just northeast of where Shaw and his mother would soon move. Islington is symbolic of the Victorian state of mind. Smith chose for his lodging "Dodd's Buildings," a smallish square containing "eleven {severely respectable} houses. {It was a quiet spot in a noisy neighborhood, and conveyed an impression that Dodd, though unimaginative as an architect, was a strictly pious man" (3). *Original wording:* **"The pavement was granite, pierced in the middle by a fountain, which with a clothes line, and a window blind inscribed 'Seedlings, Bookbinder,' afforded the sole relief to the dreary style of architecture followed by Dodd".**} Smith's knock at the door of No. 3 causes an ancient yet very Victorian sound—the scream of the mistress of the house at the servant to answer the door, even though the mistress is apparently much closer to it. Rose, the servant, is characteristically in no hurry. When a boarder complains of the continued knocking, Mrs. Froster retorts, "And do you expect me to take my servant's place, Mr. Fenwick?" (3). Mrs. Froster is more subdued upon noticing that the visitor is a gentleman, but she quickly lets her new lodger know of Rose's stubborn pride, the kind that goes before a fall. "There is a wicked devil in her. I have spoken to the minister about her" (4), explains Mrs. Froster, unintentionally explaining more about respectable, caste-ridden Victorian England than about wicked Rose. For what could be more "immature" than a system of caste that makes the purely functional opening of a door a matter of grave ceremony? Smith simply wants an open door to a minimal social acceptance, and if he becomes impatient with a way of life that makes the opening of that door an issue of morality, particularly by the likes of a Mrs. Froster, we can hardly be surprised.

Now Shaw certainly improved the original opening by replacing the one sentence indicated here, but the rest, left untouched, makes quite clear that the young author was already a master of communicating significant meaning in narrative style, partly through the sort of suggestive technique employed by all great writers to imply meaning beyond the literal. Page 1 of Shaw's first novel is the work of a very sophisticated writer, who would improve more in stylistic manner than in narrative skill or symbolic resonance. Like all the great writers, Shaw seemed to know instinctively how to invite the reader into a richly imaginative world. But of course the publishers feared that their readers would think they had been invited into a madhouse.

The narrative grows richer with each line. When later Smith is invited into the front drawing room, it is described as "Mrs. Froster's room of state, which she never let" (24). "Froster" is of course a Dickensian name, indicative of respectability's habitual chilling of all attempts at being human. Part of the chill emanates from the contents of Mrs. Froster's "room of state" her best, most pretentious, and thus most unnatural furniture, which Shaw enjoys describing:

> The table was walnut, and was covered with a crimson cloth, in the centre of which a case of stuffed birds stood on a Berlin wool mat. On the mantelpiece were an ornamental clock, a velvet watch-stand, and two plaster of Paris vases under glass shades. A convex mirror, encircled by a gilt frame of *earnestly ugly* design, hung on the wall opposite the pier glass. The win-

dow was draped with red damask curtains, which contrasted with the green
Venetian blind; and the appearance of the whole room was worthy of the
gentility to which, through many years of struggling, Mrs. Froster had never
relinquished her pretension. (24; italics added)

Shaw's "earnestly ugly" is among the more telling epithets for Victorian
respectability. The reflection that this earnest and ugly Islington was to be
Smith's home "struck cold to the heart of the tenant" (4). The man who would
later so often be accused of being "inhuman" begins his career by projecting
his lonely humanity, frozen out by those Mrs. Frosters who are *truly* inhuman, into the alienated character of his first hero.

Smith is further chilled by the ugliness of Mrs. Froster's relations with
her servant and her other male roomer, Fraser Fenwick, a down-at-heels
gentleman. When Smith is served tea, Rose handles "her mistress's china as
if it was her mistress's head" (7), then descends the stairs for a shrill argument. Shortly after, Mrs. Froster hastens up the stairs to engage the dead-
beat Fenwick in battle, the unholy noise of which penetrates the floor of
Smith's room. This fracas is followed by a visit from Fenwick, who makes
himself so disagreeable that Smith is saved from resigning his lodging only
by the opportune entrance of the intriguing Harriet Russell. The principal
point of all these encounters is the contrast between Mrs. Froster's pretensions of gentility and the ungenteel, ugly, mercantile way she runs her house.

Shaw thus sets the stage for both Smith's rebellion and a comprehensive
satire upon the whole of an immature society. Among all the symbols of the
Victorian age that have appeared in fiction, Shaw's Islington lodging house is
a worthy member. The lodging house implies that respectability is in business for itself, whatever its pretension. Being the morality of the middle class,
respectability always has rooms to let, mostly to would-be gentlemen and ladies. Roomers come and go, signifying the impermanence of this way of life.
The House of Respectability is a midway point for those on the way up (Smith)
or down (Fenwick) to the level of being either comfortably well bred or hu-
miliatingly ill bred, as the case may be. Being the straight chair for curved
spines that it is, respectability is always rather uncomfortable for the social
traveler. The true-born aristocrat or proletarian can relax in the assurance of
being in the correct place, but the rising bourgeoisie or the down-at-heels
gentleman realizes that he is no place at all, merely renting a temporary room,
and must conform to the shape of his landlady's morality just as his spine

conforms to the shape of her furniture. The House of Respectability is always more like an institution of spinal correction than a home. Small wonder
then that Smith discovers in Islington that a house is not a home, and small
wonder that he rebels against the unnatural constrictions of the respectable
way of life, a reaction that makes him wonder about the difference between
externally enforced respectability and the personal code of propriety that
drives him from within. Inherent moral sense does not seem to be reflected
in social status.

One of the important actions in *Immaturity* is that of people finding their
level. Fraser Fenwick, for instance, discovers by the end of the novel that he
belongs in a class below his birth, that he is not the born aristocrat he thinks
he is but a born shopkeeper. However, it takes him a long, painful, and embarrassing time to discover this truth. His function in the novel is largely to
help define the term "gentleman" by being so obviously not a gentleman in a
mature sense. Fenwick is all childish pride. Dissolute habits have caused him
to fall from the pampered position of his early childhood (having been raised
by Lady Geraldine Porter, a frequenter of Perspective), and now he struggles
to keep up the pretensions of refined gentility. Engaged to Miss Fanny Watkins,
the pious if somewhat rebellious daughter of a merchant, Fenwick is so haugh-
tily class conscious in his dealings with her family that the rubbing together
of aristocratic and mercantile class pretension produces an abrasive comedy
of manners. Fanny's parents are as determined to deflate Fenwick's aristocratic
ego as Fenwick is to assert his precedence. Mrs. Watkins is especially "not a
woman to be trifled with," and her own rigid code of respectability makes
Fenwick extremely uncomfortable in his genteel shabbiness. Thus Shaw uses
the Watkins–Fenwick subplot to contrast the false pride of Fenwick with the
more natural and unaffected gentility of Smith. Smith is not above a bit of
snobbishness now and then, particularly in his striving to be "correct," but
in contrast to the childish posings of Fenwick his behavior seems adult. At
least when Smith catches himself descending to snobbery, he chides himself
for this fault, or his creator steps into the breach to do so.[15]

Though immature in the manner of his rebellion, Smith is obviously justified by his creator in opposing the immaturities of Victorian society. But his
rebellion poses a question—namely, if a very intelligent and sociable young
man like Smith finds himself opposed to most of the social norms of the day
and his opposition puts him in danger of ostracism at the worst and social
disapproval at the least, what can he do to remove the opposition and con-

tinue as a functioning member of society? One answer, apparently, is that he can teach. He can rejoin the group by educating them in a way of living more acceptable to himself. It is for this reason that the Shavian hero is so often an arguer. As Rodenbeck says, "Shaw's problem . . . was to create characters who would be arguers, characters who would embody his posture of opposition, his rebellion, and at the same time stay within the realm of the thing they oppose and rebel against long enough to conduct an argument" (vii). If in *Immaturity* the principal action is the hero's search for a mature identity, one of the major devices in this search is that of argument. Smith discovers who he is by attempting to teach others through argument. His arguments with the conventions of religion, gentility, and art reveal to him by contrast what he is at the same time that he strives through argument to convert others to his way of life. This is the justification for the "discussion" in all of Shaw's works: the discussion serves art as a means of developing characterization, plot, and theme.

Significantly, of all the people available for instruction Smith picks Harriet Russell as his special pupil, thus establishing a pattern of frustration that would recur many times in Shaw's career. Harriet is proto–Candida/Ann Whitefield to this proto–Marchbanks/John Tanner. She is the Philistine female, as described by Shaw in *The Quintessence of Ibsenism*, to whom the Artist-Philosopher seems fatally attracted. The attraction is immediately physical, for Smith much admires Harriet's "extraordinary grace of movement and self-possession of manner" (12–13); he is "fascinated by the sweetness of her smile, and awed by the impression of power which he received from her fine strong hands and firm jaw" (13). He was accustomed to seeing womanly women "walk like parrots," but unwomanly Harriet moved "with the grace of a lioness" (13). She would be "poetry personified," thinks Smith, if only she were "conscious of her unaccountable grace" (54).

If the attraction were merely physical, however, it is doubtful that the intellectual Smith would have attempted Harriet's education. He sees immediately that as her body is already more "educated" by instinct than his ever will be, if he is to teach her anything the lessons must aim at the mind. He is encouraged to pursue her education by her eagerness for knowledge and her unusual reasonableness of mind. His own rationalism seems to parallel Harriet's common sense in their mutual scorn of superstition. Harriet never goes to prayer meetings, Smith discovers from Mrs. Froster, because she had been brought up by her liberal father "to believe that there is no good in such things" (26). Mrs. Froster had been scandalized by Mr. Russell's refusal to send Harriet to school "for fear she would be taught to read the Book of Books, where he said she would find nothing but bad examples" (28). Mr. Russell had told his daughter, "When you want to do whats right, youll see your way straight enough without the help of religion. When you dont, youll easily be able to invent as good an excuse as youll find in the Bible" (28). It seems Mr. Russell had brought Harriet up in the liberal tradition, allowing her to "go where she likes, except to church; and say what she likes, except her prayers" (29). With all this arrangement Smith can heartily concur, for he believes that "the majority of prayers are very little else than wishes" (23). In Smith's agreement with Mr. Russell, we have the first instance in the novels of the Shavian preference for devil's disciples.[16]

Unfortunately this apparent sympathy of minds leads Smith to misunderstand the nature of Harriet's mind, to confuse Shavian realism with Philistine realism. He does not notice at first that while his own position of rationalistic skepticism has been arrived at independently, the result of a logical-minded consideration of the discrepancy between religion's theory and religion's practice, Harriet has acquired her skepticism as an inheritance from her father, however reinforced it is by her own practical, worldly sense. It is therefore doubtful that Harriet would have arrived at this position on her own, as she is otherwise quite conventional in her opinions. Had she been born into a more conventionally religious environment, her opinion of religion would have sounded a good deal more like Mrs. Froster's than Smith's. As an example of Harriet's Philistine conventionality on the subject of sexual attraction, when Smith timidly shows Harriet his rather florid sonnet entitled "Lines to a Southern Passion Flower," inspired by a local ballet dancer, Harriet's reaction is as frosty as Mrs. Froster's would be. She is "sure {that} no woman who respected herself would . . . [dance] before a crowd of people without being decently dressed" (82).

Smith gets a good view of Harriet's Philistine limitations, particularly her inability to operate at abstract levels of thought and her dislike of fine art, when he attempts to teach her French and help her start reading books. She wants to learn French for business purposes, of course, and is disturbed by how affected it sounds when Smith pronounces it. She has a capricious memory, and Smith is confounded by its contradictions until he discovers "that she remembered perfectly all that he told her, and forgot all that she read. He found her quick to seize isolated explanations and impenetrably stupid when he endeavored to make her see analogies in the construction of the language, which he had a pedantic taste for drawing" (52). When he tries to start her on reading books, he finds to his dismay that her tastes are confined to romantic fiction and descriptive travel. She returned his precious Shelley as

"a good book, only fit for children." In revenge, he gave her Robinson Crusoe; and she, quite unconscious of the sarcasm, not only read it diligently, but contended for the truth of the narrative afterwards in an animated discussion with him. Struck by this, he followed it up with The Pilgrim's Progress, which she accepted with bad grace as having "good" characteristics, but finished nevertheless. The Vicar of Wakefield finally convinced her that reading was a pleasure, she having before considered it an irksome educational process. (56)

The gap between Smith and Harriet widens as they venture farther into the world of intellect. Smith is highly transformed by the educational process, acquiring an ever subtler insight into human nature, as he develops his potential for Shavian realism, but "meanwhile Miss Russell seemed to remain stationary" (55). She became acquainted with new facts but did not assimilate them. "Her new accomplishments, instead of changing her position in relation to the world, seemed to attach themselves externally to her, as barnacles do to a ship" (55). Her refusal or inability to budge even an intellectual inch is the despair of the rapidly changing Smith:

[He] was constantly puzzled by the contrast between her shrewdness and her simplicity. She looked on him as a very great scholar; but her admiration of his learning was tempered by doubts whether he did not know more than was good for him. She appreciated his intellectuality and freedom from vulgarity. Still, she could not believe in the real worth of attainments which left their possessor with an income and position no better than that of many ignorant persons. . . . She felt sure that he was wrong and the world right in most of their differences. . . . Being an ambitious utilitarian of strong purpose, and little sentiment, she held him in a regard which partook . . . of that pity which is akin to contempt. (56–57)

Thus it is that Shaw makes Smith understand the difference in quality between his own mind and the minds of the vast majority of human beings. Harriet may be "poetry personified" in her physical presence, but in the mind she is limited by the scope of the practical. This duality is artfully conveyed by the image of Harriet at the sewing machine. Smith comes to enjoy the sound of the rattling machine, for it keeps him company, as the vision of Penelope at the loom might comfort a wandering Odysseus. Further, the sound of the machine is the sound of industry, of commitment to a practical task, and to the professionally uncommitted Smith it has the sound of music. But gradually Smith conceives the sound of dedicated practicality to be a limitation. He discovers that Harriet lacks artistic sensibility. "That is the most insensible woman I ever saw," he concludes, "I believe she has no soul" (54).

Harriet as "soulless" Earth Mother—commonsensical, practical, and productive—forces Smith into a typical Shavian dilemma. Shaw knew that the skylarking male intellectual must flirt with the Earth occasionally if he is to retain his sanity and inspiration. After all, it is often of the Earth ("poetry personified") that the skylark sings. Shaw was one blithe spirit who recognized the need to emotionalize his mental life by occasional contact with the sympathetic Earth. Of Smith's fantasizing about the Alhambra dancer, Shaw writes, "The attraction of the dancer made Smith feel that philosophy grew monotonous if not relieved by what he called a little flesh and blood, a phrase which means, according to the nature of the individual using it, a great deal of gross sensuality, or a snatch of innocent folly" (83). For Shaw, human contact need involve no more than writing a letter to Ellen Terry or "Stella" Campbell, but at least he understood that the high and dry intellect soon withered away if it did not occasionally put down "roots" (not necessarily Freudian) into the soil of flesh-and-blood reality. The trouble with the philistine Earth is that she is woefully limited in her appreciation of the intellectual virtues, generally pooh-poohing the Artist-Philosopher's vision of Ultimate Reality, and would ground the skylark for life if she had her way. Thus he tends to guard against a complete grounding by making his relations with the Earth of the flirtatious sort. Significantly, the fourth and last book of *Immaturity* is entitled "Flirtation," the "Courtship and Marriage" being subordinated to a less climactic position, in the third book.

The metaphor of the skylark, however, is somewhat misleading. Certainly it misleads Harriet in her estimation of Smith. In contrasting the ingredients of Smith's personality with those of Scott, she decides Candida-like in favor of Scott, who despite his worldly success is the "weaker" of the two in spiritual terms. She "admired [Scott] ardently. He seemed to her thoroughly a man, susceptible, intense, and altogether different from the pale scholar of Islington, whose thoughts were like bloodless shadows of conscience and logic" (136).

It is only natural that the Earth should prefer an artist so susceptible to the beauties of her landscapes over an intellectual like Smith, who seems so ethereal in his search for Platonic realities. (In *The Quintessence of Ibsenism*, Shaw cites Plato and Shelley as principal examples of the Shavian realist.) Harriet will discover later that there's more to Smith than that (even as the more down-to-earth Ibsen was a Shavian realist too), but for the moment he does indeed seem more like an other-worldly Shelley than a this-worldly Shaw or Ibsen.

Smith's diffident search for identity naturally takes him into the society of art and philosophy to discover what sort of Artist-Philosopher he is to be. Once again he seems not to care for contemporary models, as found in Perspective society. The connection between Smith and the people at Perspective is foreshadowed not only by his writing poetry but also by his moving from Islington to Danvers Street in bohemian Chelsea to be near Cheyne Walk, the name of which "was suggestive to Smith of poets, artists, philosophers, picturesque old houses, blue and white china, wooden bridges, floating piers, and penny steamers" (88).[17]

Shaw obviously means for Smith to gauge his artistic sensibility in juxtaposition with his chief rival for Harriet's affections, the painter Cyril Scott. To make the contest more even, Scott is presented as a relatively authentic artist. Although he is not without some affectation in dress and manner, and is "superficially spoiled," it is clear that Scott is a genuine craftsman among the assorted frauds of Perspective. He could look "at the setting sun with a workmanlike attention which contrasted with the gloomy absorption affected by some others" (117). But, dominated by his sensibility, Scott is a monster of artistic pride, never relaxing for a moment his scorn of critics, amateurs, and mediocrity. "There were scarcely four artists in England whom Scott liked, and not more than two who liked him" (131). Scott is hampered in the war of art theories, however, by being "so in earnest that his own irony, labored and sometimes coarse, seemed less a weapon than a wound" (131). He has developed a reputation for being a rather blunt, uncordial sort whose aesthetic honesty will countenance no flattery, either to or from himself. Although he is beginning to win a reluctant recognition, Scott feels no gratitude, having experienced so many bitter disappointments. In short, he is the personification of Neglected Genius, a well-nourished part of the being of the obscure young Shaw. The problem for any young, unknown artist is to keep that feeling from distorting one's personality. The young Shaw, for instance, writes of Smith that it was good for him that he "received no encouragement to in-

dulge in that clamor for sympathy, the whining expression of which is sometimes regarded . . . as a sort of trade mark of genius" (83). The sort of artist
who trades on his sensibility soon becomes nothing but sensibility, or rather
its appearance.

Shaw engages Cyril Scott in an amorous debate with Harriet Russell intended to clarify the issue of sense and sensibility, their debate being an objectification of one taking place within the psyche of Smith.

Round one of this exchange occurs in a Perspective gallery, where Scott
accidentally meets Harriet as she is viewing one of his impressionistic paintings, "Fretted with Golden Fires." After much agonizing protocol, Harriet
is induced to criticize Scott's painting, unaware that it is his. Unfortunately
for the painter she has "her thimble on," meaning that the practical dressmaker is geared to see only affectation in such paintings, "as if the painter
was thinking a good deal about himself" (134). She is further dismayed to
learn that Grosvenor paid 450 pounds for it, concluding that it must have been
out of pity for the artist. Scott is momentarily floored by her criticism but
eventually comes to see the truth of it. In the course of his affair with Harriet,
he learns the lesson of his prideful and querulous nature.

In the debate between sense and sensibility, it is clear that sense has all the
advantage, for it is part of sense's character never to make a fool of herself.
Sensibility, on the other hand, never fails to make a fool of himself. This is
symbolically conveyed in a comic scene upon the river involving Scott,
Harriet, and Hawkshaw. The first of Shaw's admirably "unwomanly women,"
Harriet expertly handles the sculling of the boat until Hawkshaw's gallantry
and Scott's humiliation force her to hand over the oars. Although the two artists had been expert enough at appreciating the idyllic scenes they had been
rowed through, they are miserable failures at pulling the oars of common industry. They clumsily smite themselves with the oars and nearly capsize the
boat, saved only by Harriet's quick agility. As the two artists nurse their
wounded sensibilities, Harriet rows the boat to shore with an extra pair of
sculls.

While Hawkshaw good-naturedly luxuriates in his humiliation, Scott remains stiff-necked and pettish. Harriet points out the difference in attitude
to Scott, who defends himself with a long speech on the trials and tribulations of being an artist. The special strains of artistic creation, he argues, make
"the gratuitous worries of commonplace life doubly unendurable. Just think
of all this when you see me irritated for a moment by some trifle; and above

all, remember that it is this very sensitiveness which makes sympathy so indescribably precious to an artist" (285). Harriet replies that this need for sympathy is "nothing but a fashion. . . . People nowadays are proud of being pettish, and think it a great thing to say that they are hard to please; that they cant bear this, and cant endure that; that they are misunderstood" (286). Scott indignantly wants to know if she thinks "an artist's feelings are as blunt as those of a stockbroker." Harriet defends her class and adds a Shavian moral: "I dont see why a stockbroker should not have feelings like an artist: although he has to learn to keep them to himself, and to know his place in the world. But in any case, if an artist is superior in feeling, he ought to be just as superior in self-control" (286).[18] Many of Harriet's opinions on art and artists are quotations of Smith. He has taught her that the artist who does not know that his displays of temperament are only theatrically amusing is a great fool, and this lesson she teaches to Scott. The influence of Smith begins to spread.

Robert Hogan raises the question of the consistency of Shaw's characterizations in *Immaturity*, a recurrent theme in the criticism of all of Shaw's works. One answer I explored in an article titled "Shavian Psychology," where I proposed that in his characterization Shaw was trying to avoid stereotypes and to draw more from nature by showing his characters as torn by internal conflict, as real human beings who, unlike the characters of fiction, are naturally inconsistent. To put it in terms of the character types Shaw presented in *The Quintessence of Ibsenism,* his characters' "inconsistency" can be accounted for by the fact that "realist," "idealist," and "Philistine" principles war within their psyches, which in moments of crisis are dominated by the strongest of the principles, thus giving them a character note. An idealist can have moments of philistinism and realism, a Philistine moments of idealism and realism, and a realist, like Ibsen's Julian the Apostate, can relapse to idealism and philistinism. This idea of a struggle for psychic dominance seems to have been at work in Shaw's characterizations from the beginning, and it can account for Hogan's perception of some "wavering of line" in the drawing of Smith, Scott, and Harriet (70). Any one of them can on occasion express philistinism, idealism, or realism, but usually they are dominated by one of the three. The "wavering" may be accounted for not by a shaky hand but by Shaw's early intuition of the shakiness of personality.

The principle of character foiling can also account for some apparent "inconsistencies." For example, the clash between idealist and realist principles mentioned here can account for Shaw's creation of Scott as part artistic po-

seur and part genuine artist, but this inner conflict also serves character foiling, for Scott's not being 100 percent poseur like Hawkshaw obviously sets
up instructive contrasts. Shaw wanted to distinguish between two different
gradations of artistic immaturity for the sake of more clearly defining the
character of Smith. Scott's posing is the result of an aggravated pride and
sensibility, behind which there is real talent, whereas the posing of Hawkshaw
is the result of an incorrigible, if entertaining, dishonesty. Scott is earnest
where Hawkshaw is gaily deceiving. Scott plays the role of artist in order to
defend himself against doubts of his talent, whereas Hawkshaw assumes
the disguise of artist purely for the delight of impersonation and its social re-
wards. The point of the distinction is that Robert Smith avoids both sorts of
impersonation, for they are merely clichés, acceptable to society, that do nothing more than warp the personality of the true artist to the point where he is
more concerned with looking like an artist than with actually being an artist.
Cyril Scott comes to see (as the result of a lesson passed along from Smith
to Harriet) that he can stand alone on the product of his genius and need not
squeeze himself into anyone's image of what an artist should be. Shaw never
tired of exemplifying the point that people are what people do, not what they
look or profess to be. A true artist is nothing other than someone who creates true art. Shaw is obviously dismissing here both the commercial "hawk-
ing" kind of Shawness represented by "Hawkshaw" (an adumbration of
Oscar Wilde, some have said) and the artistic integrity monstrosity of Cyril
Scott.

The character of Harriet Russell too is more consistent than seems the case,
or at least her inconsistencies are part of the drawing. To Hogan, Harriet seems
to transform suddenly from the "merely unlearned, drably matter-of-fact, and
quietly opinionated" young dressmaker of the first book to the straight-talk-
ing, clear-sighted, rationalistic, unconventional New Woman of the rest of the
novel. Shaw started out to draw a Philistine, thinks Hogan, and wound up
drawing "the Shavian New Woman à la Vivie Warren" (48). It's true that the
Harriet of the final three books is somewhat different from the Harriet of the
first book, but that difference may not constitute an inartistic inconsistency.

For one thing, Harriet Russell takes a while to get to know. On first acquaintance, she seems a rather different person from what she becomes after
a greater degree of intimacy. Hawkshaw, for instance, had at first thought her
"made of steel, with a heart of snow, triply Scotch, the idealization of matter-
of-fact, the sepulchre of emotion, the shrine and sanctuary of canniness" (257).

To the poet she was a desert, in which the fertile sensibilities of poor Cyril would wither and die. But after the boating incident, Hawkshaw recants: "She is altogether charming. When I said she had no softness, no feeling, no sympathy, I blasphemed. Beneath the veil of her incomparable originality, she is made up of all three" (287). Thus rather than Harriet's character undergoing a change in this respect, it is more a matter of a change in opinion of her after knowing her better.

For another thing, if Harriet seems to transform from the Philistine female to the New Woman, the illusion is due largely to a change of company. Who remains always the same whatever the company kept? Shaw right from the beginning seemed to understand a subtle point of characterization (later made much of in Strindberg's preface to *Miss Julie*)—namely, that personality is relative to circumstance. What we are is often a response to where we are and with whom. It is quite natural that Harriet in the company of the "pale scholar of Islington" would be different from Harriet in the company of such poseurs as Hawkshaw and Cyril Scott. Harriet seems somewhat baffled and intimidated by the extraordinary Smith, whereas she is thoroughly competent to penetrate the foolish and transparent disguises of Scott and Hawkshaw. Whenever Smith himself acts as a poseur (the Shelleyan radical), Harriet is able to debunk him quite as thoroughly as she does the others. For the most part, Smith's hyperrationalism and hyperunconventionality make her own common sense and hereditary unconventionality seem pale by comparison, but when that same common sense and unconventionality are put in contrast with the affected sensibilities and rigid proprieties of the Perspective crowd, they do indeed make her look more like Smith than like the Philistine she essentially is. Shaw never tired either of making the point that some Philistines, especially those unconventionally raised, are easily mistaken for Shavian realists, as later Candida would often be misconstrued by the "Candidamaniacs." It is true that Harriet becomes more sure of herself after her marriage to Scott and her acceptance by society, that she is better educated (mostly by Smith) in her opinions on life and art, that she is less prissily girlish and more womanly-matronly—in short, she is wiser for her experiences—but all of these changes are the natural result of experiences recounted in the novel. She is indeed a subtly developing character, but she is not "suddenly transformed" from one sort of person to an entirely different sort. Beneath all the changes is a basic philistinism. Although Shaw's epilogue has her question the idealism of conventional marriage, just as in *The Quintessence of Ibsenism* Shaw says

Philistines think such idealism "a crack-brained fuss about nothing" (*Major Critical Essays* 49), for herself she has found marriage to be most comfortable, quite unlike both Vivie Warren and the realist of *The Quintessence of Ibsenism*. Smith speaks the part of the Shavian realist when he replies to her Philistine questioning of marriage on practical grounds with a more radical pronouncement: {"[Marriage] doesn't seem to have anything to do with me. . . . If it did not exist I should never dream of inventing it."}

Hogan believes that Harriet and Smith provide two different standards of maturity, both unconventional, against which the immaturity of the other characters is gauged (70). Harriet is a "rationalist" and Smith an austere "super-rationalist," thus making the other characters seem immature in their various kinds of emotionalism. However, Hogan also believes that both Harriet and Smith arrive at their separate kinds of maturity by paths not clearly shown in the novel. Shaw, says Hogan, "does not show Smith so much in the process of a believable change as he merely reveals a different Smith in different stages of the novel" (72).

Once again, we need to look at the detail of the characterization more thoroughly and to factor in the role of circumstance. For example, Smith's quiet flirtation with Harriet in the opening book foreshadows the later, more boisterous philandering with Isabella, but if Smith in the latter situation seems unlike Smith in the former, that is simply because Isabella, the professional flirt and "womanly woman," is quite unlike the more serious Harriet, the "unwomanly woman," who has no time for such silly games. (Smith's being more greatly attracted to the Isabella type, by the way, establishes a pattern of irony that later plagued Shaw, who, as Grene notes, while promoting the unwomanly woman was often more attracted to the womanly one.) If Smith seems more comic in the scenes with the Woodwards than with Harriet, that is because the Woodwards and their stage-Irishman butler, Cornelius Hamlet, are more comic themselves and thus bring out the comic potential in Smith. Among the Irish, Smith makes a very funny English straight man. If in the scenes with Harriet in the epilogue Smith seems wiser than at the beginning, that wisdom is less his own than a reflection of the relative maturity achieved by Harriet. Had the novel closed with a scene in which Smith revisited Mrs. Froster, Smith doubtless would have seemed as jéjune as ever. Actually, Smith is not much further along in his quest for a positive identity at the end than at the beginning. His growth is mostly negative, away from things rather than toward them, his "growth" consisting mainly of adding items to the list of behaviors he feels compelled to say "No" to. Shaw's satiric point is that Smith is going nowhere fast.

In a section of the epilogue, mostly composed of new wording that the older Shaw knew would better sum up his hero, a motherly Harriet remarks to an older Smith (who is now his creator's age, according to the original) that she doesn't think Smith was "ever really a boy at all." Smith agrees that he {"never really felt like one"}. Harriet replies, {"That is the puzzle about you. You are not a boy; and you are not grown up. Some day you will get away from your books and come to know the world and get properly set. But just now there is no doing anything with you. You are just a bad case of immaturity"} (423).

Hogan is right, I believe, in declaring Harriet to be only one standard of maturity, nothing more than an unusual Philistine commonsense type, but his assertion that Smith is "not immature, merely inexperienced" (72) is dubious. Inexperienced is certainly the case, but more fundamental to Smith is the awkward immaturity of most of his responses to life. Undoubtedly Smith seems mature in comparison with many of the other characters, but most of them are so childish that the comparison does not say much for Smith, and even his relative maturity seems restricted to his moral perceptions. A major point of the novel is that Smith, immaturely, does not know where he is going. He merely drifts. That he drifts *ambitiously* is the satiric point. Whatever identity he achieves is largely negative. He knows that he is *not* Fraser Fenwick, or St. John Davis, or Cyril Scott, or Hawkshaw, and so forth, but he does not know who Robert Smith *is*. He senses that he bears some special grace but has no idea how to activate it. That lack, incidentally, accounts for the backward push of the novel. Its principal action consists of saying "No," sometimes to models of behavior Smith's society thinks is correct, yet another reason for the discomfiture of the Victorian reader.

In revising the final action of the novel, Smith's visit to Harriet, by then Mrs. Cyril Scott with two children, after a lapse of some time (specified as five years in the original), Shaw significantly emphasizes Smith's lack of positive growth by cutting out everything that suggested otherwise and by adding a sentence that concludes the novel with Smith's shaking his head negatively. The final like the original version puts Smith in a new residence on Thurloe Square near the South Kensington tube station, but the final version is fortunately lacking the opening two pages of the original epilogue, a long introductory exposition of pure wish-fulfillment (the novel's most serious lapse of literary decorum). The original informs us that Smith has located at Thurloe Square to be nearer his government job at {"**the department of Science and Art in South Kensington**"} after passing the civil service exams and receiving a favorable recommendation from Foley Woodward. In general Smith is considerably {"**mellowed**"} and now possessed of {"**a serene temper that can afford to wait**"}. The original Smith, having given up verse-making because he has {"**nothing new to say in that form**"} and now dabbling in physics, ethnology, philology, and secularism, is described as a reasonably happy man with useful employment and {"**a fair social position**"}. {"**He no longer fancied himself at any disadvantage in that section of the community to which he looked for congenial society,**" and "**a perfect confidence and sustained interest in the progress of the world towards enlightenment replaced the old fitful bursts of enthusiasm, with their attendant impatience and despair**"}. The action that ensues, however, presents the same old Smith, still lost in negativism, and, as Grene notes (229–30), Shaw in revising fortunately recognized the contradiction, eliminating everything that suggested that Smith is cured of his emotional and psychological disabilities and adding a few sentences to emphasize Smith's ending in negativism. Shaw must have realized that his twenty-three-year-old self had nodded for two pages and drifted off to dreamland.

In the final, more aware version, when Smith departs from Harriet with the verdict of his immaturity, he stops to contemplate the contrasting patches of moonlight and black shadow beneath a Thames bridge, after which Shaw closes the novel with the sentence {"**at last he shook his head negatively, and went home**"} (424). That tiny shake of the head is a vastly summarizing action that at once dismisses the life into which Smith has been accidentally cast and points to the nature of his immaturity. In dismissing the black and white categories of his age (objectified perhaps in the patches of moonlight and black shadow), he finds himself still in quest of a "home," a permanent center of authority, as opposed to the temporary lodgings and arbitrary authorities of Islington, Danvers Street, Perspective, Thurloe Street, and St. John Davis's church. In short, the shake of the head signals Smith's plunge into a moral and religious vacuum. About that vacuum, Eric Bentley wrote, "The freedom of the tepidly Christian home made it easy for Shaw to proceed to the second stage of Victorian belief: belief in unbelief, faith in the liberating power of a No-God. For when religion is mainly negative, the rejection of religion seems mainly positive, and men can be enthusiastic about a vacuum. . . . The earliest novels, insofar as they breathe anything, breathe the agnostic atmosphere"

(*Bernard Shaw, 1856–1950* 45). In this case, however, that agnostic atmosphere is satirized by its creator. When Smith says, "My position is one of pure negation. I am an agnostic," Shaw undercuts him with "he felt like Professor Tyndall or Mr. Huxley as he spoke" (269).

That the literary descendants of Smith will find a way out of the vacuum of agnosticism is perhaps indicated by certain rather curious opinions of Smith on the subject of religious belief. Near the end of the novel, after debunking Isabella's Catholicism, Smith nevertheless opines that "every man who entertains a belief, or a disbelief, has a right to become a propagandist, both for the sake of testing himself and enlightening others" (414). This seems out of character for the diffident Smith, but notice how ineptly diffident his propagandizing is. More difficult to fit into the character of Smith is the following: when Isabella laments that "people mistake bigotry for religion" Smith replies, {"There is no real difference." *Original wording:* **"It is a wonder that so many people mistake two names for two things"**}. "The {only} man in the Pilgrim's Progress who is not a bigot is Mr. Worldly Wiseman. I would not give a halfpenny for the {**real**} faith of a votary who would not cut off the whole human race if it {**they**} differed from him" (268–69). This sounds like the mature, evangelistic Shaw, much given to overstatement, but does it fit the character of Smith? Seemingly it is not like Smith to advocate anything beyond reasonable argumentation. The justification is that in drawing Smith, Shaw intended us to see his contradictions. Smith, immaturely, only *thinks* he is a rationalist skeptic; actually, he is a young man who is prevented from becoming a thundering prophet by a critical intelligence and a diffidence that combine to stifle his many natural impulses to evangelize. Deep in that chivalric soul of his, Smith is a natural champion of the Faith. The trouble is he's not quite sure what the Faith is, although he knows what it is not. It is not anything presently organized. Like himself, his Faith still needs to be defined. If we misunderstand Smith's character on this point, it may be because Smith himself misunderstands it. And that is a subtle bit of characterization.

Thus the general charge that Shaw was inconsistent in his characterization is not, in most cases, well founded. Even less viable is the complaint, typically applied to almost all of Shaw's work, that *Immaturity* is inartistically "talky" and propagandistic. Because of Shaw's preoccupation with ideas, he is thought to be inartistic in his neglect of the traditional forms of their expression—in character and action. Henderson, for instance, accuses Shaw of being "interested in fiction, not on the score of literary technique, but as a medium for the expression of ideas" (95). Shaw did not agree with this dichotomy between form and content, believing that characters who can articulate ideas have a right to exist in literature, and that the desire to express ideas through dialogue does not preclude art.

For one thing, "talkiness" in itself can be a trait of character. For another, in a portrayal of a rather sedate society that is more noted for its talk than for its nonverbal actions, obviously the characters will be talky. Indeed, in portraying the teacup society of respectable Victorian England or the bohemian but social-climbing society of art circles, the chief action will be conversation. Perhaps in primitive, heroic societies the heart and soul of the people are its nonverbal actions, but in the drawing rooms of London the prime action is that of speaking, and no novel that presumes to portray it can succeed without focusing upon its talk. If the chief action of Shaw's characters is vocal, then that in itself is the most significant point about them. One may legitimately dislike "talky" novels, but one should not confuse that dislike with objective judgments upon the novels' art. It is quite possible to dislike a novel that is accurate in its portrayal, profound in its theme, and excellent in its art. "There's no accounting for tastes."

As for the charge that Shaw substituted propaganda for art, *Immaturity* is not very susceptible on that point. I have shown how many of the characters and incidents that seem to have no function other than to carry Shavian arguments are in fact integral to the art of the novel. On this score, nothing can be more convincing than Shaw's ironic treatment of Smith himself. If Shaw had been interested only in propagandizing Shelleyan ideas, he most certainly would not have made his spokesman look foolish and immature in the expression of those ideas.

However, there are some points on which the novel could be vulnerable to the charge of being propagandistic. Two scenes are especially questionable. One night Smith returns to his room in Danvers Street to find his landlady, Mrs. Tilly, being struck over the head with a saucepan by her drunken husband. This scene of domestic violence challenges Smith's natural diffidence until he can bear it no longer and comes to the rescue of the "damsel." Shaw undercuts the potential didacticism by showing that Smith gets no thanks for his rescue at the time, as Mrs. Tilly believes that in submitting to such a beating she was only doing her conjugal duty. But the next day she apologizes to Smith and laments the influence of spirits upon her normally gentle and loving husband: "'I wouldnt mind so much,' said Mrs. Tilly with a stifled sob, 'only for the child. I wish the government would shut up them wicked public houses, and keep honest men that would never unhappify their homes without them, from temptation'" (168-69). That speech is perfectly in character and contributes to the theme of immaturity, but it also sounds like prohibition propaganda. Here Shaw, the son of a man who "unhappified" his home with drinking, was trying to have it both ways.

In another scene, the propaganda is blatant. During Smith's visit to a cemetery, he overhears a conversation between a gentleman and a gravedigger in which the gravedigger holds forth on the evils of coffin burial. It seems a coffin will explode unless the digger drills a hole in it to let out the gas from the corrupted corpse, and the gas has been known to kill a man. After this scene Shaw in his revision appended a footnote that convicts himself out of his own mouth: "In 1878 this scene was something more than a description of the macabre side of a young man's fancy. It was a plea for cremation, which was then a much more controversial subject than it is now. And it was a repleading of Dickens's protest against the grotesque mummeries of the old-fashioned funerals" (172). Again, Shaw was trying to have his art and his propaganda too.

It is noteworthy that the two scenes described here immediately follow one another in the novel, and the same chapter relates Smith's departure from the capitalistic firm of Figgis & Weaver. Granted that all three scenes are more or less worked into the general development of character and theme, nevertheless Shaw in writing them seems momentarily to have been feeling more like a social reformer than a novelist.

The next charge, that *Immaturity* is often irrelevant in its detail, can be refuted in most cases but of course requires a page-by-page analysis. The representative sample here is chosen partly because its detail seems minor and insignificant and presumably demonstrates what Irvine calls Shaw's "clerkish conscientiousness."[19] In this scene Smith is described in the Islington lodging house unpacking his things. He has some hand-knitted socks, but {"other underclothing he had none"}. His parents "had been too poor and too careless to make him any fixed allowance," and his wages as a clerk are little more than subsistence. Among his treasures are a family Bible, a Shakespeare, and the works of Byron. In an old tool chest he keeps two toy brass cannons and some chemistry equipment, sad "relics of his boyhood, and proofs of his homelessness; for who ever removes such things from his father's house whilst any of his kin are to be found there?" Evidences of an unusual culture are a few sheets of music and a Dürer drawing "representing a knight {accompanied by Death and followed by a demon, both of them grotesquely goatish" (5–6); *original wording:* "**and a demon**"}. That this itemizing of Smith's belongings occurs in the novel for no other reason than that Shaw had not yet rid himself of the bookkeeping mentality of his former Dublin clerkship is extremely unlikely. Obviously Smith's belongings are minutely described to make the points that they are few in number, that Smith is pathetically and prematurely alone, and that, an unusually cultured young man, he carries about with him the Dürer drawing as an image of his own menaced, chivalric figure. Here as elsewhere I find evidence that Shaw knew exactly what he was doing and why he was doing it.

Several reputable critics have been extravagant in their praise of Shaw's potential as a novelist. James Huneker somewhat ambiguously opined that "for no one of his many gifts will he be so sternly taken to task as the wasted one of novelist. . . . Shaw could rank higher as a novelist than as a dramatist" ("Bernard Shaw and Women" 536). That is higher praise than Huneker knew. Another of Shaw's American admirers, Christopher Morley, praises the novels to the disparagement of the plays:

> Well, the Daemon of the Epoch did have its effect on G.B.S. Whether for good or ill, it is too early to say. With his industry (as great as Trollope's), his seriousness (as intense as John Stuart Mill's), and his mad humor (as fierce as Meredith's), he might as well—and if publishers had had half an eye, certainly would—have gone on in a series of novels that would have been unlike anything in the course of British fiction. No one can read "The Man of Destiny," for instance, without saying, What a short story gone astray! No one can read "Cashel Byron's Profession" . . . without seeing its extraordinary charm, humour and spoofing. . . . I myself regard him as a great novelist gone wrong.[20]

As late as 1930 an anonymous critic for the *New Statesman* judged of Shaw's first novel that "if *Immaturity* had been published in 1880, it is certain that the novels of Gissing and Mark Rutherford would have been richer, more confident, than it was their fate to be. . . . There are signs in *Immaturity*, as also in *Love Among the Artists*, that Shaw might, had he chosen, have taken that place in the English novel which has been unfilled since the death of Thackeray" (Henderson 112).

Huneker, Morley, and the anonymous critic may be right that Shaw was perfectly suited for the novel, but the novels suggest the opposite as well, that Shaw became increasingly uninterested in the novel the more he wrote. There seems to be a disintegration, rather than a development, in Shaw's novel form in that the novels become more and more like prose dramas with long soliloquies, and they show less and less concern with meeting conventional standards of art, so much so that one recent critic has made a plausible case for the last novel's being an adumbration of postmodernist deconstruction of the novel.[21] Only the first two novels are "finished," in the sense of having rounded-off conclusions, and even they are open-ended by the day's standards. The third and fifth novels seem to have been cut off by an impatient author before they had been properly concluded, and the fourth novel so neatly conforms to a Victorian plot cliché that the use of it seems no more than a spoof, similar to Shaw's employing of genre antitypes in his plays.[22]

It has been argued that the form of the novel was not suited to Shaw's talents. Supposedly, the necessity for narration and prose exposition conflict with Shaw's love of the purely dramatic. When Shaw writes prose, the argument goes, he writes like an essayist, a polemicist. Only when he embodies his ideas in the direct action of drama does he escape being a polemicist. In the drama his characters, but not Shaw himself, may lecture the audience. There may be something to this argument but, first of all, I do not find Shaw inept in the handling of narrative in his novels, and, second, I note that Shaw's plays have more prose exposition and narrative in the form of stage directions than those of any other playwright.[23] His need and his ability to use prose fictionally seems not to have diminished after he became a dramatist.

Others believe that Shaw abandoned the novel because, after becoming disenchanted with its conventions, he had failed to develop an effective and significantly different novel form of his own. This argument has more merit, but there are signs in at least three of his novels that, even as the Victorian novel was disintegrating in his hands, he was moving in a positive direction toward something distinctly Shavian in the way of a novel. The disintegration can be attributed to his need to destroy Victorian conventions before he could build upon his own foundations. If we can accept the "conversation novel" or the "novel of ideas" as legitimate developments, then we can better credit Shaw with a significant contribution to the development of the novel. Of course the creation of genre antitypes was also a contribution. And the possibility that he wrote perhaps the first deconstructive novel is certainly worth further consideration.

More certainly, Shaw's steadily falling interest in the novel was due to increasing preoccupation with socialism and his role as a social reformer. Doubtless he must have wondered if he couldn't do something more effective to change the existing social order than write unpublishable novels. Or perhaps, as argued in the article that presents Shaw as a deconstructor of the novel, there was something in socialism that was inimical to novel writing, the novel being an essentially bourgeois form that reinforced the very power structure socialism sought to undermine. Most convincing of all is the simple explanation that he grew tired of writing novels that no one would publish. Of course *my* thesis is that he kept going far beyond what others would have attempted largely because he was obsessed by the need to refashion himself; it's possible that he gave up the novel only when he had finished with that part of his self-fashioning that was amenable to novelizing.

At any rate, Shaw's five novels are definitely quality works, not to be placed in the first rank of his creations but superior to some of his plays. Hogan writes that "one will never understand Shaw's five novels by assuming that Shaw really condemns them, that his remarks were accurate, or that the novels themselves are jéjune work." Quite the contrary, says Hogan, "if we scrutinize the novels clearly, we will find much more than jéjune work; indeed, I think that we will find the charge of immaturity can only be made by a narrow taste or an imperceptive reading, as impervious to subtlety as it is insensitive to wit and ignorant of delight" (65). While the title of Shaw's first novel certainly does apply to Robert Smith, it does not apply, for the most part, to the twenty-three-year-old author who created him. With the exception of the first two pages of the original epilogue, there is hardly a page of this novel in which the young novelist does not display an understanding or technique that argues a maturity well beyond his years. It would be just as impossible for a truly immature Shaw to have written *Immaturity* as for a truly innocent Blake to have written *Songs of Innocence*, for as surely as innocence knows not itself, the truly immature is unaware of its immaturity. Shaw's measure to the nearest fraction of an inch of the immaturity of both society and his teenage hero suggests the insights and skills of a man nearer forty than twenty-three. The proof of this contention lies in the sudden maturity of the hero of Shaw's second novel, which he would not have been able to imagine if he had not experienced it in some measure.

$\mathcal{P}art$ 3

A Dialectical Portrait of an Emerging Superman

Unless we are replaced by . . . the Superman—the world must remain a den of dangerous animals among whom our few accidental supermen, our Shakespeares, Goethes, Shelleys, and their like, must live as precariously as lion tamers do, taking the humor of their situation, and the dignity of their superiority, as a set-off to the horror of the one and the loneliness of the other.

The only fundamental and possible Socialism is the socialization of the selective breeding of Man: in other terms, of human evolution. We must eliminate the Yahoo, or his vote will wreck the commonwealth.

John Tanner, "The Revolutionist's Handbook"

Introduction

God Being Dead, the Proper Study
of Mankind Is Superman

> The proper study of mankind is man.
> —*Alexander Pope*

> The proper study of mankind is . . . Superman.
> —*J. S. Collis*

> In trying to be more than Man,/ We become less.
> —*William Blake*

> Man is not man, as yet.
> —*Robert Browning*

Some of the most instructive parallels and differences between Joyce's *A Portrait of the Artist as a Young Man* and Shaw's novels occur in their accounts of heroic alienation, its sources and strategies. Their heroes, having experienced what Nietzsche called "the death of God," find themselves dealing with societies that do not acknowledge that death and are thus hostile to those who do so.

Joyce's novel recounts the struggles of an intellectually gifted and spiritually inclined young man to escape the burden of angelic expectations placed upon him, partly by his own lofty aspirations and partly by a church hierarchy seeking to recruit such a lofty soul, expectations that allowed no room for his "sinful humanity." Ultimately, after willfully "falling" from such lofty expectations and denying the God of his church, Stephen Dedalus refuses to "fly" again except as the godlike Dedalus/artist, soaring only in his imagination, and then not until he has founded for himself a "religion of humanity" that allows coexistence between his high-flying, angelic mind and his "sinful humanity." His lofty aspirations henceforth are to be realized in creating, godlike, through his art, "the uncreated conscience of [his] race," a conscience that will be considerably less sexually repressed than that promoted by the church.

Shaw was every bit as possessed by a sense of superiority and lofty aspiration as was Joyce. But while Joyce used the angel imagery of his Catholic upbringing to symbolize the problematics of such superiority in the face of priestly recruitment, Shaw's rather tepid Protestant upbringing, with no priestly recruitment of him to offset it, apparently allowed him to escape church tradition more easily, to experience "the death of God" less traumatically, and to invent more readily his own terms for a "religion of humanity" remarkably similar to Joyce's. In Shaw's case the "angelic expectations" were manifested as the relatively humanist Shelleyan idealism he absorbed in his late teens and early twenties, just before writing his novels, rather than as the impossibilist, antihumanist priestly idealism Joyce encountered. Shaw was thus more easily able to convert the otherworldly angel (his "Miltonic mind," as Professor Higgins terms it) into this-worldly uses. That is, Shaw's equivalent of Joyce's "angel"—"the Superman"—referred not to moral expectations of an impossibilist nature imposed from outside, largely by a church hierarchy demanding such from a potential initiate, but to his own inner moral basis, natural to him and *not in conflict* with any "sinful humanity." He thus did not feel the call to angelic or Superman behavior as a burden. The positivity of the Shavian personality derives a great deal from Shaw's possessing a more unified sensibility than enjoyed by either Joyce or perhaps any other writer of the day. Paradoxically, Shaw saw the Superman as a fulfillment of his "human" nature, not as an angel he had to wrestle.

But problems arise in understanding what Shaw meant by "the Superman" if we read his play *Man and Superman* as calling for a *literal* evolutionary jump from homo sapiens to—what? To *Homo super*? Whatever the result is called, a literal reading forces us to ask: did he mean that he had already made the jump, as an "accidental Superman?" Or did he mean that he too was short of being a Superman, in this literal sense, as suggested by his satire of his disciple John Tanner? Or did he mean simply that his being "super" was figurative, relative to the Yahoo behavior of others who had not fully realized their humanity? The problematics of the Shavian Superman begin with questions such as these, which point to confusions between literal and figurative uses of the word "Superman."

It's clear where an idea like that of the Superman (or angels) comes from. Its inspiration was one part aspiration and one part desperation. Motivated by repulsion from the world and/or attraction to an ideal, human beings on the whole seem to aspire to something beyond themselves. Largely because the world is always in a hell of a mess, more or less, with death alone making the human condition less than ideal, humankind seems to need help to rise above the mess. In some ages gods, angels, and other supernatural beings are appealed to, but in other times it occurs to certain thinkers that reliance on supernatural beings to extricate humankind from the mess and/or mortality is not justified. They are thus driven to invent more down-to-earth and, they hope, more effective substitutes for the gods and angels, such as "the hero." Monarchy and aristocracy (institutionalizations of "the hero") have been the most frequently tried alternatives to deity and angelology, but in the nineteenth century the neutralizing of monarchs and the decline of the aristocracy under the leveling impulse of democracy coincided with a scientific skepticism that emptied the skies of religion's God the Father as well, thereby creating a double vacuum that Nature especially abhorred. After declaring "the death of God" and the decadence of hereditary aristocracy, Nietzsche rushed in with his call for "the Superman," a "new" aristocracy based on specific qualities. Shaw then democratized Nietzsche's call, changing the call for a new elite into a call for evolving a universal "democracy of Supermen" (*Collected Plays with Their Prefaces* 2:755).

After "the death of God," then, it was thought that the proper study of mankind was a replacement, which Nietzsche and Shaw called "the Superman." But was that concept meant to be taken as a call for a literal evolution? As Shaw seized upon the theme of the Superman, especially in the early phases of his career, he seemed to be calling primarily for a *figurative* kind of "evolution," for a universal maturing of the species homo sapiens rather than a literal replacing of homo sapiens. In religion, politics, and other areas of our communal life, Shaw thought homo sapiens needed to "grow up" and start taking more responsibility for its social-political organization, rather than leaving things to chance ("chance" meaning "market forces" or "providence," depending upon one's bent).

Yet man seemed incapable of rising beyond a certain level of civilization; it was that limitation in fact that had without exception led to falling back on supernatural beings when things went wrong, as they inevitably did. But Shaw thought that the higher power that man needs to raise himself out of the mess and perhaps even out of mortality, resides if anywhere in himself, as a potential. When Shaw quoted "the Kingdom of Heaven is within you," he was referring principally to the evolutionary potential within man. But would realizing that potential lead to replacing man altogether or only in making man truly *sapiens* (wise) for the first time? Although Shaw conceded that the potential was genetic, he insisted, "notoriously" in the views of some, that it was also partly *a matter of the mind's acting upon the genes.* The problem was how to realize the potential through willed acts of creative moral intelligence that would bring results here and now. "Mutation" was something we could will for ourselves.

Shaw's haphazard playing with language over a long lifetime seems to be the source of some confusion over the identity of the Superman, as its denotations and connotations kept changing to meet the polemical and literary need of the moment. For a quick example, look at the quotations that begin part 3 of this book, quotations from the same work—John Tanner's "The Revolutionist's Handbook." What is Tanner arguing? Is the Superman simply man purged of "the Yahoo," man that is truly man finally, as the second quotation suggests, or is the Superman to be an entirely different species from man, as the first line of the first quotation suggests? Perhaps Tanner provides some clue when he makes it clear that he's experimenting with ideas: "the proof of the Superman will be in the living; and we shall find out how to produce him by the old method of trial and error, and not by waiting for a completely convincing prescription of his ingredients" (218).

And so, proceeding by trial and error, as does the Life Force itself, Shaw seems to have shifted ground over the years in both his terminology and his conception of the superhuman. Following his own dictum that one should grow more revolutionary with age, his shift from calling the superior being a "realist" early in his career to "the Superman" in midcareer and "the Ancient" in late career suggests the increasingly radical vision of one growing ever more exasperated with humanity, more desperate in finding ways past the mess it creates and the mortality it is saddled with. The realist of *The Quintessence of Ibsenism,* derived more from Shaw's own novels than from Ibsen, seems a relatively modest claim for superiority. Our genetic roulette does throw up heroes and geniuses from time to time, "accidental Supermen," who may possess the sort of vision Shaw meant by realism: the ability to see through appearances or to imagine things as they are without actually seeing them. One of the two "Supermen" proposed by John Tanner, the one that has "eliminated the Yahoo," would seem to be close kin to the earlier realist, to the degree that dominating one's Philistine and idealist principles is the same as eliminating the Yahoo. But the more extreme conception of the Superman of both "The Revolutionist's Handbook" and "Don Juan in Hell," involving a literal evolutionary jump, would seem to be a quantum leap past the realist to another species altogether—to *homo super.* And "the Ancient" of the later, postwar *Back to Methuselah* seems an even more extreme conception, a Superman with such *contemptus mundi* that for the first time Shaw's Superman seems otherworldly. The Ancient is far beyond just eliminating the Yahoo from man or evolving to *homo super;* the Ancient is ready to escape evolution altogether into a purely spiritual existence—that is, if we take things literally.

But it's likely that Shaw, typically thinking both of the long run and the short run, *primarily* meant the Superman to be taken figuratively, as referring to the shorter-run potential of homo sapiens to become fully human, on the assumption that we have not yet earned the right to be called homo sapiens. In this figurative sense, *homo super* would thus be code for true homo sapiens, a code necessary to distinguish homo sapiens from *homo Yahoo.* The realist, the Superman, and the Ancient may simply be increasingly exasperated expressions of Shaw's sense of the failure of man to be fully human.[1]

Such figurative meaning is supported by the four quotations that begin this chapter. What seems like disagreement among them may not be such if we translate what may be figurative language into literal. Granting Browning's "Man is not man, as yet" and supposing that "Superman" refers not literally to a new species but figuratively to the realizing of full humanity by "eliminating the Yahoo," then the study of "man" (sans Yahoo) and the study of "Superman" (true humanity) would be the same. Shaw's calling himself a Superman was perhaps partly a joking device to call attention to how much of what passes for human behavior is really Yahoo behavior, but he was as usual being earnest as well—he really did believe that he was more truly human than most.

Whatever the case, the word "Superman" as I apply it to Shaw's novels refers to the possibility, as Shaw first theorized in *The Quintessence of Ibsenism,* of educating the self to the willing of one's realist principle to dominate, *when important,* the idealist and Philistine principles insofar as they are sources of the Yahoo in man. This is a considerably more possible agenda than leaping to a whole new species. In fact, Shaw made a notable success of transforming himself in the writing of his novels, of willing the superior part of himself, as projected into his heroes, to control inferior parts, as projected mostly into other characters. "The survival of the fittest," writes John Tanner, "means finally the survival of the self-controlled" (231). Shavian self-control was not a matter of repression (as in the Freudian system the superego may repress the id and the ego) but of getting the realist principle to make the idealist and Philistine principles serve realist ends; their energy is not blocked but redirected. Of course Shaw's works show too that being truly human is nothing permanent; it's accomplished only now and then, in our best times, its chief test coming in moments of crisis, that being the stuff of Shavian drama.

In that 1892 review of his novels, in agreement with Wilde's "Life imitates art," Shaw wrote that "the business of a novelist is largely to provide models of improved types of humanity" (238). He apparently thought of the transmutation from man to Superman as an artistic process. Like an artist, the person who wishes to transmute from the Yahoo-human to the truly human may work from models—living heroes, perhaps, but more likely the heroes of art, which may have been based on living heroes. True enough, the Life Force itself is constantly experimenting on its own (through genetic roulette) with heroic types without benefit of models. But if humankind is to participate in this transmutation by contributing intelligence and imagination, Shaw thought it would pay to work from models that would exercise human faculties, which then become the "eyes" of the Life Force, heretofore blind in its stumbling drive for godhead. Artists are important to this drive because their faculties are specially developed, and they are able to embody the heroic in art.[2]

The path of Shaw's own transmutation, which presumably left behind models of improved types of humanity, is recorded in his novels. In them he was already working on the concept of the Superman, a concept related to his own struggle to overcome the Yahoo in himself and to become a more publicly effective person, capable of motivating others to overcome the Yahoo in themselves. The Superman of the novels, I theorize, refers to Shaw's sense of his own uniqueness and superiority, and to his perilous attempts to be "more than man" (that is, more than Yahoo-man) at the risk of becoming less than man. Those early heroes of the novels—Robert Smith, Edward Conolly, and Owen Jack—come close to being monsters rather than Supermen. Indeed, they are perceived as monsters by others.

The novels recount Shaw's early struggles to assert an original morality in the face of convention without losing true humanity. In placing himself outside the usual definition of a human being, the moral "saint"[3] invites classification with the outlaw, his brother in "crime." Of course the "saint" does not want to be thought criminal, but the more his moral passion extrudes beyond the fixed boundaries of humanity's socially conditioned moral code, the more "criminal" and "inhuman" he seems to others and to himself. "Inhuman" is a word that Shaw frequently used, ironically, to describe his superhuman heroes, indicating how sensitive he was to the accusation, as well as to the danger, of being inhuman. "Criminal" is another word he used ironically, for he recognized how the person of original morality appears to others as being outside the law and a threat to civilization—the "criminal" Christ being the classic Western example.

"Inhuman" and "criminal" are definitions thrust upon the Superman from outside. The novels show the young Shaw's attempt at *self*-definition. If most people are passively defined by society, Shaw at least was unwilling to accept society's definition of him as criminal or inhuman. Gradually, through the novels, he interpreted his separation from society not as the result of a loss of humanity but as the gift of a higher humanity, a true humanity. He was being ostracized (the ostracism including publishers' refusal of his novels) not because he was inhuman but because he was truly human, not because he was criminal but because society was. This was a tremendous joke, but at first the Shavian hero doesn't see it as something that can be *played* as a joke. Certainly Robert Smith can see nothing funny about his predicament. By the fifth novel, however, the Shavian hero sees the joke, accepts it, and tries to get others to recognize it as a means of reforming society. Shaw's ultimate strategy for getting conventional people to see the irony was to portray the inhuman criminal everyone thought he was in such exaggerated colors that the contrast between the burlesqued Satanism and the reality of truly human behavior would produce a disarming comic discrepancy, one that would ridicule fear of change and put people at their ease with the reformer.

The heroes of Shaw's novels constitute a rogue's gallery, a survey of desperate characters who terrorize respectable people with their "inhuman" and "criminal" opinions. At first the hero resents his classification as inhuman criminal, then sees its comic possibilities, accepts it ironically, and milks it as a deliberate joke. This strategy is quite unlike that of the aesthete who solemnly accepts his criminality as a holy trust and who ends in a tragic confrontation with the society from which he is alienated. Very much unlike "Saint Genet," "Saint Shaw" refused to remain alienated. Nor was Stephen Dedalus's "spiritual-heroic refrigerating apparatus" meant for Shaw. What was the point of creating the conscience of one's race if one stood aloof? One of the most remarkable things about the Shavian heroes of the novels is their determined friendliness toward the society they disapprove of and that disapproves of them.

Chapter 1

The Proto-Shaw:
A Monster of Propriety (*Immaturity*)

> "I suppose you are right," said Isabella, giving him up as altogether beyond her, and raising her eyes to his with an odd mixture of ridicule and admiration. "You are such *a monster of propriety* that I should be afraid to write to you even if there were none of the objections you have mentioned. Here we are at the Albert Hall. I wonder your principles did not restrain you from bringing me the longest way home." (emphasis added)
>
> —Bernard Shaw, *Immaturity*

> Have I not also a dual self—an enemy within my gates—an egotistical George Shaw upon whose neck I have to keep a grinding foot—a first cousin of Miss Lockett? And such a model of a righteous man as that George Shaw was in the days of his dominion! How resolved he was to be an example to others, to tread the path of duty, to respect himself, to walk with the ears of his conscience strained on the alert, to do everything as perfectly as it could be done, and—oh—*monstrous!*—to improve all those with whom he came in contact. . . . And here was a foundation of measureless ignorance, conceit, and weakness! (emphasis added)
>
> —Bernard Shaw, letter to Alice Lockett, September 11, 1883

Shaw's first novel, *Immaturity,* is the one that inspired the paraphrasing of Joyce's "A Portrait of the Artist as a Young Man" as an appropriate title for a study of all five Shaw novels.* The hero of *Immaturity,* Robert Smith, is a Stephen Dedalus on the lukewarm Protestant side, though further along on the path of transmutation. As Dedalus was to Joyce, so Smith is essentially the younger self Shaw was sloughing off,[1] with the same mixed attitude of sympathy and mockery. The sympathy was, in both cases, for the young man's struggle to free himself from the stifling, far-flung nets of nation, language, and religion (among others, for Shaw), those nets society throws over the individual to prevent one's attempting to develop an independent self, and that some poststructuralists doubt one can escape. The mockery mixed with the

*For those who haven't read *Immaturity,* it would help to consult the plot summary at the start of "A Relatively Mature Portrait" in part 2 before proceeding. Reading all of part 2, "The Art of the Novels," would do even more to enhance an understanding of what follows.

sympathy was aimed at the misguided ineptitude with which the young man struggled, entangled as he was in false pride as well as in those webs.

Of course the Shavian "nets" were differently characterized because they referred to different circumstances, and Shaw added the entanglements of romance and marriage to Joyce's three. And there's a major difference in the degree to which the two heroes have to struggle to free themselves. It's easier for Shaw's hero, Robert Smith, in all cases because he's more internally liberated to begin with, though Shaw gives no explanation of this. While Joyce has Dedalus struggle mightily to escape the nets of nation and religion and even has him undergo some psychological de-Hibernicizing and de-Catholicizing to prepare him for his escape from Dublin and the church, Shaw starts out with a hero already purged (deprogrammed?) of Irish nationality and religion and transformed into the most correct of Englishmen. Of course, Smith's easier escape from Irish nationality has only taken him from the Irish frying pan into the English fire, a point Shaw will develop in later works in which the Shavian will assert internationalist sympathies against a demand for loyalty to Britain. As for the struggle with the "net" of language, for Smith as with Dedalus this is mostly a campaign to redefine words (such as "moral"), to rescue certain words from orthodox connotations and make them serve the cause of self-definition. (Eventually, Joyce himself went farther than Shaw in freeing himself from the trap of language, but it was a questionable liberty in view of the severe loss of readership that it entailed, and Shaw should be given credit for challenging lexical orthodoxy when it was more difficult to make such challenges.) At any rate, even though he has it easier in escaping the three Joycean nets, Smith has to struggle just as titanically against that alienating pride he shares with Dedalus.

As Stephen Dedalus was described in terms that evoke the image of the young Joyce, so too Robert Smith's description recalls a photograph of Shaw at eighteen, except for the hair color: "He was a youth of eighteen, with closely cropped pale yellow hair, small grey eyes, and a slender lathy figure, {**neat, but lathy**}. His delicately cut features and nervous manner indicated some refinement; but his shyness {**nervous manner**} {, though fairly well covered up,} shewed that his experience of society was limited, and his disposition sensitive" (4). In his first novel Shaw allowed the world to get as direct a view of his essential, undisguised self as he was ever to give, a touchingly vulnerable self, it turns out. It was a self from which he had already evolved into a writer who could measure his former immaturity and who was taking tentative steps toward becoming the self-possessed public man known as G.B.S. In short, Robert Smith is the proto-Shavian, the raw material out of which Shaw was later to create an astonishingly varied gallery of self-portraits.

In regard to *Immaturity*, Shaw said that "there must be a certain quality of youth in it which I could not now recapture, and which may even have charm as well as weakness and absurdity" (xxxix). There is indeed a kind of innocence in this book that is touching and that makes the sympathetic reader feel rather friendly and protective toward the little lost dog of a hero, Robert Smith. It is as if Smith had been dropped from the sky, a visitor from another planet, for he is essentially parentless and nationless. He passes for English, in some respects outdoing the English themselves (one thinks of young T. S. Eliot), no doubt expressive of how immigrant Shaw himself was trying to fit in and win an English audience (see Grene 231–34). Smith makes a few bitter references to his presumably dead parents, who gave him a superficially pious upbringing, but through most of the novel he is without background, as anonymous as his name, a homeless waif whose forlornness is qualified only by an obstinate spirit of independence. Smith may be rather lost, but he has a strange way of assuming his superiority to his situation, as though, like Joyce, he was capable of "parenting" himself, a "smithy," first of all, of himself. ("Smith" is an ambiguous name, suggesting both nonentity and the creator of entity.) This Smith does not particularly assert his superiority, for it is something he seems to take for granted, however groundless it seems to be. Shaw once wrote of his younger self of the Dublin days:

> I never thought of myself as destined to become what is called a great man; indeed I was diffident to the most distressing degree; and I was ridiculously credulous as to the claims of others to superior knowledge and authority. But one day in the office I had a shock. One of the apprentices . . . remarked that every young chap thought he was going to be a great man. On a really modest youth this common-place would have had no effect. It gave me so perceptible a jar that I suddenly became aware that *I had never thought I was to be a great man simply because I had always taken it as a matter of course.* The incident passed without leaving any preoccupation with it to hamper me; and I remained as diffident as ever because I was still as incompetent as ever. But I doubt I ever recovered my former complete innocence of subconscious intention to devote myself to the class of work that only a few

men excel in, and to accept the responsibilities that attach to its dignity. (xxxiv; emphasis added)

It is this sense of unacknowledged vocation that distinguishes Smith from the heroes of the subsequent novels. He is much too shy for the role of genius. "My vanity is shyness," Shaw many years later explained (Chappelow 142). "Oh, if people only would be modest enough to believe in themselves," he said on another occasion (Irvine 58).

Smith's timidity, largely the result of an unrealized superiority, is especially apparent on social occasions. When he is invited to Hawkshaw's recital at Lady Geraldine Porter's, he greets high society "with stolidity, the effect of fright induced by his inexperience of the forms of society" (299). Even after a better job has allowed him to dress in better style, Smith feels ill at ease in society and is painfully conscious "of his own deficiencies in polite intercourse" (217). Smith's shyness in society can be attributed, as Shaw explained his own case, to a shortage of social drill in his youth, but the problem seems to go much deeper. Consider Smith's reaction when on one occasion he pays an impulsive visit to Harriet at Richmond. Harriet is genuinely glad to see him. She has had opportunity to compare Smith with the grand inhabitants of Perspective, and in such a comparison Smith has gained in stature. She feels now that her former disgust with his Alhambra dancer was unfair. To make up for this injustice she greets Smith warmly and treats him to an intimate, relaxed conversation. But Smith is plagued with doubts as to his welcome. Fearing to inconvenience her, he cuts the visit short, lying to her about pressing business elsewhere. As he leaves her apartment, he berates himself for his lack of confidence: "Why should she not have been glad to see me? How stupidly I torment myself by supposing that the commonest human feelings are suspended when I am in question!" (228). Shaw is not explicit in this novel about why Smith feels this way, and the usual explanation Shaw gave later— that his own sense of inadequacy was due to mere lack of social drill, his parents never being invited out because his father was a drunkard—seems only a surface truth. Smith's agony after leaving Harriet's indicates something more basic.

Perhaps his supposing that the commonest human feelings are suspended when he is in question is the result of his sense of being *un*common. Perhaps too that is why Shaw could not remember as a boy having been tendered love by his parents (not that he hadn't been, but that he couldn't remember it). How could his parents love anything so inhumanly different as Bernard Shaw? The fact about Smith, as about young Shaw, that nearly overwhelms him is the fact that he is *alone*. He is alone because he is different and uncommon, a mutant, the "Complete Outsider" (Preface to *Immaturity* xliv). The mere "social rawness" that Shaw usually cited as cause of his early alienation he later admitted "was complicated by a deeper strangeness which has made me all my life a sojourner on this planet rather than a native of it" (preface to *Immaturity* xliii). The agony for Smith, as for Shaw, is that he is a very social person. Such feelings provide the motive power for much of Shaw's life— the drive of the Outsider to become the Insider.[2] He eventually achieved Insider status largely by becoming the court jester who is welcome everywhere. But Smith is far from grasping that possibility, his moral dignity being incompatible, he thinks, with playing the fool.

It is in defense of his superior moral dignity that Smith becomes "a monster of propriety." Unready to accept society's presumed disapproval of him, he immaturely overcompensates for his sense of social inferiority by going to extremes of correctness. No one is more moral than Smith, as befits a future "smithy" of the uncreated conscience of his race. The point is amusingly made in several scenes with Isabella Woodward, who dubs him "a monster of propriety" in consequence.

In the dual courtship of Isabella by Hawkshaw and Smith that makes up the final book, Hawkshaw is unfavorably contrasted with Smith. Isabella, by way of Smith, has lent Hawkshaw some jewels to pay his debts. Hawkshaw's letter of gratitude is a florid affair, "which she thought greedy in its acceptance, and fulsome in its thanks" (343), betraying a weakness of character that disgusted her. Smith's letter, on the other hand, is a businesslike and matter-of-fact account of the rather unpleasant scene with Hawkshaw caused by Smith's insistence upon a receipt for the jewels. His letter reveals to Isabella the unusual probity of her father's secretary, whereupon she begins "a new romance, based on respect for virtue. The figure to which she now attributed all the qualities most opposed to those of Hawkshaw was that of her father's decorous and reserved secretary. Before sunset she had imagined a phantom Smith, above all earthly passions and associations, and was abashing {abasing} herself before it, and longing to lean on it for support, or by some act of self-abnegation to win its respect" (343). Could the angelic Stephen Dedalus ask for more of *his* inamorata?

Isabella begins her campaign for the heart of Smith upon her return to London, and Smith, not being averse to "a snatch of innocent folly," goes along with her behavior up to a point. But Smith's manner of conducting a flirtation is an example of exasperating rectitude. Isabella, engaged six times, has never had to work so hard for so little. One day she gets him alone in a corner of a greenhouse: "She was soon alone with the secretary in a damp atmosphere of earthy fragrance, where the thermometer marked eighty degrees, and blossoms of a variety of delicate hues and fantastic shapes sprang from suspended strips of board" (383). Despite Isabella's hints about Adam and Eve in a tropical Paradise, Smith imperviously discusses the ethics of the Hawkshaw affair, especially Isabella's having kept the whole thing a secret from her father. Smith had counseled telling her father, as a way to get the jewels back. Isabella had never done anything so straightforward in her life, but she took Smith's advice and was rewarded by her father's reacting in the fatherly way Smith had predicted: he raged at Hawkshaw and forgave his daughter. Smith moralizes that once again virtue has vindicated its expediency. When Isabella wonderingly asks if Smith really believes that virtue is its own reward in this world, Smith cleverly replies, "If it were not . . . it would be vice" (384). After an hour of such moralizing, Isabella finally leaves Smith, considering him {"almost a saint because he had not behaved in the fernery as Hawkshaw would have done"} (387).

Smith makes a mistake, though, when Isabella persuades him to let her read his poetry, among which is the notorious "To a Southern Passion Flower" read earlier to a disapproving Harriet. Isabella naturally believes that she is the subject of that poem, Smith's Alhambra dancer being unknown to her. The next day, so encouraged, she traps Smith in her father's drawing room. Smith uneasily comments about the "terrific weather," referring to a very heavy rain. Isabella smiles at the symbolic significance of that fertile rain, as "she made her eyes large and lustrous" (406). Suddenly feeling an urge to leave at this startling appearance of the Life Force, Smith "felt the roots of his hair stir; and his knees became weak" (406). When with pale face and unsteady voice he asks for her opinion of his poetry, "she was touched; for she had never seen such genuine emotion exhibited by a lover before" (406). Smith is now alarmed at finding that his actions are somehow escaping his control. As Isabella protests her unworthiness of the extravagant praise found in the poem, "Smith looked into her eyes, and observed, for the first time, that her eyes and hair were dark, like those of the dancer" (407). She tries to egg him on by insisting that they give up this hopeless folly and become as brother and sister. When Smith eagerly agrees to that arrangement, she tries a stronger formula, calling him by his first name: "'Well, well, be it as you will, Robert.' (Smith jumped.) 'I have no hope to give you, scarcely any heart. When next I plight my troth, it shall be as the spouse of Christ. The cloister is more peaceful; and it cannot be less happy than the world'" (408). This is too much for the humanist Smith; he begs her not to waste her life in a nunnery. But she perceives that his concern is that of a humanist, not a lover. "Growing a little impatient {**in secret**} of his scrupulously modest demeanor" (409), she presses him to consider how this affair will end. Smith counters by discussing his meager income, five-sevenths of which depends on Mr. Woodward. "It is so delightfully characteristic of you to talk about five-sevenths by way of making love," says Isabella, but "you carry conscientiousness to the most fanciful extremes" (409).

As the interview is about to be interrupted by another person, Smith, "hopelessly confused, could remember nothing but the gallant convention {**Smith forgot prudence, and remembered only**} that a man who loses the chance of kissing a pretty woman is a fool" (410). So he kisses Isabella twice and flees into the night without his overcoat and galoshes. A fecund, Lawrentian rain descends on him copiously. "'Ha! ha!' he chuckles . . . 'that was not so bad for a respectable young man like Smith. He is a gayer dog than people think'" (410). At home, he stands before the mirror and gazes "at the face which had won a woman's admiration" (411). Then "Don Juan Lothario Smith" goes to bed.

The next morning Smith accidentally meets Isabella as she is on the way to mass. At first he refuses to enter the "ecstasy shop," but Isabella promises the ceremony will be brief. The religious spectacle has no effect on him except to excite his mirth and scorn of superstition. Afterward Isabella informs him that she is obliged to travel for several months with her father and begs him to continue his suit by letter. But Smith, on his way to becoming a civil servant, expects to quit Mr. Woodward's employ and of course hopes for his recommendation. Obviously writing to her would be "impossible. I could not write to you whilst awaiting a favor from your father, knowing how he would disapprove of it. Besides, you could not write to me—at least I presume you would not care to adopt the questionable practice of writing clandestinely to a man" (416). Isabella is struck dumb with amazement {"at the morality of this inconceivable young man"} (416). When she finds her tongue, she de-

clares him "*a monster of propriety,*" and bids him adieu. Propriety or no propriety, Smith steals one last kiss and waves her goodbye. He then goes his way,
"enjoying the prospect of a long respite from further {**encounters with his
sweetheart**} {love-making, and very far from realizing the ineptitude with
which he had conducted it}" (417). Sometime later he receives a letter from
Mr. Woodward that mentions the marriage of Isabella to another, much older
man. At this Smith gives three cheers, under his breath lest he disturb the
neighbors.

That is the substance of Smith's wonderfully humorous encounters with
Belle Woodward, the point of it all being that it takes the most "immoral" of
females to bring out the inconceivable morality of Robert Smith. Granted that
some of Smith's moralizing seems put on for the sake of fending off a designing
female, it is nevertheless deeply rooted in his sense of himself as morally superior, much as Stephen Dedalus thought of himself as angelic before his "fall"
(also into the arms of Woman). Smith senses that Isabella, as a flirt, poses a
profound threat to his propriety. In coquetry there is always the delicious sense
of doing something illegal, made all the more enjoyable by the fact that flirting
is usually harmless, but Smith reacts to the challenge of the coquette as would
a saint, becoming more extreme in his own rectitude. Belle Woodward's hypo-
critical regard for the proprieties forces Smith to defend them to the point of
monstrosity, whereas with Harriet, who sincerely insists upon the proprieties,
he is somewhat more relaxed in this respect. To put it another way, Smith is
more extremely moral with Isabella because in her he senses a fellow "criminal" and thus is all the more eager to maintain his masquerade as a respectable person, lest he be found out by the world at large. In short, Isabella con-
fronts Smith with his greatest temptation, the inducement to drop his mask
of propriety and declare himself the "criminal" he feels himself to be.

The foolishness of Smith's monstrous masquerade is evident, not only in
his involuntary stealing of a few kisses but also in his sharpshooting at Isabella's
Catholicism and at religion in general, when he gives himself away anyway as
an enemy of socially approved morality. Like Stephen Dedalus, Smith seeks
to escape the net of religion so as to be able to express his natural moral self,
and he expects in doing so to be branded by the phony pious as a "criminal."
But of course his "criminality" will be that of the Christ crucified by orthodoxy. While Joyce like Wilde and Nietzsche accepted an identification with
Christ solemnly (even to madness, in Nietzsche's case), Shaw joked his way
out of its consequences.

So far Smith's craving for respectability seems to be purely negative. He becomes a monster of propriety as a compensation for both his sense of social inadequacy and his sense of being somehow "criminal." But, as with his snobbishness,[3] his extreme drive for correctness in behavior seems to be supported by positive forces in his nature as well. Just as the snobbishness is supported by an ingrained sense of superiority, the propriety is supported by a deeply ethical nature. The trouble with Smith is that he has the natural confused with the accidental, as his creator states, and thus confuses class snobbishness with individual superiority and conventional propriety with an original morality. In this novel, unlike the ones that follow, the Shavian hero is very much concerned with meeting "aristocratic" standards, however republican he is philosophically, partly because these standards are institutional codifications of his own senses of superiority and propriety. He feels a natural affinity with that class which, in theory at least, shares his contempt for the base, the mean, the inartistic. He is not yet entirely certain that this contempt is more often than not only a learned class prejudice, unsupported by the natural preferences of most aristocrats. The horrible Shavian truth, best portrayed later but displayed even in this novel, is that most aristocrats, like most of the bourgeoisie and the proletariat, are naturally common and inartistic in their preferences. Nor is their propriety the result of an understanding and love of ethical principles but only a class habit with which their real natures may violently disagree. Smith, on the other hand, is all ethics. No aristocrat has ever been so scrupulous about his behavior, and no bourgeoisie so nervously insecure as to its correctness. If the monster of propriety looks like a monster from without, from within he feels more like a timid mouse, the outward monstrosity being in direct proportion to the inward timidity.

The irony is that Smith's extreme scrupulosity does not win him the social acceptance he desires. To the contrary, his extreme correctness simply makes him seem all the more unusual. Add to this his scorn of false religion and false gentility, and Smith finds himself very much on the outs with society. If his "posture of opposition" makes him seem a rather stiff figure, his extreme propriety makes him seem even stiffer. Thus, in different ways, Smith's uncommonness forces him into the rigidity of a mechanical monster.

Smith, however, is a very friendly and kindly monster who is puzzled by his own grotesqueness. He feels that something is wrong somewhere. From his view, the monstrosities of the day are to be found in Victorian social and religious practices. Yet everyone else seems to agree that the aberration lies in Smith. Which view is correct? Smith is not at all certain, however much he likes to think he is. If he has conviction, it is not the certainty of an Elijah or a Jeremiah. The best he can do is argue and scoff a bit, look scornful, and be extremely careful to avoid any improper behavior that would support society's suspicion of his improper opinions. The discrepancy between his "criminal opinions" and his proper behavior provides a natural joke, but Smith cannot for the life of him see it, and thus he cannot use it deliberately as the joke upon others that it really is. He is not ready to play a comic Satan.

Traditionally, the solution to Smith's sort of alienation has been marriage. The young man of romantic comedy who is on the outs with society is redeemed, as society is redeemed in turn, by his acceptance of the custom of marriage. Marriage rejoins the random individual to the social group, his random behavior thereby replaced, theoretically, by the predictable conduct of the married. Further, as the young man through marriage accepts the bond of common humanity, society rejoices at this new affirmation of its collective life. As the tension between the individual and the group has been replaced by harmony, the new couple is sure to live happily ever after. The pattern of romantic comedy is attempted in *Immaturity* in the bourgeois marriage of Fraser Fenwick and Fanny Watkins, and it is imperfectly realized in the marriage of Harriet Russell and Cyril Scott, as the latter marriage's simplicity and secularity reflect ironically upon the pomp and religiosity of the former's.

It is well known that Bernard Shaw, always keenly aware of the discrepancy between theory and fact, had no use for the conventional solution of romantic comedy as it pertained to himself. He had seen too many marriages, especially that of his own parents, that belied the theory. Shaw thus added the romance that leads to marriage to Joyce's three as one of those "nets" that enslave the free-spirited, and he deliberately organized his novel in such a way as to undermine that theory. Harriet and Scott find themselves more acceptable to society after their marriage than before, in accordance with the plan of romantic comedy, but Shaw subverts this, first by closing Book III, in which the marriage takes place, with the ghastly death of St. John Davis, a disappointed suitor for Harriet, and second by following the "courtship and marriage" with a fourth book of inconclusive "flirtation." The effect of the grisly conclusion to Book III and the antiromantic substance of Book IV is to destroy, by ironic contrast, the sense of an easy or sentimental solution to Smith's alienation. As Shaw wrote to a publisher in 1880, his design was "to deal with those ordinary experiences which are a constant irony on sentimentalism, at which the whole work is mainly directed" (*Collected Letters* 27).

Furthermore, the one person in the novel who in her common sense is most like Smith, but who has accepted the conventions of marriage, concludes the novel by agreeing with Smith that marriage is probably not the solution to his problem. Smith says that he {"can't feel marriageable. And I doubt if I ever shall. Is marriage really a success?"} Harriet replies:

> "{What is the use of asking that? What else is there to do if you are to have a decent home? But it is not fit for some people; and some people are not fit for it. And the right couples don't often find one another as Cyril and I did}. The routine for most {**women**} is, one year of trying {**desperate effort**} to persuade themselves that they are happy, six months of doubt, and eighteen months of conviction that the marriage is a {**an utter and**} miserable mistake. Then they get tired of bothering themselves over it, and settle down into domestic commonplace, quite disenchanted, but not tragically unhappy. Of course, children make a great difference; but most people get quite tired of them, just as the children themselves do with a plaything when its novelty wears off."
>
> {"It doesnt seem to have anything to do with me," said Smith. "It may be all right; but if it did not exist I should never dream of inventing it. Goodnight."} (423–24)[4]

With marriage dismissed as a means for the Shavian monster-hero of rejoining society, and thus of achieving social identity, the hero naturally looks for other means of achieving identity. For that reason much of the novel is devoted to presenting the dilemma of vocation, as Smith struggles to achieve professional identity. Perhaps professional identity precedes social identity, since people don't know if you are acceptable to them until they know what your profession is. It will take four more novels before Mr. Shaw's profession is discovered.

One of the principal functions of Harriet in the early chapters of *Immaturity* is to draw out Smith on the topic of vocation. The unemployed Shaw had taken the opportunity that fiction provides authors of giving to their heroes what they themselves lack by assigning well-paid employment to Smith throughout. Smith's initial job as clerk for wholesaler Figgis & Weaver echoes Shaw's employment before he left Dublin and echoes as well his contempt

for both the job and for himself for being good at it. That Smith fancies himself a poet (as the young Shaw employed in Dublin as cashier fancied himself
an artist of some sort) gives a clue as to why he hates his job with Figgis &
Weaver, "a respectable firm to whom he attributed the most sordid views of
existence" (11). Aware of nobler things from his study of literature, he wonders if there is "any profession in the world so contemptible as that of a clerk"
(49). "He liked work; but he hated the duties of his clerkship as barren drudg-
ery, which numbed his faculties and wasted his time" (11). Furthermore,
clerks being so common, the job requires a servility that challenges the cow-
ardice of even so timid a man as Smith. It soon becomes an affair of honor to
quit the job.

Smith does not quit at once, however, for he does not know what else he
can do, poetry not being a paying thing, and even if he knew what profession
he was suited for he "couldnt afford to take it up" (92). He reasons that he
can't go into the government because passing the civil service exam would
take too much time and money. "Besides, I object on moral grounds to sub-
mit my merits to a false test. In fact, I am bound hand and foot by circumstances. I can do nothing" (92–93). This rationalizing may echo that of the
early Shaw, who also considered the civil service, but, unlike the temporizing
Smith, Shaw instinctively avoided jobs so as to remain free to practice his art
and prepare for his proper vocation.

In reply to Smith, Harriet lectures him on her favorite subject—succeeding in business by really trying. First she deprecates his cleverness. "You are
clever enough to argue for all you do; and I fear that is all the good your cleverness will ever be to you" (93). She knows from her own success "that people
who set themselves out to do it can push themselves on and make their way
in the world." "True," answers Smith, "but suppose it is not worth your while
to set yourself out to do it. Suppose you enjoy yourself more in keeping out
of the rush than scrambling in it, spending your life pushing and being
pushed." "You will be left behind, and laughed at, and be sorry afterwards.
Thats all," counters Harriet. Smith sees the impasse: Harriet's view of life
"was a view which did not fit his temperament. Besides, the imputation of
being impractical was one which he thought he did not deserve . . . it was an
elevation of taste, and not want of capacity, that had led him to contemn his
daily occupation" (93).

Nevertheless he admires Harriet for so resolutely becoming her own mistress and expresses his weariness of "seeing fools and irresolute creatures grov-

elling along in the same old track, never finding the energy to grasp their fate by the throat and lift themselves into a sphere of free activity" (94). When Harriet wonders why he does not apply this observation to himself, he assures her that his case is quite different, although he cannot explain it. He would quit Figgis & Weaver in a minute if he only knew what else he was good for. Obviously Smith is very confused by his exceptional circumstances. He is right that "his case is quite different," but by the same token he ought to see that he is not acting like a young man of extraordinary potential in slavishly and timidly continuing at Figgis & Weaver. He does not see that the new identity he wishes to carve out for himself cannot be achieved until he breaks the mold of the clerk.

When Smith finally does nerve himself to quit Figgis & Weaver, he discovers that there is danger in destroying an accustomed role, for it leaves him with a severely reduced sense of identity and makes him susceptible to complete annihilation of the self. The point is made in three scenes, in Westminster Abbey, upon a river steamboat, and in a cemetery.

After storming out of the office of Figgis & Weaver, Smith visits Westminster for the first time in his life. No longer a common clerk, he is free to breathe the atmosphere of greatness, and to romance about the aisles "with the old religious sense of their peace." Avoiding the parts of the abbey set apart for commercial purposes, he revels in "his seclusion from the bustle of the world." His "hushed step, impressed bearing, and reflective calm" marked him "as a confirmed freethinker very happy." At this point the usual Shavian commonsense qualification spoils the mood with the reminder that "As a man far removed from past ages finds a romance in history of which the persons in that history had in their time no sense, Smith could breathe the atmosphere of the cloister with an appreciation impossible to those whom it still overawed" (166).

Then Smith boards a penny steamboat and contemplates his future as he flows down the river. He imagines himself in all sorts of romantic positions— on the stage, for instance, "attired in a fur-edged coat and hessian boots singing The Heart Bowed Down to an enraptured audience." His common sense told him that this was nonsense, whereupon he grew "disgusted with his common sense, which condemned these fancies, but did not prevent their occurring to him" (167).

The next day he does something even more romantic: he wanders into a cemetery. His behavior there is generally in the great melancholic tradition, but graveyard irony occasionally inspires a Shavian gaiety unbecoming to a proper melancholic. While strolling through the multitude of tombs, he "found his sense of the ludicrous unusually stimulated" (170) by the comic discrepancy between the pious pretensions upon the gravestones and the fact of death buried beneath. When he sees a woman planting some flowers on a grave, "a perverse inclination to laugh came upon him as he conceived the idea of the transmutation of the corpse through hideous stages of decomposition into the very flowers she was handling with such solicitude" (171). Thus occurs one of the first instances of the Shavian habit, to some very irritating and unfeeling, of making of death a joke.

In these three scenes Shaw is indicating, in fairly conventional symbolism, the reaction of a sensitive young intellectual to the escape from commerce and the fact of unemployment. Smith first feels the strong pull of the cloister; then, secluded by impossibilist dreams, he floats downstream on the penny steamer of cheap romance and finally ends in the grisly abode of the brother of non-effort, namely death. These scenes rapidly and effectively bring Smith to the point of return or no return. Being the proto-Shaw, Smith laughs at death and returns to living with a search for a new job.[5]

Smith's fortuitous falling into an easy job as secretary to an Irish Member of Parliament the day after quitting Figgis & Weaver may seem like wish fulfillment, but the character of M.P. Foley Woodward and the fact of Smith's becoming his secretary have artistic justification as well. It is through Woodward and his daughters and butler that Shaw reconnects the de-Hibernicized Smith to Ireland, and the connection allows Shaw to justify his own hegira from that benighted country and to show the Irish what they missed by not making him at home there. Woodward is the personification of Irish chaos and folly, and Robert Smith is just the man to bring order out of that chaos and sense out of that folly. In no time at all Smith arranges Woodward's affairs so thoroughly that the work that once took all day now takes but part of the morning. So impressed is Woodward that he gives Smith increasing responsibility in handling his affairs. He allows Smith to write his single speech for that year and finds himself consulting Smith on matters of policy. Throughout it all Smith is quietly helpful, quietly competent, a marvel of organizational genius. Though Smith continues to torment himself with the idea that he is unworthy of acceptance as a social being, he finds acceptance and partial identity as an efficient secretary to a Member of Parliament.

This acceptance seems to encourage Smith to pursue professional identity further: at the end of the novel he quits Woodward's employ for an unspecified job in the civil service (which a deleted part of the epilogue identifies as a government job in South Kensington). From "capitalist stooge" to private secretary for an M.P. to civil servant is an ominous progression, boding a Fabian future. Smith naturally permeates the government. At the moment, however, officially he is rather apolitical, the only one of Shaw's heroes that is. Part of his immaturity consists, in fact, in his lack of political identity. Shaw himself did not achieve full integration of identity until his joining the Fabian Society allowed him to combine his social and professional identities with his political identity. Achieving such integration is apparently needed to give a human being that positivity that is perhaps the chief mark of a complete, mature individual. Of course Shaw would enjoy pointing out that such positivity is the mark of a fanatic, as well.

That Shaw understood this need for an integrated psyche at the time of the writing of *Immaturity* is indicated by a contrast he emphasizes between the evangelist St. John Davis and Smith. Davis is euphoric in his certainty that he is one of the elect, and, while Smith may classify this as arrogant humbug, he is appreciative of the value of such conviction. "No doubt every man is happy who has work to do which he likes and believes in," Smith says to Davis. Davis replies that there's "plenty of the same work for every one; and youll find youll like it" (22). Bernard Shaw did find that he liked it when he became the evangelist of socialism and the Life Force, but Smith is prevented by his rationalism from commitment to any creed, even the creed of Rationalism. However rationalist he may be, or thinks he is, Smith is no prophet of Rationalism. ("I am no prophet, and here is no great matter," says Prufrock, speaking for the uncommitted of many ages).

In the preface to the novel Shaw advises us that "there will be nothing of the voice of the public speaker in [*Immaturity*]: the voice that rings through so much of my later work. Not until *Immaturity* was finished, late in 1879, did I for the first time rise to my feet in a little debating club called The Zetetical Society, to make, in a condition of heartbreaking nervousness, my first assault on an audience" (xxxix–xl). This accounts for the curiously un-Shavian sententiousness of Smith's speech, however appropriate it may be to the character. A clue to the future, however, is to be found in Shaw's rendering of the public voice of Davis. Already he has caught the rhythms of prophetic utterance, at least in their conventional style. The eighteen-year-old Smith may feel himself incapable of such impassioned rhetoric, because it is used to convince rather than enlighten, but the twenty-three-year-old author seems tired of his previously austere worship of Truth and yearns for the ability to sway men with the power of his eloquence. Shaw was beginning to see that it was not enough to worship Truth; he had to be able to convince others that he had a vision of the Truth if he was to do anything effective in the world. Smith, however, is quite a way from recognizing any "call" to evangelize in behalf of a great cause. Smith's sense of any special grace is vague at best.

Smith is hampered in his search for identity primarily by a schism in his psyche between folly and wisdom, a schism akin to that of sense and sensibility in the debate between Harriet and Scott. Smith takes turns at being wise beyond his years and foolish beneath his years. He is alternately rationalist and impulsive, commonsensical and romantic. The priggishness of his extreme rationalist posture causes him to appear somewhat foolish even in his wisdom, and he has not yet learned to be wise in his folly. Shaw would eventually come to play the role of the wise fool as the disparate elements of his mind synthesized, but, rationalist that he thinks he is, Smith can see nothing wise about folly, and thus dreads making a fool of himself. The "fall" into an experience of common humanity that Smith needs to take is not so much Dedalus's "fall" into an acceptance of his "sinful humanity" as into a sense of himself as made ridiculous by his mechanical "posture of opposition" and stiff moral pretensions. "I managed by sheer perseverance to overcome my natural disinclination to make a laughingstock of myself," Shaw once remarked (Winsten 60). Significantly, Smith deprecates Foley Woodward as an "Irish jester" and feels nothing but shame at being the object of ridicule. His timidity and rational dignity prevent him from offering himself as a sacrifice upon the altar of laughter. Eventually, as Eric Bentley explained, Bernard Shaw, after many embarrassing failures, learned to crucify his ego on that altar, understanding that such crucifixion was the only means of winning acceptance.

That Smith's achievements of identity are largely negative signals the nature of his immaturity or incompleteness. Though his gravitation toward the governmental seems a positive force, actually it is more the result of a deepseated opposition to commercial employment. Though he writes poetry and indicates his natural affinity for the eternal society of art by residing in bohemian Chelsea, he finds himself at odds with the conventional image of an artist as established by Perspective society. Though he considers himself a gentleman and indeed practices propriety to the point of monstrosity, he cannot feel at home in the respectable society of Froster, Fenwick, and Watkins. Though he is a natural-born arguer for a religious cause, he can only scorn the contemporary examples of religion. Though he much enjoys the company of charming young ladies, he cannot see that the institution of marriage has anything to do with him. Though he has a lively sense of humor, the jesting of a Foley Woodward strikes him as contemptible.

Bernard Shaw did become an Irish jester but not in the manner of Foley Woodward. Shaw achieved gentility but not in the manner of Fenwick and Froster. Shaw became an artist but not in the manner of Hawkshaw and Cyril Scott. Shaw became an evangelist but not in the manner of St. John Davis. Shaw became a married man but not in the manner of romantic comedy. Shaw, in short, managed to create a unique personality, first by distinguishing himself from those who played conventional roles, a purely negative reaction, and then by fashioning a positive social, professional, political, and religious identity. The basis of Smith's immaturity is that he never gets further than saying "No" to conventional models of artists, philosophers, evangelists, jesters, and married men. He knows who he is not, but he does not know who he is.

There is a considerable gap between Robert Smith and the heroes of Shaw's other novels. By comparison with Smith they seem extremely mature, largely because they are positive in their actions, while Smith is negative; they are people who don't just dream about being but actually are "smithies" of the uncreated conscience of their race. Yet Smith is by far the most real of the heroes. With Smith, Shaw was looking back upon an experience of the past; with Edward Conolly and the others he was theorizing about the future. The result is that, if Smith is a monster, he is a much less imposing fright than the others. The others are creatures of the Frankenstein brain, overstatements that have about them the queer single-mindedness of allegorical figures. While Smith's monstrosity is fully human, that of the others is rather metallic, a product of the mind's workshop, psychic experiments. Smith is by far the most real of Shaw's heroes precisely because his creator has lived him, whereas the others are would-be Supermen, "models of improved types of humanity,"[6] created as Shaw struggled to embody in art, in order to realize in himself, the best of his human potential. The reader of Shaw's five novels must be aware that passing from *Immaturity* to the other four is to move from experience to theory, as Shaw abandons the Joycean obsession with the past and cultivates his own obsession with the future.

Chapter 2

Thesis: A Monster of the Mind (*The Irrational Knot*)

> I envy him sometimes myself. What would you give to be never without a purpose, never with a regret, to regard life as a succession of objects each to be accomplished by so many days' work; to take your pleasure in trifling lazily with the consciousness of possessing a strong brain; to study love, family affection, and friendship as a doctor studies breathing or digestion; to look on disinterestedness as either weakness or hypocrisy, and on death as a mere transfer of your social function to some member of the next generation?
>
> —Bernard Shaw, *The Irrational Knot*

> I had to become an actor, and create for myself a fantastic personality fit and apt for dealing with men. . . . In this I succeeded . . . only too well. In my boyhood I saw . . . a farce called Cool as a Cucumber. The hero was a young man just returned from a tour of the world, upon which he had been sent to cure him of an apparently hopeless bashfulness; and the fun lay in the cure having overshot the mark and transformed him into *a monster of outrageous impudence.* I am not sure that something of the kind did not happen to me. (italics added)
>
> —Bernard Shaw, Preface to *Immaturity*

The most remarkable thing about young Bernard Shaw was his mind. It is not surprising that in his second novel he should focus, more specifically than in the first, upon the problems of possessing an unusual mind, chiefly the gifted one's relation to his society. Because society views the expression of his intellect with such alarm, the hero is forced to ask if his is a criminal mind, as in *Immaturity* Smith is bedeviled by the question of his social acceptability. But in Shaw's second novel the hero is no longer puzzled or tormented by this; rather he begins to wonder if society is acceptable to him. Perhaps society is the criminal. The familiar Shavian game of one-upmanship and Supermanship begins in earnest in this novel.

If *Immaturity* was Shaw's *Sense and Sensibility,* then *The Irrational Knot* was his *Pride and Prejudice.* If the "pride and prejudice" of Shaw's novel is not quite true to the Jane Austen pattern, it is not merely because the object of these emotions is no more than a common workman, but because the common workman himself feels increasingly disdainful toward the supposedly higher class into which he mistakenly marries. By the end of the novel the conventional pattern of the "pride and prejudice" sort of book has been completely reversed: society (mostly in the form of presumed readers) finds itself on the outside looking in enviously at the majority of one, the self-sufficient Superman (a reversal too of the pattern of alienation found in "The Miraculous Revenge"[1]). In this case the Superman is one Edward Conolly, superrationalistic inventor of the Conolly Electro-Motor. With this character Shaw answered the question of whether his own mind was more rational than most. He at first thought this to be true, a mistake that haunted him for the rest of his life, as people like Yeats pinned the tag "rationalist" on him and wouldn't let him escape it.

The plot involving Conolly's encounter with high society is, as Woodbridge says, "better ordered and more clearly focused" than *Immaturity*'s plot (8). Since Edward Conolly is the most focused of men, it is in keeping that his aesthetic expression should be continuous and single-minded. Since Conolly is the most controversial of men, it is appropriate that the concerns and conversations of the other characters should center on him. Since Conolly is the most competent of men, it is fitting that the burden of the novel's effective action, its forward thrust, should fall upon him. In *Immaturity* the shy Smith was relatively easy to overlook, but in *The Irrational Knot* Conolly is impossible to avoid—he is everywhere, making everything happen. In a single bound, Shaw had leaped from portraying himself as he had been to portraying himself as he wanted to be and indeed was becoming, even as he wrote.

Once again Shaw's hero, although nominally an American, is essentially nationless and parentless. He makes passing reference to the fact that he has "no father" (59), meaning that his was an absent father much of the time, and he never mentions his mother. At first, while he is still impoverished and working on his invention, he is employed in the laboratory of Lord Jasper Carbury, an aristocrat by birth but a democrat by temperament, who loves to tinker in his amateur way with mechanical things.[2] Lord Carbury has hired Conolly because he respects mechanical genius and enjoys patronizing it.

Conolly's first encounter with aristocracy in the novel, however, does not take place in the laboratory. The brief opening scene shows Conolly and his sister, Susanna (in some sort of imaginative transformation of Shaw and his sister Lucy), as they are both preparing to leave their Lambeth apartment to go out for the night. Conolly is to sing for a workmen's benefit at Wandsworth sponsored by Lord Carbury's wife (just as Shaw at this point sometimes per-

formed at George Vandeleur Lee's rehearsals, accompanied his sister at amateur performances, and, a few years later, performed at socialist gatherings).
Susanna goes to the Bijou Theatre in Soho, where she transforms into the
burlesque queen Lalage Virtue (rather a caricature of Lucy Shaw's professional performances in opera, operetta, and the pantomime, but perhaps expressive of Shaw's opinion of the work Lucy did).

At Wandsworth, Conolly proves to have musical talent superior to all the
performing aristocrats, for which he wins their grudging admiration. Since
most of the major characters appear at the benefit, Conolly meets in quick
succession the many people who will become involved in his story. He meets
Marian Lind, the beauty he will eventually marry and then divorce; Nellie
McQuinch, Marian's waspish friend, an extremely advanced female;
Marmaduke Lind, Marian's jovial, Philistine, happy-go-lucky cousin, who will
live illicitly with Susanna Conolly for a while; Sholto Douglas, the proud aristocrat and type of the perfect gentleman in conventional novels, who will talk
Marian into running away with him, only to abandon her, pregnant, in New
York; the Reverend George Lind, Marian's dutiful and sanctimonious brother,
who is proud of his eloquence; and Mrs. Leith Fairfax, a busybody female
novelist of decided mediocrity and irresponsible tongue.

After turning down the man favored by her family, Sholto Douglas, because she tires of Sholto's stiff and ceremonious courtship, Marian Lind takes
a fancy to the vital Conolly and accepts his first proposal of marriage.[3] Her
father, Mr. Reginald Lind, nearly apoplectic at the prospect of a common
workman marrying into his family, tries desperately to forestall the marriage.
This incites generally amiable and dutiful Marian to walk out on her father
and marry Conolly. About half of the novel is devoted to the tying of the irrational marriage knot; the other half deals with the gradual loosening and even-
tual untying of that knot, a "knot" Shaw adds to the three "nets" that Joyce's
Dedalus finds inhibiting of genius. In *Immaturity* Shaw conceded to Victorian convention by at least marrying off the heroine, although rescuing the
hero from such a fate, but *The Irrational Knot* breaks with convention entirely
by making its subject a marriage in dissolution.

It seems that Conolly, a model of domestic efficiency, has left Marian "nothing to desire," whereupon she grows dissatisfied and imagines Sholto Douglas to possess all those romantic qualities she misses in Conolly. As Conolly
recognizes that he has made a misalliance, he does not discourage Marian's
flirtation with Douglas. Sholto's romantical rhetoric having convinced her that

the world is well lost for him, they go off on a cruise. By the time they reach New York, however, Marian has discovered that Sholto is a vacuous fraud, his aristocratic reserve having disguised a complete emptiness of mind and heart. Eventually Marian disengages herself from Sholto and prepares to abide humbly in America, in keeping with her social disgrace and what she believes to be her financial ruin.

In New York Marian conceives a "romance of penitent poverty," as one might term it, but quite unnecessarily, as Conolly has thoughtfully secured her property and money for her. Unaware that she is still a wealthy woman, Marian takes lodgings in a shabbier section of New York than her "romance of poverty" had led her to believe she would. Here she encounters Susanna Conolly, now an out-of-work performer whose alcoholism has destroyed her. Upon Susanna's death shortly thereafter, Conolly comes to New York to pay his last respects and to confront Marian with the decision of whether to return to him. Marian, pregnant with Sholto's child, thinks she ought not to remarry Conolly, for the sake of society. The novel ends as Conolly calmly accepts her decision and walks out.

In *The Irrational Knot,* as in all of Shaw's novels, the author was careful to arrange his characters symmetrically, as a principle of order. The rationalists/ realists are balanced off against the Philistines and idealists, and even the realists, idealists, and Philistines are arranged symmetrically within their own groups.[4] The opening scene, for instance, is between Conolly and his sister, both rational and realistic.[5] They balance one another in that they are at the extremes of personal control. Conolly is a monster of rational control (at least *he* would ascribe it to his rationalism, but Shaw would later identify the control as "moral passion"), whereas Susanna gradually debauches herself with drink because she lacks control. They balance, too, as the male and female of the rational view, just as Smith and Harriet gave common sense its male and female expressions in *Immaturity.* Since Susanna's affair is part of the subplot and thus not often on the page, Shaw continues the balance by introducing the character of Nellie McQuinch, whose skeptic-cynic view of the world provides female balance for Conolly. Seldom does Shaw construct a scene in this novel without the presence of Nellie, Susanna, or Conolly to provide the voice of rational criticism. Even Marian in her moments of disillusionment can speak in a rationalist voice. There is balance, too, in the arrangement of the aristocratic idealists and Philistines opposed to Conolly. Lady Carbury and Sholto Douglas are far to the right in their regard for form; Reginald and

George Lind, through their sense of accommodation, are placed somewhere near the middle; and Marmaduke and Lord Carbury, through Philistine indifference and preoccupation with other practical matters, are far out on the left wing.

As with Robert Smith, the character of Conolly had its inspiration in the external circumstances of Shaw's life and only gradually developed into a symbol of Shaw's inner condition as well. For about nine months, during the writing of the closing chapters of *Immaturity* and the opening chapters of *The Irrational Knot,* Shaw was employed by the Edison Telephone Company. Although he was perhaps the only one in the establishment who knew the theory of telephony, he was given the distasteful door-to-door sales job of persuading people in East London to allow telephone lines to be strung on their property. When Edison merged with Bell in July of 1880, Shaw was offered a job with the new firm as well, but quickly turned it down to escape the uncomfortable position of salesman. Many of the Edison Company workers were Americans, and their practical, go-get-'em approach seems to have made some contribution to the characterization of Conolly. Feeling himself unacceptable to polite society, the shabby young Shaw rather admired the contemptuous attitude of the American workers toward the useless British aristocrat. Unlike the British lower classes, the Americans showed no sense of inferiority and indeed seemed rather to consider themselves superior to the idle aristocracy. After all, they were Workers of the World, Men of the Future, whereas the aristocrats were effete creatures, doomed to extinction. Conolly comes to see that his desire to marry a lady was sheer folly, as it caused him to marry beneath himself.[6]

Yet Shaw was always the aristocrat by virtue of his superior intellect and morality, as portrayed in Conolly's being not just any kind of workman; he is an inventor, and he is careful to make others see that distinction. The inventor is the aristocrat of the working classes, and his inventiveness connects him with the creativity of the artist. "I am not a scientific man: I'm an inventor" (58), he says.[7] If Conolly's being a workman is an expression of Shaw's republicanism, Conolly's being an inventor is an expression of Shaw's sense of superiority in creative intellect.

Furthermore, Conolly is a workman of unusual culture, the product of an unusual childhood. His paternal grandfather had been an Irish sailor with such an impressive singing voice that an Italian music maestro made an opera *buffo* of him. Conolly's father was thus raised in Italy and became "first accompanist, then chorus master, and finally trainer for the operatic stage" (16). He speculated in an American tour, married there, lost his money, then returned to England. His son, christened Edoardo Sebastiano Conolly, was left behind in America as an apprentice to an electrical engineer. So Conolly, like Shaw himself, is the offspring of Italian opera, so to speak. This upbringing also accounts for his perfect manners, as he had "learnt to dance and bow before [he] was twelve years old from the most experienced master in Europe" (99). Mixing with all the counts, dukes, and queens of his father's opera company had polished Conolly's manners to perfection, and of course he could speak French and Italian fluently. Before his daughter becomes infatuated with Conolly, Mr. Reginald Lind proclaims him "altogether a man of very superior attainments, and by no means deficient in culture" (105).

Obviously Shaw was indulging in a reaction, if not wishful thinking, in creating the character of Conolly. Conolly, the very opposite of Smith, is older than his twenty-four-year-old creator; he "was about thirty, well grown, and fully developed muscularly. There was no cloud of vice or trouble upon him: he was concentrated and calm, making no tentative movements of any sort (even a white tie did not puzzle him into fumbling), but acting with a certainty of aim and consequent economy of force, dreadful to the irresolute. His face was brown but his auburn hair classed him as a fair man" (3). The "modern Ben Franklin," as Conolly is called, borders on the fanatic in his pursuit of vital economy. He "never goes anywhere without an object" (188) and never lets anyone waste his time. His favorite saying is one that Shaw repeated many times during his life: "There is no use crying over spilt milk" (229). There is no place for regret in a well-regulated life. When Conolly learns that Marian has left him, he goes cheerfully to his dinner and eats a hearty meal, as becomes the inventor of that efficiency machine, the Conolly Electro-Motor, which operates with "hardly any waste" (132).[8] As Susanna exclaims, "Ned . . . is a man in a thousand—though Lord forbid we should have many of his sort about" (172). From a woman's point of view, a man who is always right is hardly bearable and something of a bore. Since he is always blameless, he has "no variety" (304). Here an ominous fact needs to be noted in explanation of the character of Conolly. It was during the winter of 1879 that Shaw met, at the Zetetical Society, that human calculating machine and future Fabian luminary Sidney Webb. Ned Conolly is just the first of many Shaw heroes who owe something to Webb.

The authentic nineteenth-century rationalist is characterized especially by his independence of all the inefficient social ties that bind conventional people to the past—the ties of duty to church, state, or family, the same nets that would limit the freedom of the soaring Dedalus-artist. As Conolly says: "I am not one of those people who think it pious to consider their near relatives as if they were outside the natural course of things. I never was a good son or a good brother or a good patriot in the sense of thinking that my mother and my sister and my native country were better than other people's because I happened to belong to them" (98).[9] As for the church, Conolly makes it clear in his proposal to Marian that he will undergo no ceremony in, nor allow his wife to raise children in, any given religious tradition, because he is "prejudiced against religions of all sorts." She will find him "irreligious, but not . . . unreasonable" (112). The conventions of church, state, and family are, to the rationalist, merely errors of the past made habitual. "The world would never get on if every practical man were to stand by his father's mistakes" (17), Conolly informs Marian, as if to say, Progress Is Our Most Important Product.[10]

In some respects, Conolly is an enviable man. Marian, who envies him, asks Douglas: "What would you give to be never without a purpose, never with a regret, to regard life as a succession of objects each to be accomplished by so many days' work; to take your pleasure in trifling lazily with the consciousness of possessing a strong brain; to study love, family affection, and friendship as a doctor studies breathing or digestion; to look on disinterestedness as either weakness or hypocrisy, and on death as a mere transfer of your social function to some member of the next generation?" (189). The poetic Douglas replies that he could achieve all that only at the cost of his soul, a rather cheap price in fact, considering how soulless he turns out to be.

If Conolly is beginning to sound like the stereotype of the soulless scientist, he has another side that partly redeems him. Shaw was almost incapable of creating a hero who was not in some part of him an artist. Conolly wins a grudging approval from the aristocrats by being an accomplished musician, and later he proves himself a discerning, if somewhat rationalistic, critic of painting as well. In fact, upon their marriage Marian discovers him to be a veritable monster of artistic integrity. Conolly does "not like to hear music patronized" (233), and Marian gradually senses that her amateur attempts at singing and piano playing are unwelcomed by her husband. He accuses her of having "no sense at all of what was beautiful" (271).[11] Soon she stops her recitals altogether, indulging in them only when Conolly is absent.

Conolly's merely avocational interest in the arts inverts his creator's character in a way that presages a Shavian strategy. Conolly's remark "Music is not my business: it is my amusement" (15) was echoed, years later, when Shaw sometimes insisted that his real contribution was as a Fabian, not as a playwright. But such assertions depended upon mood and audience, for Shaw was equally adamant on other occasions that his artistic self was his greatest self. The mood of the young Shaw of twenty-four who wanted desperately to do something practical in the world was such that he created an inverted character, whose practical talents are given precedence over his artistic talents and whose rationality is given precedence over his creativity.

Any such inversion of the real talents of Bernard Shaw must be understood in the context of nineteenth-century aestheticism and all the follies then perpetrated in the name of "Art." For example, the fraudulent Sholto Douglas states that the true artist "instinctively hates machinery" (134). In this cliché of the Art for Art's Sake school, Douglas finds consolation for his inferiority to Conolly as an artist. Like so many of his ilk, Douglas mistakes mere prettiness for art, and, unlike Robert Smith and subsequent Shavian heroes, he cannot hear the new music in the hum of electric wires or the rhythmic clicking of railroad wheels, nor can he see the new sculpture in the bassoon shape of the factory tower.[12] The Shavian artist will be a return to an older, pre-Romantic ideal, that of the statesman-poet, the man who can be both artist and practical man of affairs. Shaw refused to participate in the Romantic alienation from bourgeois society, and the lesson of his success may have encouraged the many modern artists who have found commitment to practical tasks compatible with their lives as artists. *The Irrational Knot*, however, overstates Shaw's case for the practical and the efficient.

Since the music that is Conolly's avocation is not essential to his inventiveness, its only utility is in its therapeutic powers. Being human after all, he finds that he requires some outlet for the emotions that are otherwise so carefully controlled. The piano, organ, and voice allow him to relieve himself in politically harmless and aesthetically pleasing ways. Thus Ned Conolly is an unusual rationalist, unusual in that his rationalism in no way denies the irrational. Indeed, part of his rationality consists in the sensible way in which he allows the irrational its necessary expression. When he accompanies Marian through an artistic section of the city, he jokes about taking her on his arm, a "ridiculous mode of locomotion that . . . would be inexcusable if I were a traction-engine, and you my tender." Marian sarcastically asks what people will

think "if they see a great engineer violating the laws of mechanics by drag-
ging his wife by the arm?" Conolly replies, "I violate the laws of mechanics
. . . [because] I like to be envied where there are solid reasons for it. It grati-
fies my vanity to be seen in this artistic quarter with a pretty woman on my
arm. . . . Besides, Man, who was a savage only yesterday, has his infirmities,
and finds a poetic pleasure in the touch of the woman he loves" (194). It is
certainly an unusual rationalist who can acknowledge and give sufficient play
to the savage within.

One of Conolly's, and Shaw's, favorite doctrines is that of the holiday, a
doctrine akin to that of William James's in *Pragmatism*. Conolly's favorite type
of holiday is one that involves not beach ball or golf or horse racing but
flirtation. Like Robert Smith, he is extremely susceptible to female beauty,
and a pretty head can disrupt even the most determined of his intellectual
contemplations. More often, however, the beauties to whom Conolly is attracted prove to be, like Smith's Alhambra dancer and Harriet, intellectual
stimulants rather than intellectual drugs. Surprisingly, the two women he most
enjoys flirting with are Mrs. Saunders and Mrs. Scott, the Isabella and Harriet
of *Immaturity*. With Isabella he indulges in his love of Irish jesting, with
Harriet he discusses serious matters of business, two sides he never expresses
with Marian.

As indicated by his treating women as individuals, Conolly is not one to
maintain the double standard. He encourages Marian in her flirtations with
Douglas because "Every married woman requires a holiday from her husband
occasionally" (241), and "the attentions of a husband are stale, unsuited to
holiday time" (238).[13] Marian, believing it her conjugal duty to romance no
one but her lawful husband, is baffled by this doctrine and accuses Conolly
of not caring for her. To her indignant question "Do you like men to be in
love with me?" he replies, "Yes. It makes the house pleasant for them, it makes
them attentive to you, and it gives you great power for good. When I was a
romantic boy, any good woman could have made a saint of me. Let them fall
in love with you as much as they please. Afterwards they will seek wives according to a higher standard than if they had never known you. But do not
return the compliment, or your influence will become an evil one" (234). Poor
Marian has been raised in the romantic tradition in which love is an all or
nothing proposition, calling for complete involvement or complete indifference, and the rationalist's notion of a flirtation as a harmless play of minds is
utterly beyond her.

She is further bewildered by the contradictions of Sholto Douglas. Douglas, who is convention personified, hypocritically talks a different line when his own concerns are at stake. He tells Marian that conventional virtue is a hollow thing, something to be defied when it tyrannizes over the heart. "Trust your heart" (258), he counsels Marian, and let us "enter on a life made holy by love" (259). Uncertain of what to do, Marian discusses the problem in general terms with Conolly. Sholto has said that "to defy the world is a proof of honesty." Conolly naturally agrees. "I get on in the world by defying its old notions, and taking nobody's advice but my own. Follow Douglas's precepts by all means" (260). Conolly is virtually inviting her to abscond with Douglas, for he is more concerned about her learning to be honest than about preserving a bad marriage. When, in the final scene, Marian expresses shame at having run away, Conolly rages at her for being ashamed of "the only honest thing you ever did" (331).

According to Conolly, and Shaw, it is a question of education. Conventional schooling consists of teaching that the pretty theories that cover "ugly facts" are more real and more valuable than the facts. Unfortunately, according to the argument developed in *The Quintessence of Ibsenism*, the facts will not go away and keep tripping the idealist up. But instead of learning respect for the facts, some people, like Marian, suffer a succession of disillusionments that make no lasting impression on their deep-dyed idealism. Marian can declare on one page that "love is a myth" (190) and on another page reaffirm her old idealism by stoutly maintaining, "People do fall in love" (252). After her disillusionment with Douglas, however, she feels that the "grand passion . . . was a lamentable delusion" (282). The novel ends in disillusionment for Marian, but as she clings to her old social idealisms in refusing to return to Conolly, the odds are good that she will restore the idealism of romantic love before long. Shaw defines the idealist by his or her utter inability to learn from experience. It matters not how often Marian experiences the falsity of her ideals; she always returns to their defense. Conolly catalogs her crimes against the real in a lengthy, impassioned speech that is remindful of "Don Juan in Hell":

There is no institution so villainous but she will defend it; no tyranny so oppressive but she will make a virtue of submitting to it; no social cancer so venomous but she will shrink from cutting it out, and plead that it is a comfortable thing, and much better as it is. She knows that she disobeyed her father, and that he deserved to be disobeyed; yet she condemns other women who are disobedient, and stands out against Nelly McQuinch in defense of the unselfishness of parental love. She knows that the increased freedom of movement allowed to her as a married woman has been healthy for her; yet she looks coldly at other young women who assert their right to freedom. (242–43)

Marian seems incapable of adjusting her conception of what marriage is supposed to be with what she has experienced:

She knows that marriage is not what she expected it to be, and that it gives me many unfair advantages over her; and she knows also that ours is a happier marriage than most. Nevertheless she will encourage other girls to marry; she will maintain that the chain which galls her own wrists so often is a string of honeysuckles; and if a woman identifies herself with any public movement for the lightening of that chain, she wont allow that that woman is fit to be admitted into decent society. (243)

In the face of such blind loyalty to the ideal, the Shavian realist is torn between the desire to destroy the ideal and the wish to prevent anything cruel from happening to the blindfolded idealist, as one would care for a child.

There is not one of these shams to which she clings that I would not like to take by the throat and shake the life out of; and she knows it. Even in that she has not the consistency to believe me wrong, because it is undutiful and out of keeping with the honeysuckles to lack faith in her husband. In order to blind herself to her inconsistencies, she has to live in a rose-colored fog; and what with me constantly . . . blowing this fog away on the one side, and the naked facts of her everyday experience as constantly letting in the daylight on the other, she must spend half the time wondering whether she is mad or sane. Between her desire to do right and her discoveries that it generally leads her to do wrong, she passes her life in a wistful melancholy which I cant dispel. I can only pity her. I suppose I could pet her; but I hate treating a woman like a child: it means giving up all hope of her becoming rational. (243)

Woodbridge has suggested that the heart of this novel is the tragedy of Marian Lind. Shaw *seems* to have agreed when he wrote, in his preface, that "*The Irrational Knot* may be regarded as an early attempt on the part of the

Life Force to write *A Doll's House* in English by the instrumentality of a very immature writer" (xix). Considering that Shaw hadn't even heard of Ibsen when he wrote the novel itself, and given that *A Doll's House* was first receiving Scandinavian notice as Shaw began *The Irrational Knot,* the novel is remarkably similar to Ibsen's play in its presentation of the doll-wife. Conolly, despairing of Marian's ever reaching maturity, has begun to treat her more and more like a doll or a child. But the Shavian difference is that Conolly never consults Marian on matters of serious import, not because *he* believes that women are incapable of such matters but because Marian has been trained in this belief and acts the part. But at least she is sensitive enough to know that she is being treated as a child and robust enough to resent it. She complains to Nelly that she has nothing real to do in this world: "A courtier, a lover, a man who will not let the winds of heaven visit your face too harshly, is very nice, no doubt; but he is not a husband. I want to be a wife and not a fragile ornament kept in a glass case. He would as soon think of submitting any project of his to the judgment of a doll as to mine. If he has to explain or discuss any serious matter of business with me, he does so apologetically, as if he were treating me roughly" (202).

Nelly points out that Marian didn't like Conolly's other approach either: when he tried to treat her as a rational adult, she immediately took refuge in childish idealisms. This novel may be Shaw's *A Doll's House,* but Conolly has nothing in common with the husband of Ibsen's Nora, for Conolly, unlike Torvald, would welcome his wife's becoming a New Woman. But not all women were or are capable of this, any more than all men were or are capable of becoming the New Man. In a way, Shaw's version, unknowingly, was a reply to Ibsen in that he shows what happens to the Nora sort after she slams the door. Marian, like Nora, has been trained to behave like a doll,[14] and though Marian is intelligent and robust enough to rebel, the training is deeply ingrained. Her "tragedy" is summed up in the old formula of "realism's" favorite melodrama: the heroine, caught between two worlds, despises the one that she is born to, yet she has not been prepared for the world she longs for and is quite powerless to bring it into being.

Shaw effectively symbolizes Marian's fate through the device of a dream. The dream occurs after Marian has first encountered the drunken Susanna in the shabby New York lodging house and has been forced to make the galling and humiliating confession that she was an unfaithful wife to Susanna's brother. That night Marian dreams "that she was unmarried and at home with her father, and that the household was troubled by Susanna, who lodged in a room upstairs" (305). Marian and Susanna end up in the same lodging house because they are really "sisters" underneath it all and belong in the same house of disrepute. Even in her dream house, Marian cannot restore the ideal without a sense of the troubling presence of Susanna's reality, just as respectability depends upon the troubling presence of the disreputable for its raison d'être. You can't have repute without disrepute. The dream signifies that the "good" Marian senses, at least unconsciously, her complicity in the fate of her "evil sister." There is irony, further, in that Susanna, a faithful if illegal wife, destroys nothing but herself; whereas Marian in her idealism manages to mar the lives of half a dozen others, including Susanna. It is no wonder that in the escapist world of the dream, Susanna has become a difficult, Freudian boarder in the house of the ideal.

Nelly McQuinch is perhaps better prepared for the brave new world of women's emancipation, but in her contemporary world of assumed female inferiority she is quite a misfit. She is tolerated by Mr. Lind only because her cynicism serves as a correction to Marian's extravagance. Nelly comments, "What is the use of straining after an amiable view of things, Marian, when a cynical view is most likely to be the true one." "There is no harm in giving people credit for being good," replies Marian, whose eyes always plead for peace like those of a good angel. Nelly disagrees: "Yes, there is, when people are not good, which is most often the case. It sets us wrong practically, and holds virtue cheap" (62).[15] Such is the general pattern of the many conversations between the two girls. Nelly has a sharp eye for the flaws in reality, and, as she says, "my disposition is such that when I see that a jug is cracked, I feel more inclined to smash and have done with it than to mend it and handle it tenderly ever after" (205). Marian of course would by nature either try to mend it or pretend the crack wasn't there, but she is married to a husband who has the same intolerance of cracked jugs. In fact, Conolly forces her to break the cracked jug of their marriage and start over.

It is Nelly who forces Marian to break the cracked jug of the parental relationship. When Mr. Lind fails to back Marian in her choice of Conolly, Nelly advises her that she is fighting "the most unreasonable of adversaries, a parent asserting his proprietary rights in his child" (151). Nelly has good reason to know about such adversaries, as much of her childhood was spent combating the wrongheaded tyranny of Mr. and Mrs. McQuinch. The McQuinches believed that "when God sent children he made their parents fit to rule them."

Unfortunately, the McQuinches were no more fit to have charge of Nelly "than a turtle is to rear a young eagle" (32).[16] In this novel, says William Irvine, "the respectable mantle of John Stuart Mill is lifted and the cloven hoof of Samuel Butler becomes visible" (26). Shaw had not heard of Butler at this time, but the McQuinches do indeed seem to be close neighbors of Butler's Pontifex family.

It is also Nelly who envies the independence of Susanna Conolly. Nelly has come to see that marriage is merely the polite word for legalized prostitution, and she admires a woman like Susanna who has the spunk to live outside that institution. When Susanna shocks Marmaduke by rejecting his offer of a clandestine marriage and insists upon remaining independent by paying her own way, Marian is scandalized. But Conolly wants to know: "What has Susanna to lose by disregarding your rules of behavior? . . . She would not really conciliate you by marrying, for you wouldnt associate with her a bit the more because of her marriage certificate. . . . Believe me, neither actresses nor any other class will trouble themselves about the opinion of a society in which they are allowed to have neither part nor lot" (98–99).

However much Conolly defends Susanna's right to live her private life as she chooses, he is contemptuous of her choice of public life, of the way she has prostituted her talents on the burlesque stage as Lalage Virtue. When she is dying the slow death of the alcoholic, her performance deteriorating proportionately, Conolly advises her to hurry up and die if she is bent on killing herself. What is shocking is not that he gives such advice but that it is "the very best advice [he] could have given" (231). Susanna believes that she didn't make herself nor her circumstances and, when Ned visits her death bed in New York, he seems at least partly to agree. He explains to Marian Susanna's motive for drunkenness:

Society, by the power of the purse, set her to nautch-girl's work, and forbade her the higher work that was equally within her power. Being enslaved and debauched in this fashion, how could she be happy except when she was not sober. It was her own immediate interest to drink; it was her tradesman's interest that she should drink. . . . She was clever, good-natured, more constant to her home and her man than you, a living fountain of innocent pleasure as a dancer, singer, and actress; and here she lies, after mischievously spending her talent in a series of entertainments too dull for hell and too debased for any better place, dead of a preventable disease, chiefly because most of the people she came in contact with had a direct pecuniary interest in depraving and poisoning her. (332–33)

The shock of seeing his sister's dead body forces Conolly to abandon his kid-glove treatment of Marian. He calls for "an end of hypocrisy! No unrealities now: I cannot bear them. Let us have no trash of magnanimous injured husband, erring but repentant wife. . . . Now I refuse all conventions" (331). He speaks harshly to her about her self-deception, and she is surprised by this rough treatment from one who has treated her as a doll until now. Marian accuses him of not being himself, and he replies, "On the contrary, I am like myself—I actually am myself tonight. . . . Is it utterly impossible for you to say something real to me?" (332). When Conolly offers to take her back and be a father to Sholto's child if only she will snap her fingers at the social disgrace that is sure to meet her in London, Marian is still bound fast by her well-trained sense of duty. She thinks that she had better remain "free" and "independent," and she is baffled by Conolly's willingness to give up his freedom to take on a family again.[17] At this, Conolly makes a very Shavian speech:

Freedom is a fool's dream. I am free. . . . I once thought, like you, that freedom was the one condition to be gained at all cost and hazard. My favorite psalm was that nonsense of John Hay's:

For always in thine eyes, O Liberty
Shines that high light whereby the world is saved;
And though thou slay us, we will trust in thee.

And she does slay us. Now I am for the fullest attainable life. That involves the least endurable liberty. You dont see that yet.[18] (334–35)

This is a curious definition of liberty, a definition that leads away from nineteenth-century liberalism straight to Karl Marx (or to Roman or Anglo-Catholicism in other cases), or at least to the Shaw who insisted on the paradox that socialism was resisted because it offered people too much freedom. People, he argued, found it much easier to be wage slaves under capitalism than to run their society in a way that would allow "the fullest attainable life."

That people love to call their slavery "freedom" is illustrated by the way Marian is bound by social duty to remain "free" of Conolly. Furthermore, she does not even have the usual consolation of disappointing Conolly by refusing him and nobly remaining true to her duty, for Conolly has foreseen how he would adapt himself to that circumstance. He always faces facts. "'You are too wise, Ned,' she said. . . . 'It is impossible to be too wise, dearest,' he said, and unhesitatingly turned and left her" (336). More explicitly than the negative shake of the head that ends *Immaturity*, this exchange between Conolly and Marian, which concludes *The Irrational Knot*, dismisses the conventions of society as delusions not to be countenanced by the rational mind.

Critics have been hard put to know what to make of Edoardo Sebastiano Conolly. Woodbridge believes that the lesson of the novel "is that a man who tries to become a purely rational thinking and acting machine will wreck his own life and other peoples'" (8–9). While Shaw confessed that he could hardly abide Conolly himself,[19] he does not mean for us to judge Conolly's life as wrecked. Quite the contrary, his experience in untying the irrational knot has left Conolly stronger and more vitally aware than ever before. The conclusion leaves us with the sense that he will go on to great things because the encounter with Marian, as a test, has revealed him to himself, making him all the more confident of his own strength and quality of mind. Conolly is far from being a tragic figure.

Shaw did not mean for the wreckage of the novel's ending to be read as the catastrophe of tragedy. Conolly is only the first of a long series of Shaw characters who will triumph over tragic circumstances. As has often been noted, unalloyed tragedy is extremely rare in Shaw's world. Just as it has been argued that there is no such thing as "Christian tragedy" because the saint ultimately triumphs over his martyrdom, so too "Shavian tragedy" seems to be a contradiction in terms, for in the catastrophes that fall upon the Shavian hero there is usually the sense of ultimate triumph. The difference is that with the Shavian hero the triumph of the indomitable spirit is expected to occur in this world, not the next. Apparently Shaw was constitutionally indisposed to see himself as a tragic figure. Only in tragicomedies such as *Saint Joan* and *Heartbreak House* did he allow moments of tragic mood. He avoided Socrates and Jesus as subjects and wrote instead about the Superman behavior of Napoleon and Caesar, Caesar's play ending before the return to Rome and the assassination. Shaw allowed Dick Dudgeon to escape the noose in *The Devil's Disciple*, Barbara to escape the river in *Major Barbara*, Lavinia to escape the lion's mouth in *Androcles and the Lion;* and he wrote a playlet dealing with the trial of Jesus but ended it before the crucifixion.[20]

Saint Joan proves that Shaw did not lack tragic insight, and his conscious striving to avoid martyrdom by creating the character of the "privileged lunatic" proves that he was fully aware of the tragic potential inherent in the Socratic gadfly. But the possibility of playing the "privileged lunatic" had not yet occurred to him at the time of writing *The Irrational Knot*. If Edward Conolly is not a tragic figure, neither is he a comic figure, a "wise fool," for he dislikes being the butt of the joke as much as did Robert Smith. In Conolly's opinion, says Marian, "the greatest misfortune that can happen to anyone is to make a fool of oneself" (199). Making a fool of oneself is the mark of idealism and ignorance, the twin sources of the irrational in human affairs, and no self-respecting rationalist would allow himself such foolish postures. For Conolly, folly is an indulgence born of weakness, not a strategy for wisdom. In the early novels, the part of the fool is always given to a minor character. In this case, Marmaduke lightens the tone of the book with his "gift of drollery."

Conolly is yet another monster of propriety, in his own way even more monstrous than Robert Smith. But Conolly's propriety is not confused with an external social system; rather it develops more intensely into a private, internal sense of the correctness of certain human conduct. Shaw, as much as Hemingway, possessed a private code of conduct that he expressed literarily in the conflict between the inner-directed Shavian hero and the people who follow an external code. The Shavian hero, like the Hemingway hero, carries the code around inside him, and of course others constantly violate it because they don't know it's there. The others see only what appears to be a lawless man, who gets extremely irritated whenever they cross him by following their conventions. "They get on with the queerest makeshifts for self-respect," says Conolly, "old Mr. Lind with family pride, Douglas with personal vanity, and Marmaduke with a sort of interest in his own appetites and his own jollity. Everything is a sham with them: they have drill and etiquette instead of manners, fashions instead of tastes, small talk instead of intercourse" (270).[21] In fact, the more mannerly the Shavian hero is, the more unmannerly he seems to those who consider personal manners to be synonymous with an impersonal system of etiquette.

This confusion between the real and the ideal is most humorously illustrated by the results of the Reverend George Lind's visit to Conolly's sister. When Reverend Lind, feeling "like St. Anthony struggling with the fascination of a disguised devil," pays a visit to the voluptuous Lalage Virtue (Susanna), who meets him dressed in a harem costume, he informs her that if Conolly marries Marian, Lalage must give up her illicit relationship with

Marmaduke, as the scandal of it would then reflect on Marian. After a dazzling display of intellect in which Susanna inverts all his values, somehow managing to put him in the wrong, she seductively contrives to fall into his arms. At this the much distraught minister hastens home and composes a sermon, the general theme of which is "How can Satan cast out Satan?" Reverend Lind is referring specifically to the way people visit the Baal altars of local theaters hoping to cast out their devils through the pursuit of pleasure, which of course is satanic; more generally, his message is that "there is not left in these latter days a sin that does not pretend to work the world's salvation, nor a man who flatters not himself that the sin of one may be the purging of many" (184). To any devil that claims to have cast out many devils, the Lord scoffing shall say, "How can Satan cast out Satan?" It is a question made even more interesting by Shaw's asking it at the beginning of his satanic career.

Shaw does not address the question directly in this novel, but his reaction is implicit in everything he wrote. His answer is that the conventional mind, like that of Reverend Lind, has allowed appearance primacy over reality. It has failed to see through the satanic disguise, preferring formal piety to real piety, just as it prefers formal etiquette to real manners. This preference for illusion is best exemplified in the primacy of word over thing. "The Atheist," complains Reverend Lind, "no longer an execration, an astonishment, a curse, and a reproach, poses now as the friend of man and the champion of right" (184). Even though an atheist might be the most godly man living, the important thing to Reverend Lind is the *word* "Atheist," which he superstitiously capitalizes. That word qualifies the man as satanic and thus disqualifies him from casting out Satan. Shaw would attempt to show otherwise with his joking Satan pose.

Shaw explains in his preface that while writing *The Irrational Knot* he used Bizet's *Carmen* "as a safety-valve for my romantic impulses. When I was tired of the sordid realism of Edward Conolly . . . I threw down my pen and went to the piano to forget him in the glamorous society of Carmen and her crimson toreador and yellow dragoon. . . . The Carmen music was . . . exquisite of its kind, and could enchant a young man romantic enough to have come to the end of romance before I began to create art for myself. I still could enjoy other people's romances" (vi). Although the later Shaw did not find Conolly's realism quite so sordid, nor Bizet's *Carmen* quite so attractive, this confession shows us how far the young Shaw was from accepting rationalism as his ideal.

Indeed, Shaw seems to be implying criticism in the childlessness of Conolly's two-year marriage, whereas Marian's short episode with Douglas is quite fertile, which might be construed as a comment on "barren rationalism." On the other hand, Shaw may have been saying something more complex. Conolly is creative enough in the world of ideas, and thus his fertility is to be measured not in terms of children produced but in inventions completed. That Marian cannot conceive by him may be no more than a comment upon the incompatibility of realist and idealist.[22] Furthermore, there is poetic justice in Marian's romantic "conceptions" turning out to be fraudulent and bastardly, as symbolized by Sholto Douglas's impregnation of her. As Douglas absconds and romance disappears, Marian is left with the reality of a child. Romance may be more fertile, biologically and emotionally, but in the end the children it produces are bastards. Note that it is Conolly the realist who is willing to raise the bastard as his son.

Preparing us for the realist of *The Quintessence of Ibsenism,* Conolly's intuitive realism often rescues him from his own mere rationalism. As I have said, Conolly, unlike the rationalist of convention, is unusually aware and indulgent of the irrational. He would agree more than anyone with Marian's idea that "we should not let our little wisdoms stifle all our big instincts" (253). He congratulates her for having done the honest thing in running off with Douglas. This burst of honesty encourages him in turn to allow freer play to certain of his own impulses. At the beginning Conolly is much like Smith in following a surface propriety in his treatment of Marian. He practices a kind of deception, the kind that adults use to protect children from "harsh realities." But in the final scene he breaks loose from this habit of treating idealists like children and begins the tactic of expressing honestly his sense of the real. Idealists are no longer to be pampered or catered to; their only chance of growing up is to be told the truth. In keeping with his need to follow his own "big instincts," the Shavian hero now enters on a period of rudeness and social impropriety.

Chapter 3

Antithesis: A Monster of the Body
(*Love Among the Artists*)

> I exhausted rationalism when I got to the end of my second novel at the age of
> twenty-four, and should have come to a dead stop if I had not proceeded to
> purely mystical assumptions. I thus perhaps destroyed my brain, but
> inspiration filled up the void, and I got on better than ever.
> —Bernard Shaw, Letter to the Abbess of Stanbrook (December 23, 1924)

The young Shaw understood that the negativism of Robert Smith led nowhere, that the "posture of opposition" had to be replaced by a "posture of proposition," but the nature of the proposition was not at all clear. In his need for positive action, a need quite as fundamental as his need to oppose, Shaw attempted psychological transformation to a more positive personality. To buttress this transformation with a set of ideas, the sine qua non of the intellectual, Shaw sensed that he needed to convert conventional rationalism from a nay-saying agnosticism to a yea-saying religion of some sort, probably an impossible task. In *The Irrational Knot* he ended up with a puzzling discrepancy between the religious force of some of Conolly's actions and the total absence of a religious motivation or a religious theory that would explain those actions. That is, Conolly at times *acts* like a man with a holy cause, but nowhere in the novel is that holy cause stated or referred to. Shaw thought of religion as "that which binds men together, and irreligion that which sunders" (*Sixteen Self Sketches* 47), and rationalism, having a sundering, analytical quality, simply resisted being converted into a religion.

Shaw later came to a much different understanding of his mind, and of the mind in general, an understanding that made it much easier to connect his personal psychology with a religion. He came to see that what primarily characterized him and made him different from others was not an unusual rationality but rather the passion of his moral genius and the inspiration of his artistic genius, both gifts and instruments of the Life Force.[1] The mind of the Shavian hero continues to be rational because, as Shaw says in *The Quintessence of Ibsenism*, "Ability to reason accurately is as desirable as ever; for by accurate reasoning only can we calculate our actions so as to do what we intend to do: that is, to fulfill our will; but faith in reason as a prime motor is no longer the criterion of the sound mind, any more than faith in the Bible is the criterion of righteous intention" (*Major Critical Essays* 22). Shaw later upset the semantic apple cart even more by concluding that thought is a passion, that reasoning is an emotional act, that, as Eric Bentley summed it up in his book on Shaw, "all thinking is wishful" (Bentley 217).

Critics whose minds run along the grooves of cliché have tended to label Shaw and Shaw's heroes as "coldly rationalistic" because reasoning is supposed to be inhumanly mechanical and machines are associated with coldness. But all of Shaw's heroes and heroines, even the ones who themselves think they are cold-hearted rationalists, possess minds chiefly characterized by the intense heat and emotional nature of their rapid reasoning about events and issues. Shaw was most explicit about this in describing Saint Joan: "Everything she did was thoroughly calculated . . . though the process was so rapid that she was hardly conscious of it, and ascribed it all to her voices" (*Collected Plays* 6:37). This rapid reasoning amounts to the sort of instantaneous perception of reality that is conventionally called "vision" or "genius." There is nothing cold or mechanical about it. Having its source in the irrational unconscious, which presumably contains the entire past of the Life Force as well as its present impulses and the potential of its future, this superrational vision is like a hot, flashing light that, passing through the mind, illuminates some of the dark places. In no joking mood, Shaw once compared this action of the mind to sexual orgasm, to the detriment of the latter. He had come to understand that as blood is the very life of the brain, nourishing that field of electrochemical charges we call thinking, the mind is therefore to be understood as an organ of passion as surely as any other organ of our bodies.[2] The mind, after all, *is* body (that is, matter) as well as being that part of the body that aspires to be more than body, and that is in fact capable of creating "thoughts," which we are pleased to call "spiritual essences" insofar as they seem to exist without weight or dimension or palpability of any sort.

Conventionally, however, passion has been considered a function of the mindless body (or "the heart," as certain sentimental writers of Shaw's day would have insisted), just as reason has been considered a function purely of "the mind." Typically, caught between his unconventional understanding of things and his need to communicate with a conventionally minded audience, Shaw mostly used "the mind" and "the body" as conventional symbols of the rational and the irrational, respectively, though he also sometimes used them unconventionally to make the point that the usual dualism is not accurate. Physiologically, the mind, not the heart, is the seat of the passions. But stuck with a symbolism difficult to overturn, the only way he could see to make this point in literature was, first of all, by accepting the conventions (use of "the body" to symbolize the irrational in general), then by making "the body" a symbol of the irrationality of the *mind* in particular, confusing though it be.

A critic once accused Shaw of being "a chaos of clear opinions" (Bentley 20), in fact, but it was more a case of Shaw's being clear about the chaos. Nobody in his day had a clearer sense of the chaos that lies at the heart of both life and language, and nobody struggled harder in its toils. It is the price of admission to Shaw studies that one has to enter the struggle with Shaw in order to understand him. Symptomatically, he once declared in exasperation, "I do not deal in definitions," in the midst of a work that did nothing but deal in definitions (*The Quintessence of Ibsenism* 30). We may share his exasperation at the shiftiness of words, but we can't escape their problematics any more than he could. Here we will try to understand the problematics of the mind/body, reason/passion dualism as he confronted them in the heart of Victorian darkness and as they conditioned his attempt to understand himself in the writing of himself.

Please understand that when I term the hero of Shaw's third novel "a monster of the body," the term "body" refers, to be sure, to Shaw's extreme turn to the irrationality of physical existence in general, after becoming fed up with Conolly's equally extreme rationalism, but it refers mostly to that irrationality that has its source in the mind. To repeat what can't be repeated often enough here: *the mind, not the heart, is the seat of the passions.* Though the hero of the third novel displays a certain "wildness" that is physical, hungering for sex like an animal, for example (though disguised as proper courtship), Shaw focuses here on the irrationality of the artist's mind—that is, the "bodiness" of the mind, as it hungers for expression and for "food."

The hero of *Love Among the Artists* is one Owen Jack, a Welsh composer supposedly modeled on Beethoven in looks, manner, and artistic temperament, but an unpublished short story called "A Reminiscence of Hector Berlioz" that Shaw wrote in 1880 suggests Berlioz was as much the model.[3] Certainly in his compositions Jack is post-Wagner, thus the scorn and obloquy heaped upon him by the academics who will allow nothing after Beethoven to be called music. A major theme is the obvious one of genius neglected and genius ultimately vindicated. The point is made repeatedly by contrasting the authentic genius of Owen Jack with the uninspired craftsmanship of Adrian Herbert, a contrast echoed on the female side by the difference between Mademoiselle Szczympliça, a Polish pianist of international renown, and Mary Sutherland, a mere dabbler in art.

The title of the novel is supposed to be a humorous reminder of the old popular song "Love Among the Roses," but it is misleading if it suggests bohemian love affairs. Rather than being centered on love, the novel is concerned first with art and second with whether artists should allow love to divert their energies. These are the social terms in which Shaw projects the psychological issue of what constitutes the artistic mind and how far it can accede to "bodily" appetites.

Henderson enjoys saying that the novel is "as innocent of plot as a Sunday school tract" (98), but as usual such enjoyment comes at the expense of understanding, for the novel is far from being either plotless or a Sunday school tract. The plot is more complicated than that of *The Irrational Knot,* but its structure is fairly simple. *Love Among the Artists* has two books (in the original as well)—the first very long, the second very short—which, although without titles, might be called "Before Marriage" and "After Marriage." In the opening scene we find Owen Jack sitting on a park bench in Kensington Gardens, to which Mary Sutherland, her father, and Adrian Herbert have come to view the Albert Memorial. Fatigued, they share the bench with Jack, a stranger to them, and discuss the difficulty they've had getting a tutor for Charlie, Mary's younger brother. Owen Jack, impoverished as usual (his name is a pun on his indebtedness), astounds them by butting in to offer his services as tutor. Herbert and the Sutherlands are taken aback by the impropriety of this but promise to check his references. Jack is eventually hired for the post and gets along famously with Charlie. Unfortunately, Jack's rough manner and brutal attacks upon the pianoforte in his labors of composition constantly offend the delicate sensibilities of his employers, causing his dismissal.

Then Shaw introduces a sort of *Trelawny of The 'Wells'* subplot. On the train back to London, Jack encounters Mr. Brailsford and his daughter, Madge, acquaintances of the Sutherlands. Brailsford is a haughty, intolerant old man who tyrannizes over his daughter, a spirited girl who wants to go on the stage. Brailsford has a secret love for the stage himself, but since acting is not a respectable profession for a lady he cannot allow it for Madge. Jack and Brailsford pass the time exchanging insults and anathemas until reaching London, where Jack aids Madge in escaping from her father. Later, à la Professor Higgins, Jack instructs Madge in elocution, the first step in her slow progress in becoming a queen of the theater.[4] Mr. Brailsford eventually becomes reconciled to his daughter's choice of profession but only after a bitter interval of disowning her. When Madge finally establishes herself as a first-rate actress, she attempts a liaison with her Pygmalion, but Jack rebuffs her.

The rest of the novel is largely concerned with Jack's rise to fame, his conflict with the academicians, and especially with the contrast between the two geniuses, Jack and Mademoiselle Szczympliça, and the two would-be artists, Mary Sutherland and Adrian Herbert. The contrast is made by a familiar Shavian device, that of misalliance. The characters engage in a sort of mating dance in which various partners are tried, found incompatible, and exchanged for others (recall that *Immaturity*, similarly patterned, was originally entitled *The Quadrille*). It is through such social interaction that the Shavian hero learns about the nature of his mind, its susceptibilities, and its difference from others.

Mary Sutherland begins the series of exchanges when she discovers after a long engagement to Adrian Herbert that despite their kindred interest in art she does not really want to marry Adrian. Adrian, having become infatuated with Aurélie Szczympliça, feels the same way. The engagement is broken off, Adrian marries Aurélie, and Mary ultimately marries a Mr. Hoskyn, a promoter for the Conolly Electro-Motor. Before Mary settles for Hoskyn, however, she receives a proposal of marriage from Owen Jack, who in a moment of weakness decides to mix marriage (a concern of the "lower" body) with art (a concern of the "higher" body, or mind). He is rescued by her refusal and dedicates himself thereafter to a life of art. Aurélie Szczympliça is not so lucky. Aurélie finds her marriage to Herbert a great inconvenience to the pursuit of her art, the problem being solved only by leaving Herbert behind when she goes on tour. Herbert meanwhile has become such a slave to his love that he grows negligent in his painting. In all this the only really successful and healthy marriage is that of Mary and the Philistine mechanic, Hoskyn, who succeed largely because they never interfere in one another's business. That Genius should not marry is obviously the moral. Genius should especially not marry mere Talent. Talent would be much better off allying itself with Business Interest and Practical Efficiency.

In *Love Among the Artists*, says Pearson, Shaw abandoned rationalism and "took for his theme the degrees and contrasts of that entirely mystical (or super-rational) thing called genius" (58). Shaw believed that his reaction against Conolly was total: "Jack is just the opposite of Conolly: the man of genius as opposed to the rational man. The novel makes a *volte face* on my part. I had before kept within intellectual bounds: here I let myself go and guessed my way by instinct" (Rattray 39). But Shaw is here confusing fact with theory, for the reaction against Conolly was not so absolute as he would have us believe.

As already shown, Shaw may have intended Conolly to be a complete rationalist, but he rather failed by making the man something of an artist and something of a genius as well. The factual character does not fit the theoretical character. The same is true of Owen Jack. However hard Shaw tried to present the character of willful, abandoned genius, he succeeded only in creating another Shavian hero who partakes of his creator's unusual combination of sense and sensibility. The difference between Jack and Conolly is one of degree, not a difference in kind, as Shaw would have us believe. Yet, as said earlier, it's what a writer imagines to be true that serves him as symbols of self. Calling Conolly "a monster of the mind" and Jack "a monster of the body" reflects Shaw's belief that the latter was an absolute reaction against the former—never mind the qualifications of character that make the reaction something less than absolute.

Certainly Jack tries very hard to be the opposite of Conolly—"I hate business and know nothing about it," says he (16)—but he nevertheless drives a good bargain with the Sutherlands for his tutorship, and he calculates to the penny the money he impetuously gave Madge at the train when she was escaping from her father. When Madge comes to repay him, Jack does not refuse the money but simply refuses to touch it, and Madge hands it instead to his landlady, Mrs. Simpson. Jack's impulses are all magnanimous. He gives Madge elocution lessons at no charge, but poverty makes him conscious of the need for some efficiency in money matters. The impecunious young Shaw must have decided that poverty is the natural condition of genius, for Owen Jack is always owing "jack." It's a fit name," says Mrs. Simpson, although she concedes that "he is honorable when he has the means" (66–67). It must have been aggravating for the efficient young Shaw, formerly a crackerjack cashier at a Dublin firm of land agents, not to have any money to be efficient with; he compensated by showing his contempt for money in drawing the character of the disdainful Jack, though Jack's disdain, like Shaw's, was theoretical only.

Jack is like Conolly in other ways, too. Jack is no mechanic, but he shares with Conolly and every other Shaw hero the appreciation of the machine (see note 12 in chapter 2). On the train ride to London, Jack is exhilarated at the rhythmic clattering of the wheels and composes in accordance with their inspiration. At the first playing of Jack's magnum opus, "Prometheus Unbound," Adrian Herbert is disgusted by the total lack of melody, whereas the American mechanic, Mr. Hoskyn, thinks it a wonderful piece of music because "it reminds [him] of the Pacific railroad" (245). Later, at Lady Geraldine's, Conolly the mechanic plays some of Jack's music "much more calmly and accurately than Jack himself played it" (230). As the use of the comparative here indicates, the difference between Jack and Conolly is, as I said, a matter of degree.

Jack is perhaps most unlike Conolly in his social manner. To Mr. Brailsford, Jack says, "I am as well versed in the usages of the world as you; and I have sworn not to comply with them when they demand a tacit tolerance of oppression. The laws of society, sir, are designed to make the world easy for cowards and liars. And lest by the infirmity of my nature I should become either the one or the other or perhaps both, I never permit myself to witness tyranny without rebuking it, or to hear falsehood without exposing it" (46). Conolly would agree with this diagnosis of the laws of society, but he's far too civilized, except in the *Knot*'s final scene with Marian, to conduct a deliberate campaign of insulting people. He is normally urbane and tactful in his truth-telling. Not so Owen Jack, who is variously described as "a bear," "a bull," "a buffalo." After conducting the orchestra of the Antient Orpheus Society, Jack castigates them to another for being "over civilized . . . afraid of showing their individuality." His piece "was written to be played by a savage—like me" (138).

Long before the lessons provided by Eliot's Prufrock and Joyce's James Duffy, Shaw understood that an effective personality must descend into the brute irrational for the source of its energy. Furthermore, he came to believe that a truly whole personality was an evangelistic personality, devoted to attack and conversion. Truth was the result of conflict, a strife of wills, and it took something of the animal to engage the enemy, however intellectual the combat.[5] That is why the hypercivilized Conolly becomes the "savage" Owen Jack. Jack, however, is an overstatement; the social manner of Bernard Shaw was somewhere between Conolly's and Jack's. Jack is perhaps a confession of how far overboard the young Shaw was going, or *thought* he was going, in his attempts to gain attention. Shaw tells how he thought that on those rare occasions when invited to other people's houses in the early days, he made the impression of being "a bumptious discordant idiot" (*Sixteen Self Sketches* 57). Jack, appropriately, lives in Fitzroy Square, where Shaw and his mother had moved from South Kensington.

Jack's brutishness is not merely in social manner; it is also a physical fact. "A sort of Cyclop with a voice of bronze" (22), Jack is short and thick-chested (a brutishness projected as truncated and bullish by the tall and thin-chested Shaw). Jack's face, marked by smallpox, is extremely ugly. It is handsome Adrian Herbert's opinion that "Nature does not seem to have formed Mr. Jack for the pursuit of a fine art" (8). The smallpox reflects Shaw's experience while writing this novel in 1881 where, despite childhood vaccination, he was stricken with smallpox and almost died of it. Pearson terms the experience "a humiliating exposure of his mortality" (58). Much of the novel was written during Shaw's convalescence, and shortly after the illness he began growing the satanic red beard to cover the pockmarks. So, too, the ugliness of Owen Jack contributes to his diabolical appearance. Nethercot calls this character Shaw's "first real diabolonian" (60). He has a very wicked look that he often uses to frighten people, especially servants, and when thwarted by circumstances he shakes his fist at the sky (41).

The effect of Jack's presence is to make the delicate souls of conventional society feel their fragility. They fear Jack as a china shop owner fears a bull, for Jack is a breaker of the thin cups and saucers of social habit. Herbert warns Mary of "the injury that can be done by the mere silent contact of coarse natures with fine ones" (32). In other words, Jack is to be treated like a dangerous criminal. He fulfills the definition of the outlaw by constantly disrupting the smooth workings of social rules. Mary remarks that "Jack creates nothing but discord in real life, whatever he may do in music" (130). But there is paradox here. Jack is an outlaw in art as well as life. Herbert and the academicians rant about his "lawless composition" (129), completely void of melody. Yet Mademoiselle Szczympliça insists that it is full of melody. As for Jack's social note, the adolescent Charlie gets along quite harmoniously with Jack. Harmony and discord, it seems, are relative.

In a further paradox, while the unbound Promethean is a terror to those still bound by conventions, in his unpredictable freedom lies most of his appeal. Though scandalized by him, society finds that it cannot do without him. "'Society' found relief and excitement in the eccentric and often rude manner of the Welsh musician, and recognized his authority to behave as he pleased" (174). In the character of Jack, Shaw developed much further the phenomenon of the privileged lunatic, which he was experimenting with in person as well as on the page, in such short stories as "The Miraculous Revenge" and "The St. James Hall Mystery." He had learned already that many people escape from their ordinary selves by identifying with a social gadfly, who is tolerated expressly for that purpose.

The toleration of Jack is not unanimous, however. Lady Geraldine, for instance, "was a lady of strong common sense, resolutely intolerant of the eccentricities and affectations of artists. . . . Society, in her opinion, had one clear duty to Jack—to boycott him until he conformed to its usages" (174). When Jack strongly agrees with the commonsensical advice he has overheard Lady Geraldine giving to Mary, she is much astonished: "Well, really!" says she, "Is this the newest species of artistic affectation, pray? It used to be priggishness, or loutishness, or exquisite sensibility. But now it seems to be outspoken common sense; and instead of being a relief, it is the most insufferable affectation of all" (179). There seems to be no pleasing Lady Geraldine, but Jack is being lionized by nearly everyone else.

His partial acceptance by society, acceptance of his musical genius at least, betrays Jack into a weak desire for further acceptance. He asks, "Why have I less right to the common ties of social life than another man?" (199). Upon his shocking Mary Sutherland by a proposal of marriage, she asks him if a true artist can really have any concern for either marriage or money. He replies ironically: "No, of course not. Music is its own reward. Composers are not human; they can live on diminished sevenths, and be contented with a pianoforte for a wife, and a string quartet for a family. . . . I am a privileged mortal, without heart or pockets. When you wake up and clap your hands after the coda of Mr. Jack's symphony, you have ministered to all his wants, and can keep the rest to yourself, love, money, and all" (198–99). Earlier, without irony, he says, "When I took to composing, I knew I was bringing my pigs to a bad market. But don't pretend to believe that a composer can satisfy either his appetite or his affections with music any more than a butcher or a baker can" (198).

After such speeches from "the heart," Mary wonders if she should sacri-fice herself for the sake of Jack, but Jack reads in her face the repugnance she really feels. He speaks in a stirring voice:

> I have committed my last folly. . . . Henceforth I shall devote myself to the only mistress I am fitted for, Music. . . . I have broken with the world now; and my mind is the clearer and the easier for it. . . . *I* hanker for a *wife*! . . . *I* grovel after *money*! What dog's appetites have this worldly crew infected me with! No matter: I am free: I am myself again. Back to thy holy garret, oh my soul! (201–3)

This speech has reminded critics of the final scene in *Candida,* where the poet Marchbanks turns his back on domestic comfort and strides out into the night, secure in the secret knowledge that genius does not need love.[6] Is Shaw ridiculing Jack and Marchbanks for bravado? Jack's previous commonsense speech about the needs of the man being unfulfilled by the achievements of the artist sounds rather more Shavian, but the unpublished young Shaw, nearly friendless in great London, must have felt an equal necessity for extreme dedi-cation to his art. Shaw may have felt the call to the "holy garret" to be sincere enough, yet simultaneously ridiculous. "There are times when composing music seems to me to be a ridiculous thing in itself," says Jack (149).

Although Jack is Shavian enough to see occasionally the absurdity in his rigid attitude of artistic probity, he cannot help assuming such extreme pos-tures. He is violently intolerant of amateurs, and only fear of poverty can force him into "teaching female apes to scream, that they may be the better quali-fied for the marriage mart" (197). His is a one-man campaign against the abuses of music, especially his own. He is much given to stomping out of the theater when the orchestra improperly executes the score. So extreme is his intolerance of artistic ineptitude that even Aurélie Szczympliça reproves him for insulting "those who are less fortunately gifted than he" (145).

But if Jack is such a monster of artistic propriety, it is because, in Shavian fashion, he feels a mystical connection between art and ethics. Jack refuses a bandmastership with the army on the grounds that he would not be "the hire-ling of professional homicides" (100). Music and ethics are deeply involved with one another. There are two kinds of art, says Jack. "There is an art that is inspired by nothing but a passion for shamming" and "there is an art which is inspired by a passion for beauty, but only in men who can never associate beauty with a lie. That is my art" (330). Nethercot believes that "It is a bit of a surprise to hear Shaw's mouthpiece reiterating that beauty is truth and truth beauty, and that that is all men need to know about art. . . . It is pure art that commands his allegiance at this time—art untouched by any hint of didacticism or utility" (139). There are plenty of hints of didacticism in Shaw's novels, but Nethercot is right that Shaw's allegiance at this time is more to Keatsian theory, if not always to Keatsian practice. Such loyalty should not be surprising, as Shaw, even when he later claimed to be a didact, insisted upon the unity of beauty and truth. The "moral passion" was *not* an ugly passion.

If Jack's artistic posture strikes us as absurd, we must understand it in the context of nineteenth-century aestheticism. Jack's volatile artistic temperament seems to us a cliché, mechanical in its predictable unpredictability, but for Shaw it was an expression of revolt against the even more mechanical cliché of a contemporary ideal, as represented by Adrian Herbert. Adrian explains Jack's deficiencies in a way that is more revealing of his own. Jack "has taken up an art as a trade, and knows nothing of the trials of a true artist's career. No doubts of himself; no aspirations to suggest them; nothing but a stubborn narrow self-sufficiency. I half envy him" (109). Furthermore, Jack "is so far from possessing the temperament of an artist, that his whole character, his way of living, and all his actions, are absolutely destructive of that atmosphere of melancholy grandeur in which great artists find their inspiration. His musical faculty, to my mind, is as extraordinary an accident as if it had occurred in a buffalo" (157). The two clichés about the artistic temperament thus come head to head. It used to be possible to recognize an artist by his Agonizing Doubts, Refined Manner, Delicate Sensibility, and Melancholy Disposition; nowadays "mere brute skill carries everything before it" (296), and the true artist is marked by supreme confidence in his genius and a robust rejection of all the prescribed forms of behavior. A significant difference between the two kinds of artist is in the class pretensions of the former. When Jack enlists a trombone-playing soldier found in a local tavern to accompany him in his composition, Adrian overhears the result and is very much affected by the music until he sees the maker of it, whereupon he "despis[ed] the whole art of music because a half-drunken soldier could so affect him by it" (31).

Much the same conclusion is arrived at on the female side of the question. The three major female characters—Aurélie Szczympliça, Madge Brailsford, and Mary Sutherland—represent three different levels of artistic ability. Aurélie, at the top, is unmistakably a genius; Madge, on the second level, is a fine craftswoman with moments of genius; Mary, "a woman of force and intelligence," cannot for all her high seriousness achieve anything beyond the amateur, though her intelligence makes her a discerning critic of the work of others. Mary instinctively recognizes the weakness in Adrian's work, just as she feels the force of genius in Jack's.

Mary Sutherland, though, is a puzzling character because she takes up so much of the novel; she probably has more scenes and lines than any other character. Woodbridge notes that she is the character "who is most central in the plot. . . . Such semblage of unity as the novel has depends largely on her" (12–13). It is difficult to account for Shaw's interest in her. As Woodbridge says, since she has "nothing bizarre about her, she is not a Shavian type. She is a serious, high-minded girl, with some wit but not much fun in her, whose chief virtue is perhaps her tolerant generosity" (12). Perhaps she has the central position because Jack is such a rude, noisy, willful character that he disqualifies himself as a *raisonneur;* Shaw could not readily use him for straightforward commentary on the happenings of the novel. Though limited by her class prejudices, Mary's combination of quiet sense, honesty, and tolerant generosity provides a kind of moral norm for the book through which the other characters are reflected.

Mary is something of an emergent New Woman, mildly scornful of conventional propriety and rather masculine in her walk and her general authority. She rules her father with an iron hand. It is against this background of the mildly rebellious daughter of the upper class that we are able to measure the rebellious character of Owen Jack and of Madge. It is by means of her critical intelligence that we can gauge the relative artistry of Jack, Herbert, and the others. And it is against the extent of her tolerant generosity that we measure the intolerance of class prejudice. Perhaps this would have been a better novel if Jack had commanded the center throughout. Certainly it would have been more spirited. But apparently Shaw felt the need of an ethical center that Jack's brute behavior, overstating Shaw's case for the irrational, could not supply. If Shaw had kept Jack in the center, he might have become more like Conolly. It is significant that Conolly is reintroduced in the final chapters and provides the rational voice on the question of "love among the artists" that Mary herself cannot supply since she is involved in it.

If Shaw had come to the end of rationalism by his second novel, he had not yet come to the end of Edward Conolly. The reader gets the feeling that the really dangerous man in this novel is not Owen Jack but Ned Conolly. He poses a far greater threat to society through his practical, economic subversion of conventional values than does Jack through his merely artistic rebelliousness. Jack's brutal aggressiveness is an important qualification of the Shavian hero, but Shaw comes back to Conolly because his practical concerns are closer to Shaw's own preoccupations at this time. The heroes of the final two novels will be more like Conolly than like Jack. Conolly's influence upon genteel society has been insidious. When invited out to Lady Geraldine's, he declares himself contentedly "at home" (228). Lady Geraldine is secretly gratified at this and sensibly accepts cultured, rich tradespeople as an improvement over the old style of ladies and gentlemen. After all, she asks, "who is a gentleman nowadays?" (231).

On the question of marriage for Mary, Lady Geraldine is all for the practical Mr. Hoskyn (Hoskyn is Conolly without genius or culture). She counsels Mary that taking a husband is not "the same thing as engaging a gentleman to talk art criticism with" (233). So much for Adrian Herbert. Mary has been her father's housekeeper too long to feel uncomfortable as the wife of a practical man like Hoskyn. And "a perfect husband is one who is perfectly comfortable to live with" (232). For that reason, "Genius . . . is a positive disqualification. Geniuses are morbid, intolerant, easily offended, sleeplessly self-conscious men, who expect their wives to be angels with no further business in life than to pet and worship their husbands. . . . They are not comfortable men to live with" (232). So much for Owen Jack. Conolly then explains to Mary why she should not marry a man like himself, who has achieved her ideal of a self-disciplined man. Giving an objective account of his marriage to Marian, Conolly explains how the model husband had led his wife "to believe that he would be as happy without her as with her. A man who is complete in himself needs no wife" (237). So Hoskyn, who is far from being the complete man, and who indeed needs Mary to complement his cultural deficiencies, is the perfect mate for her. And that is the way the marriage turns out, as symbolized by their offspring. Mary's baby is a "healthy and smiling child," in contrast to the baby of Aurélie and Adrian, which always looks sad and old.

Aurélie Szczympliça is one of the most charming of Shaw's many astonishing female creations.[7] The Polish pianist is an elusive character, "as evasive as a bar from a Chopin mazourka" (Huneker 536). She doesn't really fit any of the clichés about either women or geniuses, although Shaw undoubtedly meant for her to present the female side of the character of genius. She regrets her marriage to Adrian, as she finds it interfering with her art. To her, love is the most stupid thing in the world. To Adrian she confesses: "I cannot love. I can feel it in the music—in the romance—in the poetry; but in real life—it is impossible. I am fond . . . of the bambino, fond of you sometimes; but this is not love. . . . I see people and things too clearly to love. Ah, well! I must content myself with the music. It is but a shadow. Perhaps it is as real as love is, after all" (314). Aurélie has come to agree with Jack that "it is marriage that kills the heart and keeps it dead. Better starve the heart than overfeed it. Better still to feed it only on fine food, like music" (329). Aurélie refuses to conform to the image that other people have of her. When Charlie tries to make a Candida of her by becoming infatuated with his poetic image of her, Aurélie irately tells him that he is very mistaken: "I am not what you think me to be. I am the very other things of it. I have the soul commercial within me" (337). However poetic she looks, she is at one with the unpoetic-looking Jack in having the soul commercial within her and in seeing things too clearly to love. Once and for all, Shaw seems to be saying, artistic genius is not a matter of poetic appearance or noble intentions.

Many times in the course of this and other works, Shaw repeats the lesson of the discrepancy between a naive view of the artistic life and the hard-working reality of such a life. Here, he devotes a long chapter to a detailed account of the rising career of Madge Brailsford in its several stages, revealing, by the way, his thorough knowledge of the stage years before he became a dramatist. At first Madge "ridiculed the notion that emotion had anything to do with her art . . . the matter being merely one of training" (121). A love affair then opens her eyes to the value of emotion, causing her to despise her "complete method." She goes to the opposite extreme in declaring "that study and training were useless, and that the true method was to cultivate the heart and mind and let the acting take care of itself" (121). Later she achieves synthesis when she understands that "She had had to exhaust the direct cultivation of her art before she could begin *the higher work of cultivating herself as the source of that art*" (124; italics added). That statement of synthesis explains the art of Bernard Shaw as well as any, in fact so well summing up what he was doing in his novels that, with a change in gender, it could serve as a frontispiece quotation for this study.

As Hesketh Pearson puts it, *Love Among the Artists* has no catastrophe and no ending, it just stops (58). Shaw admitted that "it was a lame conclusion; but I simply stopped when I had nothing more to say" (*Collected Letters* 217). It stops with Aurélie's disillusioning of Charlie before her tour in America, which will leave Adrian behind, and with Charlie's decision to take a job with the Conolly Electro-Motor Co. Just before this, in his only scene in Book II, Owen Jack has disillusioned Madge about the possibility of romance: "Juliet must not fall in love with Friar Lawrence, even when he is a great composer" (331). Besides, he has no need of special romance. "Romance comes out of everything for me. Where do you suppose I get the supplies for my music? And what passion there is in that!—what fire—what disregard of conventionality! In the music, you understand; not in my everyday life" (328).

Jack argues, using conventional terms, that as his art has its source in "the heart," the heart must not be killed by stuffing it with the food of love. The great artist is a hungry man, great in art because hungry as a man. At least that is what the hungry, unloved young Shaw had decided, momentarily. In his more extreme Shelleyan moments, Shaw was capable of imagining that the body of the Superman could be "fed" entirely with spiritual food, but in his saner, more Shavian moments, some of which occur even in this novel, he saw that the Superman to survive must get along on the world's terms to a considerable degree, and he protested the tendency of society to make of him a Kafkaesque "hunger artist."

If *The Irrational Knot* goes too far in the direction of rationalism, *Love Among the Artists* goes too far in the opposite direction. Doubtless the extreme thesis of *The Irrational Knot* made necessary the extreme antithesis of *Love Among the Artists.* The reintroduction of Conolly in the last part of the latter, however, suggests that Shaw had sensed a need for synthesis even before he had completely finished his statement of antithesis. Perhaps that is why he brought the novel to such a swift conclusion and proceeded to a fresh statement of synthesis in the next novel.

Chapter 4

Synthesis (Theory): The Mind and Body of the Superman (*Cashel Byron's Profession*)

> There are pugilists to whom the process of aiming and estimating distance in hitting, of considering the evidence as to what their opponent is going to do, arriving at a conclusion, and devising and carrying out effective counter-measures, is as instantaneous and unconscious as the calculation of the born arithmetician or the verbal expression of the born writer. This is not more wonderful than the very complicated and deeply considered feats of breathing and circulating the blood, which everybody does continually without thinking; but it is much rarer, and so has a miraculous appearance.
>
> —Bernard Shaw, Preface to *Cashel Byron's Profession*, 1901

The quotation that opens this chapter suggests the basis for Shaw's symbolism of "the mind" and "the body" and also clues us in to the problematics of that symbolism. Although as symbols we speak of "the mind" and "the body" as separate things, in experience they are not separate, as suggested by the similarity between fighting and thinking that Shaw calls attention to in this quotation. As "the body" stands for the whole material self, it is simultaneously the repository of "the mind," a piece of matter that can create immaterial thoughts. "The body" as symbol can refer both to the body as the fleshly repository of biological drives, motives, appetites, and physical power and to the body as the "embodiment," literally and figuratively, of the mind. The "rapid reasoning" of the mind finds an apt symbol in the instinctual response of the body, as both are swift, natural, unconscious, and marks of genius. Those who "think" with their bodies, like Owen Jack the musician or Cashel Byron the pugilist, can be as much the genius and visionary as those mental giants known as "thinkers." Indeed, Shaw's point is that genius thinkers are those who use the muscle of the brain in the same way that Cashel Byron uses the muscle of his arm—with swift inspiration. Shaw came to see that the trouble with conventional nineteenth-century rationalism was that it incorrectly assumed that the reasoning brain is exclusively a calculating machine and furthermore a "cold" machine, constantly at war with the "warm heart." Shaw instead saw the brain as being the supersophisticated, blood-bathed, electrochemically charged muscle or organ that it really is, as well as being the seat of all drives and passions.[1] The effort of *Cashel Byron's Profession*, then, is, while using "body" and "mind" as conventional symbols, to overcome stereotypical notions of mind and body as separate things by narrating a "marriage" between them that reveals their inter-relatedness.

In constructing the plot of his fourth novel, Shaw seems to have made rare concessions to popular tastes, but the concessions were either superficial or perhaps in the nature of a joke upon the popular press, of the sort he later perpetrated in writing his plays as "genre anti-types" (Meisel 141).[2] The story line is pure Horatio Alger, Local Boy Makes Good. The "orphaned" hero, Cashel Byron, runs away from school at an early age, becomes boxing champion of England and the colonies in his young manhood, marries a wealthy heiress, and discovers himself to be of noble birth. He then spends his life fighting for noble causes as a member of Parliament, living as happily ever after as people are ever allowed to do at the end of a Shaw work. Were there nothing more to this novel than the bare plot suggests, we would be justified in dismissing the novel as merely another example of Victorian pulp fiction.

But Shavian frivolity always packs a hidden wallop. And Shaw's being an inveterately autobiographical writer adds even greater weight to the apparent slightness of this novel. Critics have been misled by the hero's being an uncultured pugilist of distinctly nonintellectual habits into believing that the autobiographical element is missing in this novel.[3] Shaw's taking boxing lessons at this time suggests an autobiographical element, but otherwise Shaw and Cashel Byron seem to have little in common.[4] The misunderstanding is caused by Shaw's trying something new. In the other novels he had fixed the autobiographical element mostly upon a single, male person, but in this novel he experiments with a dialectic. Besides being themselves, the hero and the heroine are "the body" and "the mind" of Bernard Shaw, as the young man was working out their relationship. Like a good Greek humanist, his conclusion was the marriage of body and mind. Following a certain Victorian idealism about the greater spirituality of the female, Shaw made "the mind" female and "the body" male. He would later reverse that characterization in *Man and Superman*, as part of his campaign to subvert Victorian idealisms (or to deconstruct value hierarchies, as we say nowadays), but his point throughout his career was that either sex could represent either quality, as indeed in this novel each—yin and yang—has a bit of its opposite in him or her.

Here "the mind" of Shaw is principally represented by the character of Lydia Carew. William Irvine, who doesn't like rationalists, says that Shaw in creating Lydia "allowed that superlogical electrical inventor, Conolly, after nearly ruining one story, to don petticoats and scramble into the principal role of another."[5] Allowing for the physical, psychological, and social differences between male and female, that's true enough, although in her occasional sententiousness and priggishness Lydia seems to retrogress beyond Conolly to Robert Smith.

Lydia's upbringing is suspiciously like John Stuart Mill's. Her father was a writer of books intellectual and cultural. Daughter and father spent much of their time traveling, sight-seeing, reading, and theorizing. By the time Lydia is twenty-five, she has "a reputation for vast learning and exquisite culture" (24). At the novel's inception, her father has recently died and left her a wealthy woman, the heiress of a huge estate and Wiltstoken Castle, "a nondescript mixture of styles [Turkish, Moorish, Egyptian, and Italian Renaissance] in the worst possible taste" (23). "All the rooms there were either domed, vaulted, gilded, galleried, three sided, six sided, anything except four sided: all in some way suggestive of the Arabian nights' entertainments" (180). The strange Eastern architecture and interior decorations exactly accord with the lower-class idea of aristocratic splendor. Lydia finds it all rather unbearable and does most of her work on the biography of her father outside the castle. She has managed, however, to impose some of her tastes upon the furnishings. "Everything was appropriately elegant; but nothing had been placed in the rooms for the sake of ornament alone. Miss Carew, judged by her domestic arrangements, was a utilitarian before everything" (43).

The "dismal science" of utilitarianism accounts for much of Lydia's behavior. She is "interested in facts of any kind" and writes letters only when she has something factual and informative to convey (107). Echoing Conolly, she says, "Work is one of the necessaries of life" (69). Among the many "manlike proceedings" that scandalize her friends is her participation in business, including accounting. She has "a manner of making people believe she is interested in them" (174), but her interest in people seems to be an extension of her interest in facts. She has the statistician's habit of treating people as facts useful in the inductive process of reasoning. And, like later Shavian heroes, she has a realistic appreciation of human motive, never deluding herself, for instance, about the motives of friendship. "Absolutely disinterested friends I do not seek, as I should only find them among idiots or somnambulists. As to those whose interests are base, they do not know how to conceal their motives from me" (109). Furthermore, far from despising her wealth, Lydia pragmatically sets "great store by the esteem my riches command" (109).

Lydia is equally utilitarian in her attitude toward art. Her politician cousin, Lucian Webber, warns another that Lydia's "pet caprice is to affect a distaste for art, to which she is passionately devoted; and for literature, in which she is profoundly read." Lydia, however, replies, "Cousin Lucian . . . should you ever be cut off from your politics, and disappointed in your ambition, you will have an opportunity of living upon art and literature. Then I shall respect your opinion of their satisfactoriness as a staff of life. As yet you have only tried them as a sauce" (49). Perhaps humans cannot live by bread alone, but the Shavian always reminds us that survival is even less likely on art alone.

Recalling the aesthetic regard of Smith, Conolly, and Jack for the railroad, it is not surprising to hear Lydia's opinion that "Clapham Junction is one of the prettiest places in London" (79). Her companion, Alice Goff, "thought that all artistic people looked on junctions and railway lines as blots on the landscape," a thought that inspires Lydia to poetic rebuttal:

> Some of them do . . . but they are not the artists of our generation; and those who take up their cry are no better than parrots. . . . The locomotive is one of the wonders of modern childhood. Children crowd upon a bridge to see the train pass beneath. Little boys strut along the streets puffing and whistling in imitation of the engine. . . . Besides . . . a train is a beautiful thing. Its pure white fleece of steam harmonizes with every variety of landscape. And its sound! Have you ever stood on a sea coast skirted by a railway, and listened as the train came into hearing in the far distance? At first it can hardly be distinguished from the noise of the sea; then you recognize it by its variation; one moment smothered in a deep cutting, and the next sent echoing from some hillside. Sometimes it runs smoothly for many minutes, and then breaks suddenly into a rhythmic clatter, always changing in distance and intensity. When it comes near, you should get into a tunnel, and stand there whilst it passes. I did that once; and it was like the last page of an overture by Beethoven, thunderingly impetuous. . . . Abuse of the railway from a pastoral point of view is obsolete. There are millions of grown persons in England to whom the far sound of the train is as pleasantly suggestive as the piping of a blackbird. (79–80)

This seems to be the definitive word on the new relationship between art and the machine. Machines are not to be automatically disqualified as unaesthetic.

Lydia is equally Millite in her politics. Democratically, she believes that "a native distinction and grace of manner [can be found] as often among actors, gipsies, and peasants, as among ladies and gentlemen" (55). Yet as these native talents provide us with a natural aristocracy, Lydia is democratic only to get at the real aristocracy. Lydia's democracy is not of the coonskin variety any more than was Shaw's or Mill's. If she is a leveler, her method is to "level up, not down." Although she keeps servants, she allows them the run of her library in the hope that they will better themselves. She would like everyone to be as clever as she is.

As befits a progressive Victorian intellectual, Lydia is also internationalist: "In the course of my reading I have come upon denunciations of every race and pursuit under the sun. Very respectable and well-informed men have held that Jews, Irishmen, Christians, atheists, lawyers, doctors, politicians, actors, artists, flesh-eaters, and spirit drinkers, are all of necessity degraded beings. Such statements can be easily proved by taking a black sheep from each flock, and holding him up as the type" (128). Lydia will have nothing to do with theories of racial, national, religious, or professional superiority, for superiority is purely an accident of nature, concerning individuals alone.

With beliefs like these, Lydia finds herself rather alone in class-conscious England. The Tory Lucian argues that their marriage would be compatible enough because her opinions "are not represented by any political party in England; and therefore they are practically ineffective, and could not clash with [mine]." Lydia replies that "such a party might be formed a week after our marriage—will, I think, be formed a long time before our deaths. In that case I fear that our difference of opinion would become a very personal matter" (111–12). As a matter of fact, Shaw's Fabian Society was only about a year away from being launched.

One is made to wonder, however, if Lydia's lack of political commitment is due to the absence of a party to which she can give her allegiance or to the intellectual habit of noncommitment. Her idea of truth is not particularly compatible with political action. She believes that "reticence is always an error" (110). Truth must always come out. The trouble is that she has a rationalist's rather than a pragmatist's idea of truth. That truth is relative, circumstantial, and a matter of consequences she will not admit. An Ibsenite before her time (that is, as Ibsen was misunderstood by his disciples), she is sure that the consequences of lying are always the same: "The one convicton she had brought out of her reading was that the concealment of a truth, with its resultant false beliefs, must produce mischief, even though the beginning of that mischief might be as inconceivable as the end. She made no distinction between the subtlest philosophical sophism and the vulgarest lie" (188).

Yet when the police are pursuing Cashel Byron for illegal boxing, Lydia hides Cashel and lies to the police. She even causes her footman, Bashville, to lie. During it all she "felt as if the guilt of the deception was wrenching some fibre in her heart from its natural order" (185). After the police have left, she declares that "the very foundations of my life are loosened" and bids Cashel never to darken her door again. She drops Cashel not so much because of any crime he has committed but because he is an impostor (she is unaware of his prizefighting) and has forced her to lie in his behalf.

> The evil of Cashel's capture was measureable, the evil of any lie beyond all measure. She felt none the less assured of that evil because she could not foresee one bad consequence likely to ensue from what she had done. Her misgivings pressed heavily upon her; for her father, a determined sceptic, had left her destitute of the consolations which theology has for the wrong-doer. It was plainly her duty to send for the policeman and clear up the deception she had practised on him. But this she could not do. Her will, in spite of her reason, acted in the opposite direction. And in this paralysis of her moral power she saw the evil of the lie beginning. She had given it birth; and Nature would not permit her to strangle the monster. (188–89)

Obviously Lydia Carew, with her rationalist's regard for the police, is a long way from becoming a political revolutionary, although she is making some progress toward that end. Later, when for the first time she tells a very small social lie for the sake of sparing another's feelings, she fancies "that she was beginning to take a hardened delight in lying" (202). Still, it is Cashel and not Lydia who ultimately goes into politics, for Lydia is of the type who can never sacrifice without discomfort her notions of absolute truth to the compromisings of political action.

But Lydia is not merely a scholarly recluse, bumbling, inept, and timid in all matters requiring action. In her own sphere of social action she is quite competent. Although she lives without ceremony, "whatever Lydia did was done so that it seemed the right thing to do" (54). Her little bourgeois companion, Alice Goff, wonders at Lydia's "secret of always doing the right thing at the right moment, even when defying precedent" (170). But there is a significant change from the manner of Jack, Conolly, and even Smith in the way Lydia feels about her mastery of propriety. She agrees with Mary Sutherland (now Mrs. Hoskyn) that there is a difference between good manners and conventional manners, but, she says, "one can hardly call others to account for one's own subjective ideas" (96). This statement is not in keeping with the proselytizing spirit developed in the other novels, and Shaw may not be approving it. Rather, this may be one more example of the deficiencies of an intellect uninspired by evangelical passion.

Lydia understands quite well the deficiencies of her rationalism, thus her motive for marrying Byron. She declares herself "sick to death of the morbid introspection and ignorant self-consciousness of poets, novelists, and their like" (221). "If one could only find an educated man who had never read a book" (79), she exclaims. Such outbursts of anti-intellectualism are understandable as reactions against the scholar's life, which Lydia, like many another scholar, is willing to undersell. Believing herself "not good at intuitions, womanly or otherwise" (111), she "thought herself a well-taught plodder in comparison to the genius of Mrs. Byron [Cashel Byron's mother, Adelaide Gisborne, a famous actress]" (155).

Lydia is confirmed in her self-devaluation by a letter left to her by her father to be read after his death. During their lives the relationship of father to daughter had been one of scholar to amanuensis or clerk, but in the letter the scholar struggles to express his "heart." He begins by acknowledging that he belongs "to the great company of disappointed men" (27). Lest Lydia develop a sense of injustice at the apparently selfish use he made of her, he wants to justify himself. He explains the egotistical character of her mother, whom he divorced after six unbearable years of marriage. He then explains that although he made use of Lydia without scruple, he never did so without regard to her own advantage, as he never imposed a task of no educational value on her. In time, the promise of his young daughter brought pleasure to a life that he otherwise thought barren and wasteful. He began to be concerned about her future, as "the world has not yet provided a place and a sphere of action for well-instructed women" (29). However, he does not counsel accommodation to the world:

In my younger days, when the companionship of my fellows was a necessity to me, I tried to set aside my culture; relax my principles; and acquire
common tastes, in order to fit myself for the society of the only men within
my reach; for, if I had to live among bears, I had rather be a bear than a
man. The effort made me more miserable than any other mistake I have
ever made. It was lonely to be myself; but not to be myself was death in
life. Take warning, Lydia: do not be tempted to accommodate yourself to
the world by moral suicide.[6] (29)

As for choosing a husband, the late Mr. Carew's counsel is heavy with a
sense of the futility of advising anyone in matters of "the heart." He has only
one prejudice: "Beware of men who have read more than they have worked,
or who love to read better than to work. . . . Self-satisfied workmen who have
learnt their business well, whether they be chancellors of the exchequer or
farmers, I recommend to you as, on the whole, the most tolerable class of men
I have met" (30). Such is the advice of a man who calls himself "an educated
stone," "an overcivilized man" (30). Much later, when Lydia is wavering over
the question of marriage, she comes across a Christina Rossetti poem that her
father had marked as a favorite:

> What would I give for a heart of flesh to warm me through
> Instead of this heart of stone ice-cold whatever I do!
> Hard and cold and small, of all hearts the worst of all.

Lydia recoils at these words, and, after long thought, speaks to herself in
conventional terms: "If such a doubt as that haunted my father, it will haunt
me, unless I settle what is to be my heart's business now and forever. If it be
possible for a child of mine to escape this curse, it must inherit its immunity
from its father, and not from me—from the man of impulse who never thinks,
and not from the rationalizing woman, who cannot help thinking. Be it so"
(204).

"The man of impulse who never thinks" is Cashel Byron. As proof that
he never thinks, "there isn't a more cheerful lad in existence" (203). Lydia
describes him as "a man who had never been guilty of self-analysis in his life—
who complained when he was annoyed, and exulted when he was glad, like a
child and unlike a modern man—who was honest and brave, strong and beautiful" (222). When she first comes across him training in the woods behind
Wiltstoken, she feels as though "she had disturbed an antique god in his syl-

van haunt" (36). He is like a beautiful Greek statue who delights her by coming alive. (In contrast, Byron thinks Lydia a ghost, or an angel, and her house a fairyland.) Byron as sylvan god is reminiscent of the innocent Donatello in Hawthorne's *The Marble Faun,* except that Byron does not lose his essential innocence. He remains a child, and Lydia treats him as the greatest of her children.

Even though he does not lose his innocence, Byron at the outset does lose his "home." Rather, he never really seems to have had a home. He is another disconnected young Shaw hero who as a child abided, against his will, in the orphanage-like boarding house that is the Moncrief House school for sons of gentlemen. He does, however, have one living parent, unlike any other Shaw hero in the five novels, but that parent might as well be dead. His actress mother, Adelaide Gisborne ("Mrs. Byron"), alienated him as a child by her changeable, hot-tempered treatment, causing him to reserve his affection for the servants. Quite early in his life she farmed Cashel out to a boys' school, visiting him only on rare occasions (a situation that perhaps reproduces Shaw's own sense of abandonment by his mother). When the master of the school summons Adelaide for an interview regarding the deportment of her son, she makes no effort to understand Cashel's side of the argument and agrees with the master that her son is a bad boy. After this interview, Cashel exclaims, "I hate my mother!" (8) and runs away from the school, scaling the wall in the best prison-break fashion. (This escape, by the way, may be a wishful reversal of Shaw's experience with his mother, who in 1873 ran away from him, in effect, when she abandoned his father.)

Cashel stows away on a ship bound for Australia, becomes a sailor for a while, then meets Ned Skene and his wife, Skene being a former boxing champion who now operates a gymnasium. The Skenes become his adopted parents,[7] and from then on he speaks of Mrs. Skene as his real mother, even after Lydia engineers a partial reconciliation between Cashel and Mrs. Byron. In short order Skene makes a champion of Cashel and together they return to England.

To be a boxing champion had not been Cashel's first ambition. His original ambition, to go into the army, was quite respectable. But when his flight from Moncrief House makes him a sort of escaped convict, he decides "to go to sea, so that if his affairs became desperate, he could at least turn pirate, and achieve eminence in that profession by adding a chivalrous humanity to the ruder virtues for which it is already famous" (10). Here again is the chivalric rogue whose involuntary outlawry prevents him from taking his rightful place among the respectable professions of society. Like the professions of the later Mrs. Warren and the "immoralist" named Shaw, the professions of piratry and prizefighting are outside the sphere of acceptable occupations. Yet the "chivalrous humanity" and essential gentlemanliness of Cashel create the paradox of the *chivalric* outlaw. Lydia comes to the realization that, after all, "Ivanhoe was a prizefighter." This in turn makes her wonder if "some romancer of the twenty-fourth century will hunt out the exploits of my husband, and present him to the world as a sort of English nineteenth-century Cid, with all the glory of antiquity upon his deeds" (219). Shaw of course has suggested this possibility by naming his hero "Cashel Byron," thereby evoking both Lord Byron, the very epitome of romantic exile and moral outlawry, and the Rock of Cashel in County Tipperary, which was the very emblem of Ireland's fighting spirit. But Cashel Byron, unlike the poet, fights only for "cash," thus suggesting a pun on the name "Cashel" that undercuts the otherwise heroic associations. Cashel Byron does not become the sort of fighter that Shaw prizes until he enters Parliament as a wealthy man and fights for noble causes without concern for recompense.

Cashel's basic superiority to the society that at first ostracizes him is well illustrated in two different scenes. In the first scene, as a test of their natures, Cashel deliberately insults Lucian Webber and invites Lucian to take a poke at him. Lucian is a relatively puny intellectual who lives in terror of physical violence of any kind, yet "his point of honor, learnt at an English public school, was essentially the same as the prize-fighter's" (217).[8] Fear of dishonor ultimately overwhelms the fear of physical injury, causing Lucian to take a wild, harmless swing at Cashel, who then congratulates him for showing pluck and cheerfully bids him good day. But Lucian is sickened by the revelation of his inner self; he sees "no escape from his inner knowledge that he had been driven by fear and hatred into a paroxysm of wrath against a man to whom he should have set an example of dignified control" (218). Lydia is ecstatically happy when she discovers that Cashel did not retaliate. She had wondered whether the brutality of Cashel was evidence of his deepest nature or merely professional. Now she knows: "He has beaten you on your own ground, Lucian. It is you who are the prizefighter at heart; and you grudge him his superiority in the very art you condemn him for professing" (224).

Another scene that points up Cashel's moral superiority occurs near the end of the novel. After having been shamed by causing Lydia to lie in his behalf, Cashel gives himself up to the police and stands trial. The result is an imposture of a trial. However illegal it is, the establishment of boxing, like that of prostitution, is generally winked at because of its secret popularity. The defense of the miscreants against the charge of boxing is brilliantly sophistic, carried on by "an eminent Queen's counsellor, whose spirits rose as he felt the truth change and fade whilst he rearranged its attendant circumstances" (228). After the defense had completed its case, Cashel "was awestruck, and stared at his advocate as if he half feared that the earth would gape and swallow such a reckless perverter of known facts" (228). The judge himself had handled the gloves in his youth, and he along with "the more respectable persons in court, became extraordinarily grave, as Englishmen will when their sense of moral responsibility is roused on behalf of some glaring imposture" (228).[9] Cashel and his opponent are found guilty of a common assault and are given a suspended sentence and a promise of being fined if they fight again in the next twelve months. As Cashel leaves the trial a free man, he exclaims, "By Jingo . . . if we didnt fight fairer than that in the ring, we'd be disqualified in the first round. It's the first cross I ever was mixed up in; and I hope it will be the last" (229).[10] Byron had complained to Lydia earlier, when she accused him of being antisocial in his profession, that it was unfair for him to "be put out of decent society when fellows that do far worse than I are let in. . . . If all these damned dog-bakers and soldiers and pigeon-shooters and fox hunters and the rest of them are made welcome here, why am I shut out like a brute beast?" (135–36).

It is a question that Lydia is very hard put to answer. For all her advanced opinions and philosophic radicalism, Lydia still shares some of the prejudices of her class, one of them being that prizefighters are not gentlemen. She is confused at first by the contradiction between the natural gentility she senses in Cashel and the brutality he displays in the ring, not yet understanding that the brutality is more that of Ivanhoe than of Attila the Hun. Upon being invited to one of Mrs. Hoskyn's "at homes" as a celebrity, Cashel rather incongruously harangues his drawing room audience for five solid pages on the necessity of "Ivanhoe's" possessing an "executive power" (a passage that will later find its echo in *Major Barbara*):

> We have been told that if we want to civilize our neighbors, we must do it
> mainly by the example of our own lives, by each becoming a living illustra-
> tion of the highest culture we know. But what I want to ask is, how is any-

body to know that youre an illustration of culture? . . . *You want an execu-tive power;* thats what you want. Suppose you walked along the street and saw a man beating a woman, and setting a bad example to the roughs. Well, you would be bound to set a good example to them; and, if youre men, youd like to save the woman; but you couldnt do it by merely living; for that would be setting the bad example of passing on and leaving the poor creature to be beaten. What is it you need to know, then, so as to be able to act up to your ideas? Why, you want to know how to hit him, when to hit him, and where to hit him; and then you want the nerve to go in and do it. . . . thats whats wanted worse than sitting down and thinking how good you are. . . . Dont you see? You want *executive power* to set an example. If you leave all that to the roughs, it's their example that will spread, and not yours. (87; italics added)

Later Cashel will have a chance to test this philosophy when Lydia bra-zenly walks through a disreputable section of London and is molested by a tough. As Cashel just happens to be passing by, he comes to her rescue. Al-though Cashel is not eager to fight, the tough wants a brawl until he discov-ers the identity of the champion and chooses the better part of valor. That's "executive power," and a much more powerful lesson in it will be given by Andrew Undershaft to his daughter and Adolphus Cusins in *Major Barbara* when he explains why "good people" should control politics by getting ex-ecutive power. Lydia Carew, the intellectual without a party and almost with-out a political conviction, feels frustrated by the "incommunicability of ideas," and, while she intellectually understands that to communicate even the no-blest idea "one must take one's gloves off" (62), she is temperamentally dis-inclined to enter the arena herself. After their marriage, it is Cashel who fights for her ideas in Parliament. It is the ignoble "body" that must go out to do battle in the name of the noble "mind."[11]

"Ivanhoe's" executive power makes him nearly unbeatable, but Shaw ad-mits a set of circumstances that can defeat even the genius with executive power. Byron twice boxes a savage named William Paradise. The first exhibi-tion is stopped when Paradise tears off his gloves, rushes Cashel before he can do likewise, and sinks his teeth into Cashel's shoulder.[12] The second af-fair is the bare-knuckle bout that was broken up by the police. In both cases Cashel beats Paradise to a bloody pulp, but Paradise refuses to fall. Shaw explains in the preface: "There is a well-known way of defeating the pugilistic genius. There are hard-fisted, hard-hitting men in the world, who will, with the callousness of a ship's figurehead, and almost with its helplessness in defence, take all the hammering that genius can give them, and when genius can hammer no more from mere exhaustion, give it back its blows with interest and vanquish it" (xviii).

Although Shaw was temperamentally disinclined to think much about defeat, he shows here an early awareness of the tragic potential in the career of genius, awareness that not all the moral genius in the world, fully equipped with executive power, can guarantee the subduing of the brute in creation.

But the brute must be fought, and it can be fought only on its own terms. When Cashel engages Paradise, Shaw writes that in Cashel "there was no chivalry and no mercy" (165). When Ivanhoe is fighting the Black Knight, he is foolish to abide by the chivalric code. Lydia struggles to understand this. Byron's "perpetual fighting metaphor" indicates to her his attachment "to the modern [Darwinian] doctrine of a struggle for existence . . . life as a continual combat." Byron agrees: "Just so. What is life but a fight? The curs forfeit or get beaten; the rogues sell the fight and lose the confidence of their backers; the game ones, and the clever ones, win the stakes, and have to hand over the lion's share of them to the moneyed loafers that have stood the expense; and luck plays the devil with them all in turn. Thats not the way they describe life in books; but thats what it is" (99–100).

Keeping in mind that pugilism is a metaphor for the fighting spirit and executive power that Shaw felt necessary to the noble cause, this view of life as a strife of wills is central to the Shavian philosophy; but its difference from the Darwinian "survival of the fittest" is that it does not define "the fittest" as merely the physically strongest. By "fit" Shaw means fit for human society. Furthermore, as the strife can bring out the best in human beings and make life more meaningful and more clearly defined, people should be encouraged to participate.[13] At least this is the view of the young Shaw who was about to abandon his role as spectator and become an amateur Fabian, taking on all comers in the debating ring, with every intention of rising to the level of the top professional in his field.

There is another paradox here. Our Shavian hero is an Ivanhoe fighting to make the world a better place, but only because such struggle is natural to him. According to Cashel Byron: "All this struggling and striving to make the world better is a great mistake; not because it isnt a good thing to improve the world if you know how to do it, but because striving and struggling is the worst way you could set about doing anything. It gives a man a bad style, and weakens him. It shews that he dont believe in himself much" (91). Here Byron is repeating the realization that came to Adrian Herbert at the end of *Love Among the Artists.* "Nothing can be what you might call artistically done," says Byron, "if it's done with an effort. . . . The more effort you make, the less effect you produce. . . . Ease and strength, effort and weakness, go together" (91–93). As an example, Byron points to a painting by Adrian of St. George and the dragon. St. George is in conventional fighting posture, but Byron argues that "one touch of a child's finger would upset him . . . because he's all strain and stretch" (92–93). Byron illustrates his point more graphically by gently placing his hand against the breast of Lucian, who has pugnaciously challenged his opinions, whereupon Lucian "instantly reeled back and dropped into the chair" (94). This lesson is an important qualification of the strife of wills: it seems there is an art to striving, and the quickest way to fall short of the goal is to force one's art. In short, a person who isn't a natural-born world-betterer should find something else to do. Shaw's chief objection to "do-gooders" is that they try too hard.

The lesson is universal, it seems. Alice Goff, Lydia's hired companion, finds it to be true in social matters.[14] When Lydia first engages her, Alice is insufferably bourgeois. She believes that good manners are measured by their stiffness and formality. Proper behavior is the very opposite of natural behavior and therefore something to be struggled for. Propriety seems to consist largely in being as uncomfortable as possible. Alice's salvation is that she is a robust young country girl who longs "for swift motion and violent exercise," and under the tutelage and example of Lydia she comes to understand that what natural grace she possesses in her mere physical presence is superior to and more trustworthy than the artificial poses of conventional etiquette that she has relied upon. She comes to understand that these poses are prescribed by etiquette because the bourgeoisie are insecure in their social manner, not trusting themselves to act correctly by behaving naturally. By the end, Alice finds the great commercial middle class to be "all a huge caricature of herself—a society ashamed of itself, afraid to be itself, suspecting other people of being itself and pretending to despise them for it, and so stifling and starving itself" (171).[15] Alice now understands that instead of being well-mannered she was merely self-conscious. She sees the distinction between "the most mannered [and] the best mannered." It is thus "true that effort defeated itself—in personal behavior" as well as in boxing (171).

The lesson of *Cashel Byron's Profession* is chiefly a physical one. Figuratively speaking, it is a much-needed boxing lesson that Shaw is giving first to himself (even as he was taking literal boxing lessons) and second to all who share his awareness of evil and his impotence to fight it. Far from being a frivolous book, this novel is rather profound in theme and philosophy. One of its chief lessons—that effort may defeat itself—sounds rather like a tenet of Zen Buddhism.

Shaw's novel moves along on at least three levels, one of which is clearly autobiographical. First is the objective story of the local boy who makes good, the sentimental assumptions of which Shaw undermines with a contradicting content. On another level is the general and rather explicitly symbolic story of the clash between the Millite "mind" and the Darwinian "body" then occurring in Victorian society, with the marriage of that mind and that body being Shaw's solution. On the final level is the autobiographical confession of the synthesis, or dialectical relationship, between "mind" and "body" that Shaw was working out in his own being.

Shaw ends the story on the first level by adding a joke in his revision of the novel. Lydia had decided to marry Byron as "a plain proposition in eugenics." "I believe in the doctrine of heredity; and as my body is frail and my brain morbidly active, I think my impulse towards a man strong in body and untroubled in mind a trustworthy one" (223). But Lydia discovers that "heredity is not so simple a matter as her father's generation supposed" (231)—or as Shaw had thought when he wrote the original. In the revision she bears four precocious children, all of them smarter than their father, "the boys disappointing her by turning out almost pure Carew, without the slightest athletic aptitude, whilst the girls were impetuously Byronic" (232). So much for eugenics.

On the second level, Shaw suggests in the original version that the marriage of the Millite "mind" and the Darwinian "body" is, like most partnerships, an unequal affair, for "the body" is really quite helpless, a child at heart, and relies heavily upon "the mind" for judgment, moral strength, and information. There's no doubt that Lydia controls Cashel and that all the trouble in dealing with the family is hers. But there is one benefit for her: taking care of such a troublesome family leaves her little time to think about herself. The morbidity of the Millite mind is healthfully transformed by preoccupation with the strategic matters of directing a family and a parliamentary career.

The autobiography of Shavian being, the third level, concludes on a triumphant note. The novel ends with a sense of relative wholeness, as if in preparation for a mighty endeavor that will require a whole person. Shaw has finished with the measuring of his mind and the training of his body; now he is ready for battle. All that he lacks is a religious impulse to set him going, and in the next novel the very reverend Karl Marx will provide that.

Chapter 5

Synthesis (Practice): Mr. Shaw's Profession
(*An Unsocial Socialist*)

A little past midnight . . . I was turning from Piccadilly into Bond Street, when a lady of the pavement, out of luck that evening so far, confided to me that the last bus for Brompton had passed, and that she should be grateful to any gentleman who would give her a lift in a hansom. My old fashioned Irish gallantry had not then been worn off by age and England; besides, I was touched by the similarity of our trades and predicaments.
—Bernard Shaw, Preface to *The Irrational Knot*, 1905

With my egotism, my charlatanry, my tongue, and my habit of having my own way, I am fit for no calling but that of saviour of mankind.
—Bernard Shaw [Sidney Trefusis], *An Unsocial Socialist*

By the time Shaw embarked on his fifth novel, he had come to a far better understanding of himself and was ready to declare his profession, that of "unsocial" socialist, in a new ironic voice. He had come to see that the difference between himself and most others was a difference in degree, not in kind; he was a mutant perhaps but not a Martian. His mind was just further developed than most, not in being more rational but in possessing a keener moral intelligence and a certain kind of artistic genius. These special qualities of mind made him unusual, certainly, and distrusted, but they did not make him the monster from outer space he sometimes felt himself to be. His difference from others was more like the difference between the realist, on the one hand, and the idealists and Philistines on the other, a difference that he would later draw out in *The Quintessence of Ibsenism;* even if they were at different stages of evolution, they were all at least members of the same mortal species. Furthermore, if anything, the realist was inclined to be *more* moral, not, as often charged, *less* moral or even amoral. With this understanding he could better see the humor in the way certain people acted as though he *were* a monster, and thus he learned to play his presumed monstrosity as a deliberate joke. Far from being a handicap, his "monstrosity" provided him with a wonderful comic device to instruct people in the difference between the real and the apparent. Further, the ironic acceptance of his role made him considerably more at peace with himself, on the one hand allowing him to escape the ivory tower for a life of moral action while, on the other hand, preventing him from becoming the sort of fanatic whose scourging of the world always ends in the world's striking back with martyrdom for the fanatic.

Of the kinds of fanaticism, two of the purest are that of the detached intellectual who in scorn isolates himself from the world (see Joyce's "A Painful Case" in *Dubliners*) and that of the Savonarola type of crusader who attempts by brutally coercive methods to impose his moral obsession upon society. In either case, the mark of the pure fanatic is the willingness to sacrifice life for the sake of his ideal. In the first case, the zealot is willing to endure a living death for the sake of remaining undefiled by the corruption of common humanity; in the second case, the obsessed is willing to kill others for the sake of removing the source of corruption. Most of us are able to release our lesser fanaticisms in relatively harmless ways, but for the extraordinary person such as Bernard Shaw, who is "fit for no calling but that of saviour of mankind," the possibility of pure fanaticism is always present and seldom harmless.

Shaw's five novels reveal that the question of "unsocial" fanaticism was a very real issue to him. Characters like Robert Smith, Owen Jack, Ned Conolly, and Lydia Carew express an early tendency on the part of the lonely, introverted young Shaw to withdraw in contempt from the world of vain flesh, a tendency redeemed only by his social instincts and the Shavian habits of common sense and good humor. As the novels indicate, the struggle to extrovert himself was long and arduous. Though with hindsight we may declare the outcome inevitable, to Shaw himself at the time the struggle must have seemed very uncertain. Though we may find it difficult to imagine Shaw residing all his life in an ivory tower, the young Shaw who was devoted to Shelley might not have felt this way.

Yet the novels suggest that the sort of fanaticism that would provide the greatest threat to Shaw was not the suicidal zeal of the ivory tower intellectual (that was Joyce's temptation) but the murderous mania of Savonarola, "fit for no calling but that of saviour of mankind." We see tendencies in the Shavian hero that, once he has found his faith, could lead to extremes of intolerance.[1] We need look only at the history of this century to see the path of blood followed by other disciples of the very holy and blessed St. Marx. It is thus with a sense of relief that we discover in *An Unsocial Socialist* a Shavian hero, fully extroverted and religiously motivated by Karl Marx, whose blend of common sense and good humor qualifies his revolutionary zeal sufficiently to avoid fanaticism of the Leninist stripe. The hero, Sidney Trefusis, luckily sees himself as a clown-prophet rather than a scourge-fanatic, whose task is to convert through ironic role playing and friendly persuasion rather than through bloody purgation of the body politic. His "unsocialness" is a joke.

Of his fifth novel Shaw once said, with characteristic thoroughness, "people who will read *An Unsocial Socialist* will read anything" (x), thereby relieving himself of the burden of defending it. Defending it *as a novel* is indeed a burden. There is first of all a discrepancy between Shaw's professed intentions and the seemingly different results. In writing the novel he had resolved "to give up mere character sketching and the construction of models for improved types of individual, and at once to produce a novel which should be a gigantic grapple with the whole social problem. But, alas! at twenty-seven one does not know everything! When I had finished two chapters of this enterprise—chapters of colossal length, but containing the merest preliminary matter—I broke down in sheer ignorance and incapacity" ("Mr. Bernard Shaw's Works of Fiction. Reviewed by Himself," in Lawrence 313). According to this account, *An Unsocial Socialist* is merely the first two chapters of an unfinished work. Perhaps taking Shaw's cue, critics have dismissed the novel precisely for being no more than "the merest preliminary matter." Henderson calls it "a brutal burlesque, full of mad irresponsibility and cheap levity" (107). Weintraub says that, in writing it, "the gaily paradoxical Shaw had overreached himself, attempting to erect his ponderous economic edifice on a foundation of whipped cream" (*An Unfinished Novel* 12). Among its earlier readers, the Macmillan critic declared it "a clever trifle" and hoped that Shaw would try something "more substantial" (Henderson 116–17).

In reply to Macmillan, Shaw shot off a letter protesting the charge of trifling: "Your reader, I fear, thought the book not serious—perhaps because it was not dull. If so, he was an Englishman. . . . You must admit that when one deals with two large questions in a novel, and throws in an epitome of modern German Socialism as set forth by Marx as a makeweight, it is rather startling to be met with an implied accusation of triviality" (*Collected Letters* 111). If the older Shaw thought that the novel was no more than the merest preliminary matter, the young Shaw who did the writing thought that he had created something quite substantial, however preliminary.

The problem is further complicated by a criticism of Woodbridge's that insists that "The book does not square with this account of its origin. It contains indeed a considerable amount of socialist preaching, but it is also a good story, with a plot as unified and symmetrically developed as any which Shaw had produced, and with some of his best drawn characters. The fact seems to be that in spite of himself he was still more interested in the characters and what happened to them than he was in his socialist theories" (18). That the characters, supposedly created for the sake of demonstrating an economic theory, nevertheless come to life and exist independently of their intended economic allegory may account for the sense of frivolity that many critics detect. The characters do seem rather startled by the heavy Marxist intrusion, and the economic situations into which the author throws them so as to demonstrate his theory seem so ludicrous that the only response to this farcicalizing of Marxism can be laughter. So wildly disconnected seem theme and character that readers of such ponderous tomes as Marx's *Capital* and Henry George's *Progress and Poverty*, or even the Fabian tracts, must by comparison think Shaw's work a Peacockian *jeu d'esprit*.

But there's another possible reason why Shaw's characters and many of the situations in which they find themselves are indeed farcical: they may be expressive of the crossing of a serious satirical purpose with a recent uplifting of the author's mood. On the one hand, a satirical contrast is drawn between the gay, irresponsible world of English society and the dark crime of social mismanagement of which it is guilty. The lighter and gayer the spirit of the English rich, the heavier and sadder the crime of unbrotherliness it is committing. The satirical point is precisely in the contrast between upper-class levity and the economic burden of the poor. On the other hand, Shaw's first response to this contrast is typically not one of burning indignation and frothing at the mouth. He is so deliriously happy at having the matter brought to his attention that he can think of nothing but bringing it to the attention of others as the great joke that it really is, and the darker comedy of the satire is thus lightened by the gaiety of Shaw's recently uplifted spirit. It is fitting that the most socialistic of Shaw's novels should also be his gayest. As Irvine puts it, "Gaiety is his natural artistic medium. Moreover, he had found a new faith. He was exuberantly happy in a dazzling new certainty."[2]

To illustrate his certainty, Shaw wrote a novel in which the most frivolous situations and characters are shown to have heavy economic significance. The "whipped cream" of social manner is weighty with hidden economic motive.

Shaw did not need to go into the manufacturing jungles of Manchester or Liverpool to make his economic point; that would have been too easy and too obvious. So utterly confident was he of the Marxist point of view that he dared to show its relevance in the places and situations farthest from Manchester— in a country school for girls and on the rural estate of landed gentry. You would expect to find Marx in a Manchester factory, but what the devil is he doing in the drawing room? In short, the critical confusion has been caused by another Shavian paradox: the relevance of Marx is most substantial where the life of England is most insubstantial.

William Archer says that the first time he met Shaw, in the reading room of the British Museum, Shaw was reading almost simultaneously from Marx's *Capital* and Wagner's *Tristan and Isolde* (*Collected Plays* 1:37). There, in a nutshell, is Bernard Shaw, and *An Unsocial Socialist* echoes the juxtaposition. Much of the comedy of the book, in fact, comes from the juxtaposition of romance and economics, and the dizzying rapidity with which the hero moves from one to the other. This is not to imply that the two are unconnected; they are juxtaposed because their ironic reflection upon one another contributes to a unified theme. A recent feminist and poststructuralist reading of this novel by Eileen Sypher, although it misinterprets my "juxtaposition of romance and economics" to imply no connection between the two, nevertheless argues cogently that "the novel exposes economic relations in the most unlikely place: at the level of everyday domestic gender relations, the scene of the Victorian novel. *An Unsocial Socialist* is a novel which powerfully and subtly links capital with patriarchy . . . which suggests that the position of workers, who sell their labour, is linked with that of middle and upper class women, who sell themselves in the marriage market" ("Fabian Anti-Novel" 242). Sypher goes on to argue that Shaw was ultimately frustrated in his politically radical and deconstructive agenda by the built-in patriarchal and antisocialistic bias of the Victorian novel (243). Such an exclusively feminist/idealist reading ignores contradicting detail (detail that, for example, points an accusing finger at a matriarchal bias behind the Victorian novel as well). Such a reading also ignores Meisel's demonstration of how Shaw drew satiric strength from his permeation and subversion of Victorian genres; it provides, however, a way of accounting for Shaw's abandonment of the novel that deserves further investigation.

At any rate, the opening scene certainly is an unlikely one for a novel purporting to be a Marxist analysis of a rotting capitalist society. The novel begins, in 1875, with three schoolgirls sliding down the banister at Alton College, Lyvern, the banister serving as a launching pad for a certain feminine rebelliousness that Shaw hoped would support his socialist agenda. The schoolgirls are Agatha Wylie, a spirited nonconformist whose talents of mimicry, ventriloquism, and candor keep her forever in trouble with the authorities; Jane Carpenter, a stout, practical, simple-minded creature whose inevitable comment on everything is "I never heard of such a thing"; and Gertrude Lindsay, a self-conscious young woman who insists a bit too much upon her good breeding, the mark of the underbred. The hero, Sidney Trefusis, manages to find time to romance all three and ultimately marries their ringleader, Agatha.

Before that development, the millionaire Trefusis busily works his Marxist wiles among the English peasantry, making converts and generally laying the groundwork for the revolution. He has just run away from his new bride, Henrietta Jansenius (who curiously shares Shaw's birthday), and has assumed the disguise of Jeffrey Smilash, humble peasant, who abides in an equally humble cottage near Alton College. As Henrietta's father, a wealthy merchant, is also the guardian of Agatha Wylie, Trefusis does not long remain undetected in his disguise. When Agatha is threatened with expulsion for her banister launch, Mr. and Mrs. Jansenius, accompanied by their newly deserted daughter, Henrietta, visit Alton College to plead for Agatha's reinstatement. Trefusis/Smilash has by this time made the acquaintance of Agatha and has been hired to do odd jobs around the college. Not long after arriving, Henrietta recognizes Smilash as her recently lost husband and faints in his arms. While Agatha, the only observer of this scene, scurries for help, Trefusis grabs Henrietta and runs for cover. After eluding a posse, Trefusis at great length explains to his lovely young wife why he had to desert her. Briefly, Marx and marriage do not mix (as art and marriage did not mix in the previous novels). Henrietta is simply too distracting. Although he somehow talks her into returning to London without giving away his disguise to the others, he is eventually captured by the police for abducting her. Fortunately, a telegram from Henrietta in London assuring her safety argues his acquittal.

Agatha meanwhile has been conjuring up a romance about the mysterious Smilash. In her presence Trefusis frankly drops his yokel accent and speaks as the well-bred son of an aristocrat of trade that he is, a technique that causes Agatha to imagine all sorts of heroism. The romance is heightened when one stormy night Trefusis bangs on the door of Alton College and pleads for hospitality for a peasant and his family whose flimsy house was destroyed in the storm. Such heroism causes Agatha to fall adolescently in love. Trefusis as Smilash encourages her with some pretty words, calling her his "golden idol" (104). This is harmless flirtation so far, but trouble ensues when Agatha writes a letter to Henrietta confessing her secret lover. As Henrietta knows who Smilash is, she immediately embarks for Lyvern in a rage to confront her husband with the incriminating letter. Trefusis explains the harmlessness of his philandering, protests his undying love, and packs her off back to London.

As this all occurs on the coldest day of the year, Henrietta comes down with pneumonia and shortly, as well as conveniently, dies. Trefusis returns to London for the funeral but behaves in a most scandalous way. He quarrels with Jansenius over his hypocrisy and over the matter of a tombstone epitaph. To make an economic point, Trefusis searches for a mason who will provide a tombstone at a fair price. When he refuses to attend the funeral, he quickly develops the reputation of a beast, exactly what would be expected of a socialist. Agatha meanwhile has learned the truth and in her horror and disillusionment withdraws into herself. After several seasons in London society she remains unmarried.

The novel was originally divided into two books, a division unacknowledged in the 1932 edition except by a shift of scene and the lapse of a few years. As Irvine describes the change, "Sylvan fairy tale becomes Marxist-Ibsenite social drama. . . . Shavian intellectual drama is obviously struggling to be born" (32). Most of the action of the second part takes place either on the estate of Sir Charles Brandon, baronet husband of the former Miss Jane Carpenter, or at the family mansion of Trefusis, called Sallust's House (no doubt to evoke the licentious Roman). After Jane developed into a handsome, ample woman, Sir Charles married her, under the delusion that her beauty and sensuous charms promised great sympathy with his own artistic aspirations. Jane is still stout in mind, however, and she quickly disillusions him as to her sexual and intellectual talents, at which Sir Charles tries "to drown his domestic troubles in art criticism" (187).

The Brandons first encounter Trefusis leading a pack of laborers in a march across one of Brandon's fields, claiming it as a right of way. Jane "never heard of such a thing," but she is so susceptible to Trefusis's flirtations that she invites him to visit her. A bit later she also invites Agatha and Gertrude, ostensibly for a class reunion but in fact to rescue them from a life of maidenhood.

The rest of the novel is concerned alternately with the evangelistic attempt by Trefusis to convert Sir Charles and his poet neighbor, Chichester Erskine, to socialism and with the involved philanderings of Trefusis among the women. Gertrude mistakes his intentions and plans suicide when she learns that he has proposed to Agatha, but Trefusis sweet-talks her into marrying Erskine, who all along has been harboring a tragic love for her. The novel ends with an ironic letter to the author from the "real" Sidney Trefusis, appended to the 1888 "cheap edition," protesting that Shaw has misrepresented him as a heartless brute. The letter congratulates Shaw for his talent, however, regretting that Shaw has no better employment for it than the writing of novels.[3]

Sidney Trefusis is the driver of this plot because he is himself a driven man, his motives rooted in overcoming family circumstances. He seems to be aware of his parentage only because of its economic significance. One of the earliest examples of the ruling-class recruit to socialism in the Victorian novel, Trefusis has inherited from his parents a considerable wealth and has a sense of guilt or moral discomfort about the way in which the money was collected.[4] His father "was a shrewd, energetic, and ambitious Manchester man, who understood an exchange of any sort as a transaction by which one man should lose and the other gain. He made it his object to make as many exchanges as possible, and to be always the gaining party in them" (68). As a cotton manufacturer the elder Trefusis was responsible for the involuntary slavery of many wretched Englishmen, and now his son is left with the awful burden of a wealth he did not earn, "whilst the children of the men who made that wealth are slaving as their fathers slaved, or starving, or in the workhouse, or on the streets, or the deuce knows where" (71).

The guilt is further compounded on his mother's side of the family, landed gentry. His mother's father had inherited considerable land that had first been settled by a fairly prosperous race of peasants, who paid him enough rent "to satisfy his large wants and their own narrow needs without working themselves to death" (73). But Trefusis's maternal grandfather was a shrewd man. "He perceived that cows and sheep produced more money by their meat and wool than peasants by their husbandry. So he cleared the estate. . . . he drove the peasants from their homes" (73). If anything, this is more wicked than what Trefusis's father did, for his grandfather was born free and wealthy and could at least have lived and let live. His father, on the other hand, "had to choose between being a slave himself and enslaving others. He chose the latter, and as he was applauded and made much of for succeeding, who dare blame him? Not I. Besides, he did something to destroy the anarchy that enabled him to plunder society with impunity. He furnished me, its enemy, with the powerful weapon of a large fortune. Thus our system of organizing industry sometimes hatches the eggs from which its destroyers break" (204).

The destroyers of capitalism are in such a minority, however, that they have first to build an engine of destruction—namely, a party of revolutionaries. Candidates for such a party are, according to Marxist theory, to be found among the exploited proletariat—thus Jeffrey Smilash, recruiter. The pretext for the Smilash disguise is that Trefusis is hiding from his wife, but there is no reason why some other disguise would not have accomplished the same purpose, nor even a reason why any disguise at all is needed. In fact, Trefusis becomes Smilash really because, in Shavian fashion, he has decided to play the economic fool to the madness of King Capitalism, a strategy that is not recommended in Marx.

Trefusis explains, in Shaw's final revision, that he chose the name Smilash because he thought it gave a pleasant impression: "It is . . . a compound of the words smile and eyelash. A smile suggests good humor; eye lashes soften the expression and are the only features that never blemish a face. Hence Smilash is a sound that should cheer and propitiate. Yet it exasperates. It is really very odd that it should have that effect, unless it is that it raises expectations which I am unable to satisfy" (104). The name exasperates because, although it suggests genial servility, Trefusis the ironist protests too much his peasant humility. He aggravates the ladies and gentlemen by constantly stressing his inferiority through the sarcastic use of drawing-room clichés about the poor.

For example, Smilash is deliberately reckless with the truth, for he is "of the lower orders, and therefore not a man of my word" (35). He confesses to one of the Alton College teachers that he is a "natural born liar—always was. I know that it must appear dreadful to you that never told a lie, and dont hardly know what a lie is, belonging as you do to a class where none is ever told. But common people like me tells lies just as a duck swims" (97). When hired to do a menial job, Smilash advises his employer: "I am honest when well watched" (39). When a local parson protests that paying Smilash too much for a job "would only set him drinking," Smilash humbly agrees and argues that a lesser wage will keep him drunk until Sunday morning, which is all he desires until religion can take over. After all he is a common man, who "understands next to nothing," and since "words dont come natural to him," he can expect nothing more than the other dumb brutes of creation (39–40). As for the accusation by a neighboring farm boy that Smilash had been seen kissing Henrietta, Smilash effectively refutes it by reminding the police that "a lady . . . dont know what a kiss means" (60), as physical stuff like that is practiced only by the lower classes. And of course the poor's indulgence in sex is directly responsible for their poverty, in the form of mouths to feed, so they've no one to blame but themselves. "Reverend Mr. Malthus's health!" toasts Smilash (90).

The poor have gotten themselves a bad character, and Smilash "humbly" agrees that it is largely a result of their lack of thrift. After rolling the lawn at Alton College for a few pence, he announces that he's going to "put up all this money in a little wooden savings bank I have at home, and keep it to spend when sickness or old age shall . . . lay their 'ands upon me" (39). But when he uses some of Sidney Trefusis's saved money to improve the dilapidated peasant's cottage he has rented to go with his disguise, the landlord warns him that the rent will be raised, as "a tenant could not reasonably expect to have a pretty, rain-tight dwelling house for the same money as a hardly habitable ruin" (82). Struck by the truth of this, Smilash later chides the rector of Alton College for "flying in the face of the law of supply and demand" by overpaying him "threppence." "If you keep payin' at this rate, there'll be a rush of laborers to the college, and competition'll soon bring you down from a shilling to sixpence, let alone ninepence. Thats the way wages go down and death rates goes up, worse luck for the likes of hus, as has to sell ourselves like pigs in the market" (64). The Smilash sarcasm is beginning to show through bitterly here, a revelation that contributes to his acquiring a bad character. A teacher warns him to mend his ways if he wants to get a better character. Smilash replies: "I am grateful to your noble ladyship. May your ladyship's goodness sew up the hole which is in the pocket where I carry my character, and which has caused me to lose it so frequent. It's a bad place for men to keep their characters in; but such is the fashion. And so hurray for the glorious nineteenth century!" (40–41).

Perhaps because the relatively understated irony of the "humble" Smilash persona was not really his style, Shaw soon developed the opposite strategy of playing the "arrogant" devil's disciple, overstatement being more natural to him. But the principles of ironic impersonation and smiling attack were consistent in both guises, and at least Smilash was an interesting experiment in impersonation. "G.B.S." is not fully born at the end of this novel, but Trefusis/Smilash is clearly the penultimate stage in that birth.

The Smilash disguise may have been dismissed, for one reason, because it does not allow for a direct enough attack. At times Trefusis finds that he must abandon his Smilash disguise to speak directly, as when he explains to Henrietta about the clichés with which they have been brainwashed. "At Cambridge they taught me that [my father's] profits were the reward of abstinence—the abstinence which enabled him to save. That quieted my conscience until I began to wonder why one man should make another pay him for exercising one of the virtues" (71). Beyond that was the question, what did his father abstain from? "The workmen abstained from meat, drink, fresh air, good clothes, decent lodging, holidays, money, the society of their families, and pretty nearly everything that makes life worth living. . . . Yet no one rewarded them for their abstinence. The reward came to my father, who abstained from none of these things, but indulged in them all to his heart's content" (71). The only thing his father abstained from "more and more as he grew richer and richer" was work. As for his father's argument that his fortune was the reward for "his risks, his calculations, his anxieties, and the journeys he had to make at all seasons and at all hours," Trefusis came to realize that this argument would better fit a highway robber (72).

Trefusis is a kind of advanced Shelley who sees that the masks of anarchy have shifted from the faces of kings to the faces of capitalists. He has no use whatsoever for the old style liberalism, as represented by the poet Erskine, author of *The Patriot Martyrs*.[5] Erskine is eager to show that he is just as revolutionary as Trefusis: "Is it not absurd to hear a nation boasting of its freedom and tolerating a king? . . . I admire a man that kills a king. You will agree with me there, Trefusis, wont you?" Trefusis certainly does not agree: "A king nowadays is only a dummy put up to draw your fire off the real oppressors of society, and the fraction of his salary that he can spend as he likes is usually far too small for his risk, his trouble, and the condition of personal slavery to which he is reduced. What private man in England is worse off than the constitutional monarch?" (199). He then goes on to detail the trials and tribulations of being a modern king. Fifty years later Shaw would expand this paragraph into a play entitled *The Apple Cart*, in which King Magnus gets his way with his cabinet by threatening to abdicate and run for office. Shaw was then accused of turning Tory in his old age, but this novel proves that his contempt for the old-style antimonarchical liberalism was there from the beginning.

Erskine also provides Trefusis the occasion for debunking artistic affectation. Erskine believes "that the sole refiner of human nature is fine art,"
whereas Trefusis believes "that the sole refiner of art is human nature. Art
rises when men rise, and grovels when men grovel" (165). Trefusis heatedly
denounces "the tyranny of brain force" by which less clever men are enslaved,
the artist being "the worst of all." "No men are greater sticklers for the arbitrary dominion of genius and talent than your artists" (74). "[An artist] wants
to be fed as if his stomach needed more food than ordinary stomachs, which
it does not. . . . He talks of the higher quality of his work, as if the higher
quality of it were of his own making . . . as if, in short, the fellow were a god,
as canting brain worshippers have for years past been assuring him he is. Artists are the high priests of the modern Moloch." And Shaw adds to the 1887
version, in corroboration of Yeats's "tragic generation": "nine out of ten of
them are diseased creatures, just sane enough to trade on their own neuro-
ses" (74–75). Shaw was interestingly medieval in his willingness to consider
the possibility of genius being a gift that, as Trefusis says, "costs its possessor
nothing; that it was the inheritance of the whole race incidentally vested in a
single individual; and that if the individual employed his monopoly of it to
extort money from others, he deserved nothing better than hanging." Trefusis
exclaims that artists were foolish "in fancying themselves a priestly caste when
they were obviously only the parasites and favored slaves of the moneyed
classes" (135). Though he trimmed his share-the-wealth program a bit later,
here is proof that Shaw was inclined toward sharing before there was anything
like Fabian policy. At this point, anyway, he believes that exceptional gifts,
whether they be gifts for writing novels or gifts for making money, should
not, in the socialist state, be rewarded by exceptional salaries.

Trefusis illustrates his contempt for the merely artistic by his neglect of
Sallust's House. When Erskine and Sir Charles visit him for a lecture on socialism, they are scandalized by the state of disrepair of the old, ornate mansion. It seems Trefusis has contributed to the normal decay by using the statu-
ary for target practice. To the horror of his visitors, he demonstrates his icono-
clasm literally by taking out a pistol and decapitating a statue of Hebe.[6] He
further startles these art lovers by declaring photography the art form of the
future. In photography "the drawing counts for nothing, the thought and
judgment count for everything; whereas in the etching and daubing processes,
where great manual skill is needed to produce anything that the eye can endure, the execution counts for more than the thought" (159). In Trefusis' own

photographic collection is proof of the superiority of photography over paint-ing. He converts Sir Charles to socialism, at least temporarily, by overwhelm-ing him with seemingly matter-of-fact photographs of working-class condi-tions, the effect being heightened by a contrast with photographs of his father's immaculate stables full of well-fed horses. Another collection is devoted to pairs of identical faces, one of which belongs to the nobility, the other to the peasantry, thereby illustrating "the fact that Nature, even when perverted by generations of famine fever, ignores the distinctions we set up between men" (205). A third collection contrasts the noble faces of "Nihilists, Anarchists, Communards," and such with the coarse, vapid faces of European royalty, thereby illustrating "the natural inequality of man, and the failure of our ar-tificial inequality to correspond with it" (206). Sir Charles is much impressed by the thoughtful art of Trefusis's photography, but the conversion is not clinched until he is apprised that Mr. Donovan Brown, the famous artist, is also a socialist. Donovan Brown is obviously based on William Morris, who for Shaw was the symbol of the regeneration of art through political com-mitment.

When Erskine earlier calls upon Trefusis for his opinion of the future of the arts, Trefusis responds with a vision of the future that anticipates *Back to Methuselah:*

Photography perfected in its recently discovered power of reproducing color as well as form! Historical pictures replaced by photographs of *tableaux vivants* formed and arranged by trained actors and artists, and used chiefly for the instruction of children! Nine-tenths of painting as we understand it at present extinguished by the competition of these photographs, and the remaining tenth only holding its own against them by dint of extraordinary excellence! Our mistuned and unplayable organs and pianofortes replaced by harmonious instruments, as manageable as barrel organs! Works of fiction superseded by interesting company and conversation, and made obsolete by the human mind outgrowing the childishness that delights in the tales told by grown-up children such as novelists and their like! [The next sentence was added to the 1887 edition:] An end to the silly confu-sion, under the one name of Art, of the tomfoolery and make-believe of our play hours with the higher methods of teaching men to know themselves! [Returning to the original text:] Every artist an amateur, and a consequent return to the healthy old disposition to look on every man who makes art a

means of money-making as a vagabond not to be entertained as an equal
by honest men! (160–61)

It is easy to explain this as a young novelist's reply to the Victorian art establishment that would not let him publish, or even as an expression of his
recent conversion to the new pragmatic politics, which had small use for pure
art, but Shaw returned in his sixties to the notion that all works of art are no
more than dolls for children (see *Back to Methuselah*, part 5). Doubtless here
he is having a little joke at his present state of being unpublished, but he also
really meant it. In the short run Shaw was as much the "Artist" as the "high
priests of the Modern Moloch" denounced by Trefusis, but in the long run
he envisioned the ultimate disappearance of art (as the production of commercial or museum objects) from the list of man's serious occupations. Whenever Shaw exaggerates or deflates the importance of the artist, it is relative to
either the short run or the long run.

Trefusis combines the visionary quality of the Shavian futurist with a sometimes straight, sometimes comic involvement in the present. After a long dissertation on the future of the arts or the future of England under capitalism,
he can abruptly turn to the practical work of political conversion or to the
frivolous play of flirtation. In the latter case, he has a way of making females
think that they are his favorite. In regard to women, Trefusis curses himself
for being unable to "act like a rational creature for five consecutive minutes"
(98). Women, brought up on the idea that the only interest a man can have in
woman involves matrimony, are often misled by his trifling. "He had no conscientious scruples in his lovemaking, because he was unaccustomed to consider himself as likely to inspire love in women" (239). More to the point is
his love of a holiday. Trefusis's "natural amativeness" is heightened by the
sternly ascetic work of the political revolutionary, so that holidays are essential to his health. Trefusis tells Henrietta that he has left her because "I have
too much Manchester cotton in my constitution for long idylls. . . . The first
condition of work with me is your absence. When you are with me, I can do
nothing but make love to you. You bewitch me" (77). But the separation is
not to be permanent, for he will occasionally return to her for a holiday. A
solemn feminist reading of this as patriarchal backsliding on Trefusis's part
is less than a half-truth; Trefusis's flirtatious nature mostly exemplifies the
susceptibility of certain men to beautiful women and has much less to do with
gender politics than with biology and the wily workings of the Life Force.

But gender politics is not entirely excluded. Though the idea of a sexual holiday is part of a permanent Shavian attitude—Shaw's Caesar will trifle for a moment with Cleopatra, just as King Magnus will enjoy a romp with Orinthia—yet in the first flush of his conversion to the new economics, Shaw allows his obsession to turn some of this flirtation into didactic occasions, though he keeps it within the characterizations. Anticipating the gender politics of the coming age, Trefusis's objection to monogamy is that it is monopolistic. After the death of Henrietta, he makes some of his flirtations occasions for lectures on socialism (in which today's reader will find automatic sexism): "If you want to make a cause grow, instruct every woman you meet in it. She is or will one day be a wife, and will contradict her husband with scraps of your arguments. A squabble will follow. The son will listen, and will be set thinking if he be capable of thought. And so the mind of the people gets leavened" (215–16). Further, Trefusis is genuinely shocked when Gertrude Lindsay mistakes his philanderings for a serious proposal because, as far as he is concerned, his attentions to her are only a means of liberating her from her false pride. He believes that she has good instincts that only need instruction to cause her to throw off the bondage of "convention, laws, and lies" (matriarchal as well as patriarchal) that fence her round (192). His attentions are to make her see that the formal and false "Miss Lindsay" is the bitterest foe of the natural "Gertrude," in that the aversions of the conventional Miss Lindsay are forever contradicted by the natural sympathies of Gertrude.[7] Miss Lindsay looks with disapproval upon "Bolshevists," but Gertrude is powerfully attracted to Sidney Trefusis. In this she should trust Gertrude. "I used to flirt with women," says the "reformed" Trefusis; "now I lecture them, and abhor a man-flirt worse than I do a woman one" (216). This is hard to swallow, but Trefusis *has* undergone some sort of change.

The distinction between Trefusis's first and second marriages seems based on a change of attitude toward "romance." The marriage to Henrietta was a horrible mistake because it was supported only by romance; the marriage to Agatha has a better chance because it is grounded more in reality. Agatha succeeds with Trefusis because she is instructed by the outcome of her first, teenage romance with him. Both had believed in the grand passion of the other but knew that they felt nothing of the sort themselves. "That is the basis of the religion of love," Trefusis explains, "of which poets are the high-priests. Each worshipper knows that his own love is either a transient passion or a sham copied from his favorite poem; but he believes honestly in the love of others for him. Ho, Ho! Is it not a silly world, my dear?" (114). Of all the women Trefusis knows, Agatha is "the only one not quite a fool" (224). He decides to marry her upon the sudden realization that he "was made to carry a house on his shoulders" (225). The proposal is more like Ned Conolly's or John Tanner's than the early Trefusis's. The couple will spend their honeymoon at a socialist conference in Geneva. Agatha has one month to prepare for the wedding.

We should not be surprised to find exaggeration and obsession in this novel. It is the work of a young man just rescued from the vacuum of Victorian nihilism and a bit drunk on a conviction after a long abstinence. Shaw is seeing the world differently, and not the smallest detail escapes his new economic vision. But his lively sense of the comic anticlimactic feeds on his own obsession. Although as a Marxist he knows the seriousness of the economic motive, as a comic novelist he knows the absurdity of the economic obsession.[8] For example, Shaw is surely poking fun at Trefusis for liking orchids because "a plant that can subsist on a scrap of board is an instance of natural econ[omy]" (167). By 1888, when he wrote the joking postscript for the Swan Sonnenschein "cheap edition," Shaw even seems to have realized that his straight presentation could have been misconstrued, for the postscript consists of a letter from character Trefusis to author Shaw complaining that the novel had been taken as a satire on socialism. It definitely was not so, but Shaw had gone enough overboard that his enthusiasm could have been misread as comic exaggeration for satirical purposes. Certainly it would not have been his last satire on socialism.

One wonders how joking the 1930 preface is as well. The Shaw of 1930 declares, "The contemplated fiction is now fact. My unsocial socialist has come to life as a Bolshevist; and my catastrophe has actually occurred in Communist Russia. The opinions of the fictitious Trefusis anticipated those of the real Lenin" (v). The opinions perhaps did so, but hardly the character. The differences between a Trefusis and a Lenin are profound. While both were thought "Machiavellian" in their ethics, Trefusis inherits from Robert Smith and the other Shaw heroes an aristocratic sense of propriety that is anything but Leninist in its concern for the proper way of doing things. For example, when Trefusis violates the conventional code of truth-telling by going back on his promise to Erskine that he would not take the same train Gertrude is on—he is still not violating his own, higher moral sense. He has misled Gertrude to the point that she may ruin her life, so he feels obligated to restore her by selling the marriage to Erskine. Fancy Lenin feeling any such obligation or performing any such task. The deception of Erskine was a harmless way to prevent him from ruining Trefusis's campaign in Erskine's own behalf—hardly a Machiavellian ploy.

Shaw seems to have rejected several other Marxist-Leninist attitudes and principles right from the beginning. Trefusis talks in campaign style about a revolution, but his methods are strictly pre-Fabian. By nature he is a permeator, permeation being an evolutionary rather than a revolutionary method. Through the processes of argument and debate, the "body politic" is gradually to change its mind until it becomes something quite different in character. Bleeding of the body politic is to be avoided. According to Trefusis, "Socialism is often misunderstood by its least intelligent supporters and opponents to mean simply unrestrained indulgence of our natural propensity to heave bricks at respectable persons" (79). Trefusis is also quite unconventional in his refusal to adopt the Marxist melodrama of villainous capitalists and virtuous proles. According to the formula, his father should be a villain, but Trefusis instead congratulates him for avoiding the common lot of slavery and bringing order out of chaos. Furthermore, he does not romanticize the working classes as virtuously heroic but sees them as individuals. When one of the laborers apologizes to Sir Charles for the protest demonstration led by Trefusis, Trefusis calls him "a grovelling famine-broken slave" (148). He will go "as gently as you please with any man that is a freeman at heart . . . but slaves must be driven, and this fellow is a slave to the marrow" (149).

As for the wage-slaves employed in his inherited Manchester factories, Trefusis is not about to set them free, for if he did they would simply become the slaves of some other factory owner undoubtedly less interested in their ultimate welfare. Worse yet, by freeing his wage-slaves, Trefusis would himself become a slave and lose the opportunity his money affords to carry on the work of reform. If the old commandment was "Give all that ye have to the poor and follow me," the new commandment is "Keep all that you have and work for the establishment of socialism," for the poor will ultimately benefit more from that than from private charity. People who misunderstood socialism liked to accuse the wealthy Shaw of later years of not practicing what he preached, as if socialism were a private ethic that the individual could practice in isolation. Shaw apparently understood from the beginning, when he was yet a very poor young man, the principle that if wealth is to do any lasting good it must be invested in economic reform, not diffused by transient charity (however much he contradicted the principle in practice). When Erskine chides Trefusis for not selling all and giving to the poor, Trefusis replies:

> A man cannot be a Christian in this country. I have tried it and found it impossible both in law and in fact. I am a capitalist and a landholder. I have ... shares ... and a great trouble they are to me. But these shares do not represent wealth actually in existence: they are a mortgage on the labor of unborn generations of laborers, who must work to keep me and mine in idleness and luxury. If I sold them, would the mortgage be cancelled and the unborn generations released from its thrall? No. It would only pass into the hands of some other capitalist, and the working class would be no better off for my self-sacrifice. Sir Charles cannot obey the command of Christ; I defy him to do it. Let him give his land for a public park; only the richer classes will have leisure to enjoy it. Plant it at the very doors of the poor, so that they may at least breathe its air, and it will raise the value of the neighboring houses and drive the poor away. Let him endow a school for the poor, like Eton or Christ's Hospital, and the rich will take it for their own children. . . . Sir Charles does not want to minister to poverty, but to abolish it. No matter how much you give to the poor, everything except a bare subsistence wage will be taken from them again by force. All talk of practising Christianity, or even bare justice, is at present mere waste of words. (212–13)

Because one cannot be a Christian in modern society, Trefusis finds that it is easy enough to be a "Christ." In his final version Shaw draws out the potential for martyrdom in his original characterization by having Trefusis say, "With my egotism, my charlatanry, my tongue, and my habit of having my own way, I am fit for no calling but that of saviour of mankind" (104), the trouble being that mankind doesn't have much use for saviors except to crucify them and take their name in vain. Trefusis has already had a taste of this reaction: "The British workmen showed their sense of my efforts to emancipate them by accusing me of making a good thing out of the Association for my own pocket, and by mobbing and stoning me twice" (206). Then comes the distinctly Fabian touch: "I now help them only when they show some disposition to help themselves. I occupy myself partly in working out a scheme for the reorganization of industry, and partly in attacking my own class" (206). Yet in Shaw's case the attack on his own class was that of the clown-prophet.

There are perhaps more differences than similarities between the characters of Jesus and Bernard Shaw, but no difference is more significant than the attitude toward martyrdom. Shaw's strong sense of anticlimax (one might almost say "antimartyrdom") was directly responsible for his long life. After scarifying the Romans and Pharisees in a very Christ-like manner, he would always relieve the tension with a joke, thereby winning acceptance or at least toleration rather than "crucifixion."[9]

Quite the fashion in modern criticism is the theme of "mask" and "face." "The man and the mask" approach implies a "real" face behind a "false" mask, the mask merely serving a public function that the face is too sensitive to endure or too earnest to handle. Shaw criticism is full of this sort of apology for the "real" Shaw—the shy, gentle, gracious hermit of Ayot St. Lawrence. Archibald Henderson assures us that the real Shaw of his infrequent visits was nothing like the imaginary creature of common fame. Shaw himself chimed in with a debunking of "G.B.S.," claiming him to be a fantasy of journalism. And the epigraph of Part 1 of this book declares the clown character of his public performances to be "a fantastic character" deliberately created for the purpose of making himself "fit and apt for dealing with men." There is much truth to all this, but it is rather misleading and partly fallacious in its psychology.

Recall how literature of the J. D. Salinger variety was once celebrated for its exposure of "phonies," people caught "playing the role," the implication in some Salinger criticism being that role playing is psychologically dishonest. The confusion is brought about, I think, by a misunderstanding of the art of personality. Hypocrisy is pretending to be something you are not, whereas Bernard Shaw pretended to be something that he really was and then for strategic reasons pretended that he was only pretending. He really was the clownish, aggressive, loquacious G.B.S. as surely as he was the shy, careful Robert Smith. The principle of antinomy accounts for their coexistence, as Yeats loved to point out in his own behalf, and neither was more real than the other. If anything, Shaw's public character was more real than the private if we define "the real" in terms of intensity and lasting quality. If, however, we define "the real" as that which exists legitimately within the individual being, then certainly Robert Smith was as legitimate to the being of Shaw as Ned Conolly, Sidney Trefusis, Owen Jack, Cashel Byron/Lydia Carew, or G.B.S, even if less intense than they.

Shaw called himself a "born actor," and to the actor within him the many parts included in the general role of G.B.S. were quite natural. They provided a repertoire within the limits of which he almost always remained. He very well understood that to go outside this repertoire was to invite failure. He has recorded at least one attempt at a false impersonation, as he was just beginning *An Unsocial Socialist* and the experiment with the Smilash persona. Speaking of a book ghostwritten for Lee, Shaw said: "I dramatized myself as George Vandeleur Lee, not very successfully, as the impersonation was false and foreign to my nature" (Henderson 946). Even as he was playing with the Smilash role, Shaw understood that it was an act of hypocrisy to play a role illegitimate to one's being; illegitimacy is the source of the "phony." In going outside the limits of his own rightful being, the phony invades and violates the character rights of others by creating the impression of falsity about the general character he is impersonating, which after all may be legitimate to someone else.

Bernard Shaw seemed sometimes to understand what I have been saying about the reality of his mask, but at other times he seemed not to. Occasionally he would declare his public self to be a sham, a "mere" fiction, a deliberate calculation in his propaganda war against folly.[10] He would fight folly with folly. But that is not the whole truth. Eric Bentley explains it as well as anyone:

> True to Shavian formula the force that moved Shaw without his knowing whence or why was wiser than his conscious intention. If one can see this, one can see that even the creation of the "fantastic personality" was not merely the mistake of a bad strategist. Shaw's creation of "G.B.S." was not solely the deliberate, Machiavellian creation he tells us about. It too was created by the Life Force, by the World's Will. By all means it is a mask. But then it is part of the Shavian philosophy that life offers us not a choice between face and mask but only a choice between one mask and another. The "natural character" which he calls "impossible on the great London stage," the stammering blushing young Protestant from Dublin, this also was a "role," though a bad one. Silly and self-defeating as "G.B.S." can be, he too has his divine spark. "Every jest is an earnest in the womb of time"— even the jests of a foolish-looking mask (217).

The distinction is thus between mask and mask, not between face and mask. Bentley's distinction is valuable in that it avoids the true and false connotations of face and mask. What is objectionable is the idea that the mask is somehow less real than the face behind it. Yeats would have understood this perfectly as it applied to himself, and it is one of the great misfortunes of this period that he did not realize that it applied to Shaw as well.[11]

Bentley feels that it is more accurate to speak of the alternation or juxtaposition of masks rather than of the mask overlaying the face. For example, there is a scene in *An Unsocial Socialist,* when Smilash goes into the cottage and seconds later Trefusis comes out, that particularly reminds one of the "Superman" comic strip routine in which Clark Kent, "mild-mannered reporter," disappears into a phone booth and seconds later out pops Superman, with red cape and bulging biceps. But which is the disguise? We are told that Clark Kent is really Superman and that Smilash is really Trefusis; but is it not equally true that Superman is really Clark Kent and Trefusis really Smilash? Bentley's way out is to declare both versions impersonations.

I have said that Smilash is an expression of Shaw's decision to play the economic fool to the madness of King Capitalism. Eric Bentley explains this perfectly in another context: "If modern life was as unreasonable as King Lear, Shaw would cast himself as the Fool. Trace the word 'mad' through his plays and you will find that many of the finest characters and the finest actions have it applied to them. . . . Bernard Shaw resorted to some very bizarre shifts. Living in this queer, disgusting age he found he had to give the impression that his highest quality—a sort of delicate spirituality, purity, or holiness— was fooling when what he meant was that his fooling was holy. The devil's advocate was almost a sort of saint. The clown was something of a superman" (210–11).

Conclusion

The Romance of the Real, Or, The Adventures of the Irishman in His Search for God

> The Webbs . . . will be remembered by their work. As I have said, the prophet of the race will be the political economist. There is nothing like prosaic work. I had a grand time on the vestry worrying about drains, dust destructors, and instituting women's lavatories. The Webbs made *a romance of reality*. . . . When a person takes you aside and asks you what rent you pay and whether your boots pinch, you know that he is interested in you. The Webbs had that curiosity about life in a magnanimous spirit; they missed nothing and saw everything. Charlotte got to know them because she wanted to do something with her money. (italics added)
>
> —Stephen Winsten, *Days with Bernard Shaw*

> The chief objection to fictitious romance is that it is seldom so romantic as the truth.
>
> —Bernard Shaw, *Immaturity*

Jacques Barzun well summed up a principal Shavian agenda: "Shaw belonged to a generation of artists uncommonly cursed by alcoholism, disease, drugs, and degrading sensuality. Yeats, we know, thought that a special curse had descended on his generation of gifted men; Shaw's moral intention is to restore a belief in the fact that an artist can be sane" (272). In the "sick" atmosphere of late nineteenth-century aestheticism and the artist's alienation from bourgeois society, which found a number of artists openly identifying with the crucified Christ (as Wilde did in *De Profundis*), Bernard Shaw did everything possible to disconnect himself from the "pure art" movement. He saw in its narrow concern a rejection of at least half the life legitimate to a human being, and in that rejection a primary cause of its "sickness." The perfect emblem of the time was indeed Oscar Wilde, the Marlowe of the New Drama, driven by a death wish. Shaw sympathized with and tried to help Wilde but, figuratively speaking, crossed to the other side of the street, the sunny side, where most people lived their daylight lives.

However, Shaw's strategic publicizing of himself as the very opposite of an aesthete led critics to misunderstand his art. Eric Bentley explains the cause of the misunderstanding:

> When he himself writes in an encyclopedia: "Mr. Bernard Shaw . . . substituted the theatre for the platform . . . as his chief means of propaganda," Shaw is making his excuses. Having chosen art rather than propaganda as his profession, he tries to make up for it by making his art as propagandistic as possible, or rather—which is a different thing—by *saying* that his art is as propagandistic as possible. . . . Not that there is anything untrue in the statement that Shavian drama is didactic and public. But it is personal and expressive as well, a fact which Shaw has been at some pains to conceal. . . . Shaw's drama expresses his nature much more than it champions particular doctrines. It even mirrors Shaw's life rather closely in a series of self-portraits. (203–4)

But if Shaw's art is more "personal and expressive" than public and informative, why did he abandon the novel for the more public arrangement of the theater? Among other reasons, could it be that the novels were *too* private? Without mentioning the novels, Bentley explains the perfect fitness of the theater:

> It is the very peculiar mixture of the public and the private which the theatre affords that makes it so apt to his needs. A play is a public occasion like a political meeting; it is a celebration like a church service; it is a performance like a concert; and it is a work of art communicated by impersonations, by masks. The theatre is a magical world within a world, more satisfactory to Shaw's purpose and temperament than any other. . . . He had . . . entered the theatre because it was a world apart. The paradox of Shaw's art is that he spends his energies in refusing to let the theatre remain a world apart. If his artist's nature made him a theatre critic instead of a statesman, his puritan conscience made him use his critical articles for attacks on the conventions of art, on the pure artist Shakespeare, and on defenses of reality. If his artist's nature drove him to the "unreality" of the theatre, his puritan conscience drove him to take "reality" with him. (204)

Perhaps, as Bentley implies, the craving for public participation in his private story was a prime motivation for Shaw's substituting the drama for the novel. As far as Shaw's drama is personal and expressive, his theater takes on the aspect of a confessional, but insofar as it is public and informative, his theater takes on the character of a pulpit. In either case, pulpit or confessional, it serves an essentially religious function. Perhaps one of the drawbacks of the novel is that it was too secular and too private for the religious purposes of Shaw. The novel can easily lend itself to attacking religion, as Joyce used it in *A Portrait of the Artist as a Young Man,* but, G. K. Chesterton and Graham Greene notwithstanding, it does not support a religious agenda as well as drama can. The novel lacks the sense of communion that the group participation of drama gives, and it lacks the persuasive magic of liturgical performance. Drama, further, gives much greater reality to such affective devices of the preacher as gesture, facial expression, and tone of voice. Shaw's use of the theater as pulpit, confessional, and ritual performance[1] suggests that he was driven by an essentially religious purpose, that he saw his private story as an exemplum of the divine story. He would show how the Will of God could be done on earth without incurring the fate of the crucified Christ.

Taking a cue from one of his own titles, *The Adventures of the Black Girl in Her Search for God,* Shaw's work and life can perhaps be best understood as indeed an adventure in search of "God," the ground of Being, Authority, Motive, and Reality. Such a search was both complicated and made necessary because "God is dead," as Nietzsche famously put it, referring to standard theological and popular notions of deity. In the preface to *Immaturity,* Shaw referred to himself as a "fatherlandless fellow" (xxxv), and as was true of James Joyce, the loss of fatherland seemed to incur the loss of other fathers as well, from literal to spiritual. God the Father being dead, so to speak, the Superman must create himself. His literal sire being unworthy of fatherhood and thus psychologically dead to him, the Shavian hero, like Joyce's Stephen Dedalus, commits what amounts to autogenesis—he creates himself.

We have seen how the Shavian hero is always essentially parentless and nationless. Cashel Byron's mother is the only one to survive Shaw's general devastation of parents in the novels, and even she is alienated from her son. Further, Mrs. Byron is the living example of the neglect symbolized by the almost total absence of parentage in these novels. Their young hero or heroine is always alone, independent, and essentially homeless, either a lodger in someone else's house or the reluctant owner of some Palace of Art as unreal as Wiltstoken Castle or Sallust's House, a Heritage of the Past that is foreign to his or her nature and in which he or she resides very uncomfortably. In short, the Shavian hero or heroine is a person without a father, without a fatherland, and without a Heavenly Father. There is no "home," no center of authority, to consult or appeal to. They are their own authorities. If there is to be any authority in the world, it must proceed from the self-controlled Superman, compelled by his own moral nature to lead humankind to a better world. The Superman lived dangerously, however, for the resentment of the disruptive "world-betterer" has always gathered lightning, and all the more so in the modern democratic world where everyone must be equal and must not stand out.

The question of Shaw's "fatherlessness" has of course intrigued biographers. What is the source of the Shavian "orphan?" Personal experience or public strategy? A particular childhood or simply the human condition? B. C. Rosset's *Shaw of Dublin: The Formative Years* stirred up some fascinating speculation in 1964. Rosset's controversial thesis, which he admits is ultimately unprovable, is that George Bernard Shaw was named not after George Carr Shaw but after George Vandeleur Lee, the third party of the putative *ménage à trois* that lasted in the Shaw family from sometime shortly before Bernard's birth (1856) until Lee and Mrs. Shaw decamped separately to London in 1873, leaving George Carr and George Bernard behind. This scenario has his mother and his "real" father abandoning their "love child" when he's sixteen, a possibility that seems unlikely. There were, however, suspicions that Shaw was the bastard son of George Vandeleur Lee, Rosset believes, on the part of both George Carr (thus his insistence upon calling his son "Bob") and G.B.S. (thus his hatred of the name "George"). Rosset, further, reveals Shaw's obsession with the theme of "the fascinating foundling" (the title of one of his playlets) by counting up the impressive number of times the theme appears in his plays, letters, and conversations. The total would be astounding had not Shaw's novels left on our doorstep such "fascinating foundlings," so to speak, as Robert Smith and Harriet Russell, Ned Conolly, Owen Jack, Cashel Byron and Lydia Carew, and Sidney Trefusis (not to mention a score of minor characters).

Rosset has made his case overwhelmingly suggestive, but he does not make nearly the capital with the novels that he could have, as I have already shown. After passing reference to Smith's anonymous father and Smilash's "Mebbe I warnt born at all," Rosset goes into detail only with *Cashel Byron's Profession.*

In that novel, Mrs. Byron makes a rather odd statement in answer to a question concerning Cashel's relatives: "'I am the only relative he ever had, poor fellow,' said she, with a pensive smile. Then, seeing an expression of astonishment on the doctor's face, she added quickly, 'They are all dead'" (3). According to Rosset, "Attention to Shaw's phrasing will show that Mrs. Byron is actually saying that her son never had any relatives (other than herself) and amending it a moment later to say that the relatives he never had were dead. . . . Shaw struck precisely the note he desired in an artful suggestion of an unknown father" (141). Cashel knows nothing about his people, for, as he confesses to Lydia, his mother "boxed my ears one day for asking who my father was, and I took care not to ask her again" (137). When Lydia attempts a reconciliation between Cashel and his mother, Mrs. Byron at first rather contemptuously dismisses Cashel's pretensions to the hand of Lydia: "*You* marry Miss Carew! . . . Do you know, you silly boy, that—." Unfortunately Cashel interrupts her with, "I know all about it . . . what she is, and what I am, and the rest of it," so that we never discover what she and her son knew (211). But after she sees that her son is determined to marry Lydia despite the implication that he is baseborn, because either he is illegitimate or his father was lower class, she reverses her strategy and divulges the secret that Cashel will shortly be the heir of considerable property in Dorsetshire upon the death of Old Bingley Byron, his father's bachelor brother, thus contradicting both her previous statement that all his relatives were dead and the possible implication that his father was also baseborn. When Byron wonders about his title to the estate because people used to insinuate that his mother was never married, Mrs. Byron theatrically expresses great indignation and surprise that there could be any doubt. Cashel seems convinced by this of his noble birth, and the novel ends with our trueborn Ivanhoe marrying Princess Lydia in what, for Shaw, was an incredibly never-never-land ending. Rosset believes that the ending was pure wish fulfillment. While I agree that psychic necessity rather than a willingness to conform to Victorian fiction patterns was responsible for this ending, I am not so sure that it was simply a symbolic playing out of Shaw's desire for a literal legitimacy.

As far as Rosset is concerned, Shaw's father was George Vandeleur Lee, a man Shaw was very ambivalent about. That may be so, but of course the foundling theme can be accounted for in other ways. It may be no more, and no less, than an expression of the homelessness of genius amidst the decay and death of the old Victorian father figures. Indeed, I am sure that is the case. That explanation does not exclude the possibility that a literal bastardy may be the source of some of Shaw's art, but surely more important to the adult

Shaw than the search for a literal father was the search for a fatherland and a Heavenly Father. If he had suspicions about his parentage, he used them as materials for an artful expression of his lifelong quest for a "home" in society and a religious justification. Karl Marx (via the Fabian Society) promised the "home" of universal socialism, and the Life Force provided the religious justification, but only after Shaw had placed under suspicion all other kinds of fatherland and Heavenly Father.

The novels help us a good deal in understanding the search by the Irish immigrant for a "fatherland," a society that would both tolerate him and allow him to feel at home within it. As Victorian London seems no more hospitable to genius than the Dublin he has just abandoned, the immigrant seeks whatever hospitality he can find in supranational societies. At first Smith is just plain lost, at home nowhere really, least of all in Islington or Perspective. But Ned Conolly by virtue of his American inventiveness finds a home in the society of Intellect. Owen Jack manages to find some solace in the society of Art. Cashel Byron is quite comfortable in the society of Physical Action, although he rightly marries Intellect in the person of Lydia Carew before attempting Parliament, where he transforms Physical Action into Executive Power to pursue a career of Ethical Activism. Finally, the Marxist society provides the only home that Sidney Trefusis cares to reside in, far preferring it to Sallust's House. As these societies have in common an international or supranational character, their real premise is the abolition of all fatherlands. The new "fatherland" of universal socialism depends upon the removal of the old nationalistic fatherlands. We are all parents and children of one another, Shaw always insisted.

Because of their criminal opinions, disreputable behavior, or shabby appearance, the Shavian heroes find themselves ambivalently ostracized by conventional society, the same society that occasionally lionizes them for their talents. There is no progression in the essential homelessness of the Shavian hero—always outside, literally and/or figuratively, the presumably genteel society of his birth—but there is progression in the way these Outsiders meet ostracism by placing themselves in larger societies that find them acceptable.[2] From the society of Intellect to the society of Art to the society of Ethical Activism to the Marxist society is a progression from extreme detachment to extreme commitment. The novels tell the story of how a very social young man, rendered outlaw by his original morality, becomes an "unsocial" socialist bent upon teaching a lesson in better manners to those who had rejected him. This is in essence what Shaw meant by "socialism." The new "fatherland" of universal socialism would be a kinder, gentler, more mannerly "motherland" as well and would consist of a brotherhood/sisterhood of gentlemen and ladies, not the least of its attributes being more civilized relations between the sexes.

Shaw eventually came to see that the founding of a universal fatherland/motherland was not enough and that a Heavenly Father/Mother was needed to sanction human deeds. But the kingdom of heaven was within us, as potential, not in the sky, so Shaw's effort was bent on searching that potential. Although the novels do not tell the whole story of Shaw's religious development, they do show us the kind of young man who would require religious purpose to set him in motion. *An Unsocial Socialist* records his temporary celebration of the secular religion offered by that communist saint, Karl Marx. Yet not even the Marxist gospel escapes the critical debunking of the young devotee; almost immediately Shaw began casting suspicion upon the divinity of Papa Marx. His debunking of the class war, for instance, must have been one of the first to come from within the movement. Understanding the fallibility of Marx, Shaw cast about until he came up with the male/female Life Force, the Einsteinian "E" in $E = MC^2$, a sacred impulse at the heart of existence that gave considerably "higher" sanction than Marx to Shavian behavior. Marx helped him establish his theory of the new international fatherland/motherland, but the Life Force gave him the Heavenly Father/Mother he needed to authorize Shavian evangelism. The story of the Life Force, though, is reserved for the plays.

Shaw's novels mainly display the hero's *lack* of religious motive. His motives are ethical and sane enough, but they include no consciousness of religious meaning. The hero is ethical and sane for the sake of being so, not because ethics and sanity are part of a religious comprehension. As Shaw himself put it, "I . . . needed only a clear comprehension of life in the light of an intelligible theory: in short, a religion. . . . It was the lack of this last qualification that lamed me in those early days" (*Immaturity* xliv).

Yet, as I have shown, the heroes of the novels are natural-born champions of Faith. Smith argues for a faith he cannot name, Conolly argues for Rationalism and Realism, Jack argues for Art, Byron argues for Active Good or Executive Power, and Trefusis argues for Socialism. The novels, in short, reveal Shaw's search for "an intelligible theory" of life by way of Rationalism, Realism, Aestheticism, Ethical Activism, and Socialism, all pieces of the puzzle but not sufficient in themselves. While these secular creeds gave Shaw motive power and reasons for living the good life, they failed to supply the divine sanction he naturally craved.

That is why the Shavian hero always seems a chivalric figure off on a quest. The adventures of the hero in search of God involve him in a kind of romance, which, following Shaw's lead, I call the "Romance of the Real." In the epigraph to this section, Shaw describes the life of the Webbs in a way that accurately fits himself: "The Webbs made a romance of reality." This accomplishment parallels his own ability to find transcendent meaning in the midst of human detail and material living; to convert a prosaic vestry meeting, say, into a chivalric episode; or, in Joycean terms, to locate the spiritual *quidditas* in the humblest of human activities. Shaw's works brim over with Joycean "epiphanies."

Robert Louis Stevenson seems to have understood the underlying chivalry of Shaw's novels better than most. After reading *Cashel Byron's Profession* he wrote to William Archer about the young Shaw: "Let him beware of his damned century: his gifts of insane chivalry and animated narration are just those that might be slain and thrown out like an untimely birth by the Daemon of the Epoch. . . . if he only knew how I had enjoyed the chivalry!" (*Cashel Byron's Profession* xix). A bit later Stevenson wrote again to Archer: "It is all mad, mad and deliriously delightful; the author has a taste in chivalry like Walter Scott's or Dumas's, and then he daubs in little bits of socialism; he soars away on the wings of the romantic griffin—even the griffin, as he cleaves air, shouting with laughter at the nature of the quest—and I believe in his heart he thinks he is labouring in a quarry of solid granite realism" (*Letters of R. L. Stevenson* 48–50). Stevenson was sharper than most in appreciating the discrepancy between the seemingly "realistic" intent of Shaw's novels and the romantic results. He did not quite understand, however, that "realism" was coming to mean something different for Shaw than literary realism, nor that, unlike Scott's and Dumas's, Shaw's romance was *in* the realism. Shaw's new sense of realism was the envisioning of a reality imbued with transcendent meaning.

Stevenson was compared to Shaw in a nineteenth-century article that sheds light on Shaw's "romance of the real." In perhaps the first review of *Cashel Byron's Profession* (*Our Corner* May 1886), John MacKinnon Robertson very perceptively noted that the novel was of a new, hybrid type, but most of the review expresses Robertson's confusion over what that type might be. He rightly sees that the combination of "realistic" style with satire and comic fantasy has created disjuncture, but he's reluctant to consider this disjuncture as a valid and meaningful literary style in itself. Rather he takes it as a failure of some sort to write "true fiction," which he is inclined to believe is "realistic" by definition—"fiction in the sense of *criticism of life by the representation of it.*" Still, struggling with his own aesthetic idealism, Robertson asks "whether it is right to demur to such a fresh book as this because it does not fit into a particular aesthetic formula. Certainly there is a place in literature for *romance which is not Radcliffian, and which lays its scene in familiar postal districts rather than in hypothetical castles. There is, indeed, an obvious opening for a very valuable development of what we may call the intellectual romance*" (302–3; italics added). Robertson then goes on to compare Shaw's novel unfavorably with other examples of this genre, such as the work of Stevenson, but at least Robertson clearly sensed, as early as 1886, Shaw's predilection for finding romance in reality, a predilection very similar to the later Joycean agenda of imbuing the mundane with the miraculous.

Literary romance traditionally has two foci—the male quest to save the land and male adoration of Woman, who inspires the quest—and Shaw employs both, though in revisionary ways that include a fair amount of feminizing of the myth. The central role of Woman, not as actor in her own right but as motivator of the male, of course creates problematics for today's gender politics, which Shaw anticipated but only partially addresses in his novels. In romantic theory, although the chivalric figure ultimately serves God, he serves God principally by serving Woman, for it is in her service that he is called upon to exercise all those virtues that mark him as a godly man. Woman, further, symbolizes all those qualities of beauty and perfection that are attributes of deity, as well as fulfilling other sacred functions such as the bestowing of "grace" and "beatitude" and the creating of life. Most important, it is through her constant inspiration that the hero is encouraged to persevere in his quest for the ideal life, which in a sense involves a search for God or some divinely blessed magic that will return godliness to a godforsaken land.

The pattern of chivalry appears often in Shaw's novels, in very modernized forms, and is perhaps best illustrated by *Immaturity*. Smith is identified as a chivalric figure, first by the Dürer drawing of a threatened knight that he keeps with him, and second by his reaction to the presence of Woman. No sooner does he encounter Harriet Russell than Smith conceives a romance. However homeless he may feel otherwise, the Shavian hero always finds hospitality in the romance of Woman and can abide even in the heart of Victorian darkness if only it be illuminated by the smile of a likely female. Obviously Smith's response to Woman is conditioned by his need for encouragement. "Smith began to crave for a female friend who would encourage him to persevere in the struggle for truth and human perfection during those moments when its exhilaration gave place to despair" (83).

Smith conducts three different romances during the course of the novel—with Isabella, with Harriet, and with the prima ballerina at "a very wicked place" called the Alhambra. Harriet at first failing to give him the encouragement he desires, Smith increasingly frequents the Alhambra to adore the young lady who is the only inspired performer in an otherwise very uninspired ballet, significantly entitled "The Golden Harvest." His adoration of the dancer has a wonderful effect on him: "The dancer, instead of occupying his imagination to the exclusion of everything else, became a centre of mental activity, and caused one of those ruptures of intellectual routine which . . . are valuable as occasions for fresh departure in thought" (78). He becomes learned in the history of ballet and the traditions of the opera, and begins "to entertain notions of becoming a composer" (78). Reminiscent of Shaw's later affair with Ellen Terry, Smith's worship of his beloved dancer thrives on aesthetic distance. He never meets her. Because of its obvious artificial quality, Smith's imaginary love affair alternately exhilarates and disgusts him.

The romance comes to an end when Smith is fed a sordid tale about the real life of the dancer that bitterly disillusions him, a development that occurred only after Shaw revised the novel to draw out a moral that was incompletely realized in 1879. The revised version: {"Smith believed it all because it made him feel completely disillusioned. Men easily mistake the shock of disillusion for the impact of brute truth. As a matter of fact the whole tale . . . was a shameless fiction"} (125). Had Smith known the real story of the dancer, that of a struggling young artist trying to uphold the tradition of the grand school of Italian dancing, perhaps {"Smith would have fallen in love with her more hopelessly than ever."} The Shavian moral is that {"the chief objection to fictitious romance is that it is seldom so romantic as the truth."} The experience was probably for the better, as it made Smith {"realize that the dancer was a human being, and his dreams about her something that could never be realized even if he rescued her every night from a runaway hansom"} (126). Obviously, Shaw's revisionist version of romance as a romance of reality is already under way.

Shortly after Smith's disillusionment with the dancer, the Alhambra erupts into a volcano of flames and burns to the ground (a catastrophe that recalls the complete demolition of the Islington lodging house after Smith leaves. Smith leaves nothing behind!). With perfect timing, however, the spirit of romance rises phoenix-like out of the ashes of the Alhambra in the person of Isabella Woodward, an Irish colleen. Though the name "Isabella" continues the Spanish connotation of the name "Alhambra," and though Isabella's eyes remind him of the dancer's, Smith's romance with Isabella is of a quite different sort, as the impossible romance of the ideal dancer is replaced by the very possible romance of the very real Isabella. Iberian romance by way of earthy Ireland is a very different thing from Iberian romance pure in spirit. The romance of Isabella is the romance of a real human being, complete with sexual contact (a few kisses in Smith's case). Its character is that of flirtation because it is essentially a holiday affair, not to be taken seriously. Marriage violates the courtly sense, which sees in marriage the death of love. That is why marriage seems to have nothing to do with Smith, and why he would never have dreamed of inventing it. The true chevalier cannot bear to deny any attractive female his romantic patronage. The more devoted he is to his Lady, the more devoted he is to all ladies.

Smith is momentarily entertained by the romance of Isabella, but he concludes it with relief. It is revealing that Shaw ended the novel with Smith's return to a Harriet "married with children," thereby adding even greater reality to his romance. Smith's pilgrimage to Harriet for the verdict of his immaturity signifies Shaw's own psychic preference for realism in human affairs, which the young author had made plain enough but the older author chooses to emphasize in revising. Even in the original the young Shaw's preference for realism was dramatized when Harriet returns to Islington after her trip to Richmond and Smith, seeing her on the stairs, compares her with the Alhambra dancer: "Her appearance in the morning sunlight made him feel as though he had just stepped from that vile-smelling midnight vision of gilt sheaves, painted skies, and electric radiance, into a real harvest field, full of fresh air, noisy birds, and sunshine" (80). If Smith is already developing a Shavian preference for reality over "romantic" illusion, it is only because reality is more *"romantic," that is, inspiring and quest fulfilling.*

Of the three romances of Robert Smith—the romance of Ideal Beauty, the romance of Real Beauty, and the romance of the Real—the romance of the

Real is both first and last. Romantically speaking, the book begins and ends with Harriet. The romance of Ideal Beauty (the dancer), exhilarating while it lasts, ends in disgust and disillusionment; the romance of Real Beauty (Isabella) ends in flirtation; the only romance that endures is the romance of the Real (Harriet), which doesn't necessarily involve marriage. Smith's adoration of Ideal Beauty is a serious enough thing, as becomes a devout Shelleyan, but by its impossibilist nature it can only end in disgust and disillusionment. That conclusion to such adoration is inevitable unless one has the courage to meet the Alhambra dancer and convert her romance into a romance of the Real. As Shaw says, that would have been more romantic.

Smith's flirtation with Real Beauty is strictly a holiday thing, as it partakes of the ephemeral excitements of lovemaking. The reality here is the reality of playtime, of the child in man. It is satisfying for a while, but as it is by nature impulsive and inconstant, it is not to be taken as anything more than recreation. Ultimately Smith comes to prefer the romance of the Real as more romantic than the other two. The romance of the Real not only yields both the intellectual stimulation and the emotional encouragement provided, respectively, by the other two, but it also avoids the disillusionment of the one and the tedious hedonism of the other. At first, however, Smith lacks an appreciation of the Real. The Real naturally has imperfections, and the adorer of Ideal Beauty for a time finds them insurmountable in the continuation of his romance. Later, just as Harriet reconsiders her judgment of Smith, Smith too raises his estimation of Harriet. Harriet's sensible remark about marriage—"What else is one to do if one is to have a decent home?"—is the sort of realistic comment about human affairs that Shaw admired for its frank acceptance of life and its implied willingness to make a romance out of that reality. At the same time, the remark indicates a clear-sightedness that will not allow any delusions harmful to either mind or body.

These three types of romance seem to correspond to the three types of people Shaw classified in *The Quintessence of Ibsenism*. The romance of Ideal Beauty is the one for idealists, the romance of Real Beauty for Philistines, and that of the Real is the type for realists. That Shaw could indulge in all three types of romance is perhaps recognition of the fact that he contained within himself all three types of people.

Certainly, despite his preference for the Real, Shaw throughout his lifetime managed to carry on all three kinds of romance. The early adolescent part of his life was dominated by the Shelleyan intellectual's romance of Ideal Beauty, his young manhood by the philanderer's romance of Real Beauty, and the middle-aged Shaw by the domesticated husband's romance of the Real. His relationship with Ellen Terry, conducted by letter, is much like the romance of Ideal Beauty, although Ellen Terry herself had some of the qualities of Harriet, the real. Shaw knew this and tried to convert his relationship with the actress into a romance of the Real, but he did so only halfheartedly, as they both seemed to rather enjoy their remoteness: he watched her on the stage, and she peeked at him through the curtains. As Ellen Terry appealed to the most youthful part of Shaw, he must have been reluctant to give her up. His later philandering with "Stella" Campbell is very similar to Smith's romance with Isabella, even to the point of fleshly contact out of wedlock, and his affair with Charlotte Payne Townshend is similar to Smith's romance with Harriet, although in Charlotte's case Shaw took Harriet's advice ("What else is one to do if one is to have a decent home?") and married her. While Shaw fruitlessly worshiped Miss Terry from afar and merely philandered with Stella, he married the Real and lived with her for many years, falling off the marriage wagon fewer times than most. That is, while Shaw's diverse personality seems to have required all three kinds of romance, his preference and his most lasting affection was for the Real. The other types could be conducted better by post.

Perhaps we can get closer to understanding what is meant by "the romance of the real" if we focus on romance's quest rather than on the woman who inspires the quest. Jacques Barzun provides the following clue:

> Perhaps an iconoclast is always a man who destroys cheap images rather than ancient ones. At any rate, it is one of the oldest of all Western ideas—the idea of Christianity—which is in Shaw the central and lasting one. Shaw is a fundamentalist Christian; only, he insists that the traditional words be compelled to carry an active meaning. For him Sin, Revelation, the Communion of Saints, the Life Everlasting, the necessity of Gospel Love, are truths of experience. But they must be kept empirically true by continual re-embodiment, resisting time's burial of live meaning under the crust of habit. Charity, for example, can no longer mean giving coins to beggars; it must mean *making war on poverty*. Finding the means to the end is the task of the righteous, God's work. (270–71; italics added)

That is, if the quest of romance was, in thematic terms, to bring salvation back to the wasteland, in the modern world that might mean "making war on poverty." The elimination of poverty was as likely to heal the wounds of the body politic as any other grail. However badly the "war on poverty" has turned out so far, that war was clearly central to Shaw's chivalric vision. The war was an attempt to make Christian "charity" real in the modern world, and the quest for that reality was considerably more *"romantic," that is, quest fulfilling,* than the fictions of formalized religion, just as Shaw found the reality of political and economic engagement more romantic than the fictions of Walter Scott. Religion for him was something that happens in the street, not a ritual calisthenic to be exercised indoors on a Sunday morning, and the happening in the street is much more *romantic, that is, inspiring in its heroism,* than any number of exercises in organized religion's spiritual gymnasiums. (However, to the degree that Shaw's plays were themselves religious exercises intended to motivate action in the street, it should be noted that, while the early character Robert Smith heartily enjoys his visions of "destroyed churches and confuted priests," Shaw came to feel as he matured that the "calisthenics" perhaps did some good after all, provided that they were looked upon as *preparations* for religious action rather than as the whole of religion.)

Perhaps it was in the municipal realities of Fabian socialism that Shaw found his greatest romance. For Shaw, socialism was a political, social, and economic system for the regeneration of society, to be sure, but it also was a metaphor for something else. It was unlike Shaw to give his allegiance to something so ephemeral as a social system unless that system expressed a more permanent aspect of human affairs. Socialism was a figure of speech that referred to the only possible public response that a nineteenth-century "Christian Gentleman" (in Barzun's sense) could make to industrial capitalism and positivist science. These forces had made a mockery of traditional charity, not to mention all the other values of the traditional Christian gentleman. When private charity availed not, it was necessary to organize charity as part of the system. Eric Bentley explains this well:

> The socialism of Carlyle, Ruskin, Shaw, of what I have called the British "aristocratic" line, is not scientific; it is ethical. Their belief in humanity is not faith in the common man but in the gentleman. For the gentleman is a synthesis of the democrat and the aristocrat, the follower and the leader.

He is a living symbol of the fact that aristocracy is not something to be superseded but to be included in democracy, that the nobleman, if he has ceased to be a robber baron, is welcome in the new age, that we, as much as Louis XIV or George III, need men of light and leading. Moreover the gentlemanly ideal is the golden mean between two rival types—the priest and the soldier, the Pope and the Emperor or, in more recent language, the yogi and the commissar. That is why the British genius, which is for temperance, did not wait for Shaw before it formulated this ideal. Not only Carlyle and Ruskin, but such contrasted doctrinaires as Burke, Newman, and T. H. Huxley were spokesmen for it. (34–35)

In an off-the-cuff speech addressed to the National Liberal Club in 1913, Shaw said:

What is the ideal of the gentleman? The gentleman makes a certain claim on his country to begin with. He makes a claim for a handsome and dignified existence and subsistence; and he makes that as a primary thing not to be depended on his work in any way; not to be doled out according to the things he has done or according to the talents that he has displayed. He says, in effect: "I want to be a cultured human being; I want to live in the fullest sense; I require a generous subsistence for that; and I expect my country to organize itself in such a way as to secure me that." Also the real gentleman says—and here is where the real gentleman parts company with the sham gentleman, of whom we have so many: "In return for that I am willing to give my country the best service of which I am capable; absolutely the best. My ideal shall be also that, no matter how much my country has given me, I hope and I shall strive to give to my country in return more than it has given to me; so that when I die my country shall be the richer for my life." The real constructive scheme you want is the practical inculcation into everybody that what the country needs, and should seek through its social education, its social sense, and religious feeling, is to create gentlemen; and, when you create them, all other things shall be added unto you. (quoted in Bentley 35–36)

As we search for literal meanings for Shaw's figurative Superman, we should give serious consideration to the possibility that one principal reference was to the gentleman of the Renaissance humanists' conception. This concept was itself a derivative of the earlier chivalric ideal, and both were products of the synthesis between the best in Christian and pagan thought (see Ibsen's *Emperor and Galilean*). Shaw's call for "a democracy of Supermen" was perhaps primarily an attempt to restore both civilized, "gentlemanly" values in an age in which worth was leveled and lowered by the bourgeois democratic impulse and a sense of cohesion in an age in which life was fragmented by the practice of Social Darwinism and the capitalistic impulse.

Of course Shaw said a lot of harsh things about the English "gentleman," but all were in the same vein as his being antiromantic, anti-Christian, or anti-art: a way of distinguishing the false from the real, the dead from the living. If Yahoos call themselves "gentlemen" (sexism being part of Shaw's time), then true gentlemen have no choice but to call themselves "no gentlemen," "unsocial socialists," or "Supermen." If irreligious people identify themselves as "religious," then truly religious people can only call themselves "irreligious." If aesthetes claim to be "artists," then true artists must turn themselves into "propagandists." If crooks style themselves "pillars of society," the only name for true citizens is "enemies of the people." But Shaw recommended such misidentification with a laugh, "because by laughter only can you destroy evil without malice, and affirm good fellowship without mawkishness" (*Our Theatres in the Nineties* 1:vi).

That is the story of Shaw's novels. They show us the romance of a young Christian gentleman, possessed of the gift of irony, gradually distinguishing himself from his Victorian surroundings, discovering the cause of his outlawry, and devising the strategy of the ironist. The Superman—the Christian gentleman in desperate disguise—pretends to be the Satan that everyone thinks he is, thereby giving intelligent persons a chance to recognize and laugh at the discrepancy between the true man and the reputed devil.

The novels, thus, deal with the special problems of young, unproved genius in adapting to a hostile environment, an adaptation that involves him in a birth sequence as he passes into the womb of art before emerging a reasonably effective adult. *Immaturity* records the impregnation of the Shavian idea, Robert Smith being appropriately fetal in his undefined shapelessness and anonymity, but at the same time a "smithy" capable of autogenesis. The next three novels recapitulate the shaping of genius through the stages of intellectual development, emotional development, and the synthesis or balancing of mind and body. The final novel records the birth of a relatively complete but multifaceted human being, Trefusis/Smilash, who is not Shaw/G.B.S. exactly but well on the way to Shaw/G.B.S. The appendix to *An Unsocial Socialist* can be read as the cutting of the cord. Fittingly coming at the end of Shaw's incubation period at home and in the British Museum reading room, the last novel marks the opening of his public career. Shaw had worked out in private art the basic design of his public future, fulfilling his own dictum, "No person is real until he has been transmuted into a work of art."

Notes

Preface

1. The letter in which Shaw first signed himself "G.B.S." is dated November 29, 1880 (Laurence, *Collected Letters* 1:36). The account of his beard growing and hair styling is to be found in the preface to *Immaturity* (xx–xxvi).

Part 1: Introduction to the Novels

1. Loewenstein's *History of a Famous Novel* gives a somewhat different and apparently erroneous account of the editions of *An Unsocial Socialist*.

2. Holmes, *Some Bibliographical Notes on the Novels of George Bernard Shaw*.

3. See Berst's account of how in *Passion Play* "the rational and poetic views literally come together" (*Shaw and Religion* 18).

4. See Winsten's *Jesting Apostle: The Private Life of Bernard Shaw*.

5. For a further elucidation, see my article "Shavian Psychology" (149–71).

Part 2: The Art of the Novels

1. For an attempt to probe the modernist prejudice against Shaw as an artist, see my article "Shaw and Yeats: Two Irishmen Divided by a Common Language."

2. Grene's article (227–28) also made plain that the footnotes Shaw appended to *Immaturity* were less innocent than they seemed, for they supported the illusion that he had left the text untouched.

3. When he was working on the novel for publication in his *Collected Edition*, Shaw had a typescript of the manuscript prepared but omitted from the typescript two mice-chewed chapters and the first two pages of the epilogue. As the original handwritten manuscript is difficult to read, having numerous cross-outs and write-ins (which must have contributed to the reviewers' bafflement), the typescript has been extremely helpful.

4. For another appreciation of the art of Shaw's novels, see Berst's "*The Irrational Knot*: The Art of Shaw as a Young Ibsenite" (222–48).

5. See MacLochlainn's "Shaw's Mice" (10–11).

6. For examples of Shaw's contradictory remarks about the novels, see Hogan (63).

7. Incidentally, George Meredith as a reader for Chapman & Hall recommended that *Immaturity* be turned down. Not surprisingly Shaw considered Meredith's novels to be fifty years out of date the day they were written.

8. See comment on John MacKinnon Robertson in the Conclusion of this book.

9. An unpublished dissertation that attempts to establish a distinctly Shavian theory of fiction seems to have moved in that direction. See Judith Vincent's "George Bernard Shaw, Novelist: The Right Man in the Wrong Place?"

10. That the handwritten manuscript has pasted-over chapter numbers suggests that the thirty-nine chapters of this novel (plus epilogue) were originally numbered consecutively rather than being divided into four books. But the pasting-over could have transpired in 1879 or soon after.

11. This point is more gradually led up to and given more context in the original, which has Smith first meet Perspective society at the end of Book II, when he is called upon as Woodward's secretary to deliver letters to Woodward as a guest at Perspective. This episode was in one of the two mice-chewed chapters cut from the end of Book II, unfortunately so because it provides a richly comic view of Smith's timidity and discomfiture in society when a servant concludes by his dress that he is "either a poet or a pickpocket." It also shows a view of his pedantic reaction to discovering the fraudulent nature of the bohemian art world. The chapter concludes with Smith literally fleeing from Perspective at high speed. Even though there is an allusion in Book III to the earlier visit to Perspective, the loss of the chapters makes questionable Smith's relative self-assurance at the end of Book III, in which he meets Perspective society at Lady Geraldine's Wilton Place after the marriage of Cyril Scott and Harriet Russell.

12. Years later, in *Pen Portraits and Reviews* (22), Shaw summed up his view that "a play is a vital growth and not a mechanical construction; that a plot is the ruin of a story and therefore of a play, which is essentially a story . . . in short, that a play should never have a plot, because, if it has any natural life in it, it will construct itself, like a flowering plant, far more wonderfully than its author can consciously construct it." Such quotations point to Shaw's inclination for Romantic theory, but Shaw's practice as a novelist and playwright reveals a counterallegiance to classical methods. Although his works are almost always indirectly personal and self-expressive, and his constant theme is the Romantic one of genius in conflict with system, Shaw did not use the Romantic instrument of the directly confessional novel, nor did he realize the Romantic doctrine of following the motions of the mind with such startling innovations as internal monologue. Even had the Joycean method occurred to Shaw, he probably would not have used it because of his deeply ingrained habit of representing reality in literature externally, by means of surface character, surface action, and objective correlative, supplemented by the objective analysis of the omniscient narrator. In theme and inclination Shaw may have been Romantic, but in habit he was thoroughly classical. You will not find in Shaw any subjective presentation of the poet's mind through the use of first-person narrative, let alone any direct confessions of the poet's mind; rather you will find the poet's mind expressing itself by projecting into surface reality in the classical manner.

13. Rodenbeck, however, would call the plot Mozartian. See his ingenious comparison of *Immaturity* to *Don Giovanni* in the first chapter of his dissertation.

14. Rodenbeck (v). See Rodenbeck (24–30) for a comparison of Smith to the traditional hero of ironic comedy, the *Pharmakos*, who as a *Neinsager* either analyzes, condemns, and repudiates the vices of a sinful society or suffers as the victim of the same vices. Rodenbeck derives the expression "posture of opposition" from Richard M. Ohmann's study of Shaw's expository prose style, *Shaw: The Style and the Man* (107). Shaw was such a rebel, says Ohmann, that "the habit of saying No seems to have a life of

its own in Shaw's style, over and above its utility." Ohmann suspects that the posture of denial precedes Shaw's code of beliefs, and *Immaturity* would seem to bear him out, but I question whether the nay-saying Shaw was really more fundmental than the yea-saying Shaw. The basic explanation is that people tend to know what they *dis*like before they know what they like, partly because there are so many more examples of the former to see. That doesn't mean that the attraction toward the positive isn't ultimately stronger and more fundamental to Shaw than the repulsion from the negative.

15. Although Smith has many superior instincts, he has contracted a few inferior habits, such as his snobbishness. He is consoled by the smallness of his pay at Figgis & Weaver because it is at least a wholesale business, the vulgar retail trade being beneath him (11). When Davis gives him some sound advice, Smith refuses to listen because {"he could not believe that a man who dropped his aitches could have anything to teach him. He was only eighteen"} (22). Smith took the job with Woodward because, among other reasons, "Queen's Gate was a more refined sphere than the City" (173). When Woodward's butler tries to be familiar with his employer's new secretary, Smith, "desiring to maintain a distance between them," responds coolly (180). Later, after describing Harriet to Isabella, he is asked if he is related to Harriet in any way. At first Smith vigorously denies any relation, "discovering by his feelings at this question that he was not so thorough a republican as he had believed himself to be" (223). Obviously Smith, like Shaw, was trained in snobbery, whoever his parents were, and his republican principles are sometimes overpowered by his "aristocratic" habits, as the Shaw who has considerably overcome those habits delights in pointing out. This is perhaps the first sounding of a constant Shaw theme—that one of the chief signs of immaturity is the inability to act independently of habits inculcated by parents.

16. Grene argues (234–35) that Harriet's father "as recalled here is a wishful transmutation of Shaw's own. The drinking is made something flamboyant, reckless and enjoyable, instead of being, as it was in the case of Mr. Shaw, secretive, guilty and depressive. Shaw had suffered in childhood from what he felt to be neglect by both his parents: in the vicarious childhood he gives Harriet, the mother is significantly suppressed altogether and the indifference of the father turned into a positive libertarianism. Shaw liked later to heighten the unconventionality of his own family background, insisting particularly on his parents' lack of traditional religious belief. Yet there is counterevidence, which Shaw plays down, that his father tried to bring up his family as conventional churchgoing Protestants, and that his failure to do so may have reflected merely weakness of character rather than committed agnosticism. The strategy in *Immaturity* enables Shaw either to blot his parents out altogether, as in the case of Smith, or to remake his pathetic, shameful, drink-sodden father as the first of his paradoxically appealing devil's disciples."

17. Incidentally, Cheyne Walk was the residence of the Lawsons, very nearly the only people who invited Shaw to their at-homes in those early London years. Cecil Lawson was a landscape painter who stood as model for Cyril Scott. Shaw relates how he often stood outside their house, suffering agonies of shyness, before getting up nerve to knock. Shaw and his mother lived just to the north of Chelsea, in South Kensington. (See *Collected Letters* 29, 220, and the preface to *Immaturity* xliii.)

18. Shaw later insisted that the Superman would be known by his self-control rather than by his control over others or nature. See my article, "Shaw and the Passionate Mind."

19. Irvine (24). The scene Irvine refers to is that of Mrs. Froster's drawing room, the description of which I have already defended.

20. Quoted in Henderson (129) from Morley's introduction to *Nine Answers*. Morley was referring to a letter of Robert Louis Stevenson's that Shaw quotes at the end of the preface to *Cashel Byron's Profession* (xix): "let him beware of his damned century: his gifts of insane chivalry and animated narration are just those that might be slain and thrown out like an untimely birth by the Daemon of the Epoch."

21. See Sypher's "Fabian Anti-Novel: Shaw's *An Unsocial Socialist.*"

22. Meisel's *Shaw and the Nineteenth Century Theatre.*

23. For a review of critics who think Shaw wrote novels like a dramatist or dramas like a novelist, see Weintraub, "The Embryo Playwright in Bernard Shaw's Early Novels" 327–29.

Part 3: A Dialectical Portrait of an Emerging Superman

Introduction: God Being Dead, the Proper Study of Mankind Is Man

1. In *Here Comes—There Goes—You Know Who* (175), Shaw's disciple William Saroyan put it this way: "When I speak of the human race, I speak of the *concealed* human race, the *still* concealed human race, which is trying to come out from under, as it has been trying for a million years or more. Will it come out from under in the next thousand? Well, the answer is that it is already out in myself, and we know the slob I am, the crook, the liar, the fool, and all the other things we want to come out from under. The habit of uselessness is strong, it persists even after the element of the accidental in one man has enabled him or driven him, to come out from under. And that doesn't matter. We want the human race entire and whole. Man doesn't have to be suddenly something different or brand-new, entirely. Just partly, just in *addition to.* And if I have come out from under, at my best, there are surely others who have as well, by the thousands, most likely, although they may not be writers, communicators, makers of influence, setters of precedents, tellers, blabbermouths. They may keep it to themselves, not necessarily out of selfishness or indifference, but for want of a means by which to communicate."

2. Jorge Luis Borges poses an interesting aesthetic problem: "Can an author create characters superior to himself? I would say no and in that negation include both the intellectual and the moral. I believe that from us cannot emerge characters more lucid and more noble than our best moments. It is on this opinion that I base my conviction of Shaw's pre-eminence." (See Borges's essay on Shaw in *Other Inquisitions*, 207–10.)

3. A.E. (George Russell) called Shaw "the last saint sent out from Ireland to save the world" (quoted in Holroyd, ed., *The Genius of Shaw: A Symposium*).

Chapter 1. The Proto-Shaw: A Monster of Propriety (*Immaturity*)

1. Smith was named Robert probably because as a small child Shaw was called "Bob" and/or because Shaw wanted to associate Smith with Sir Robert Shaw of Bushy Park, the

relative Shaw always cited to underscore the aristocratic heights from which his "downstart" side of the family had fallen. As for the name "Smith," the connotations of anonymous Englishman and creative "smithy" probably account for it, but note also this passage in *Sixteen Self Sketches* (5), where "Smith" is used generically to denote the subject of auto-biography: "And here comes my difficulty as an autobiographer. . . . What earthly interest is there in a detailed account of how *the illustrious Smith* was born?" (italics added). Refer-ring to himself as "the illustrious Smith" may have been an accidental generic reference, but it may also have been caused by a remembrance (perhaps unconscious) of his first novel.

2. See the commentary on "The Miraculous Revenge" in my Introduction to Part 1.

3. For examples of Smith's snobbishness, see this book's "The Art of the Novels," n. 16.

4. In the original wording, Smith and Harriet have been discussing the ruinous mar-riage of Fraser Fenwick, and Harriet concludes:

> "Poor fellow! Why *will* people marry?"
>
> "What!" cried Smith. "Are you denouncing matrimony?"
>
> "The more I see of the world," said Harriet, "the more I am convinced that Cyril's case and mine is an exceptional one. The routine for most women is, one year of desper-ate effort to persuade themselves that they are happy; six months of doubt; and eighteen months of conviction that marriage is an utter and miserable mistake. Then they get tired of bothering themselves over it, and settle down into domestic commonplace, quite disenchanted, but not tragically unhappy. Of course, children make a great difference; but most people get quite tired of them, just as the children themselves do with a play-thing when its novelty wears off."

5. These three episodes reveal further that the diverse impulses of Smith's psyche—the romantic and the commonsensical—are unresolved except in the collision that pro-duces his strange and rather harsh sense of the ludicrous. This sense of the ludicrous will never entirely leave Shaw and is always the source of his harsher comedy, but in later years he will often achieve a more integrated psyche, in which romance and common sense will not constantly be at war but rather will combine to form the romantical common sense and commonsensical romanticism that is peculiarly Shavian.

6. Smith's greater reality may also be accounted for by Shaw's comic treatment of him. As he wrote, rather misleadingly, in the preface to *Cashel Byron's Profession* (vi), "The only characters which were natural in my novels were the comic characters, because the island was (and is) populated exclusively by comic characters." The heroes of his other novels are considerably less comic, with the exception of Sidney Trefusis when he is playing the clown.

Chapter 2. Thesis: A Monster of the Mind (*The Irrational Knot*)

1. As he was finishing *The Irrational Knot* or shortly thereafter, apparently, Shaw wrote the short story "The Miraculous Revenge," which expresses how deeply alienated from society he still felt, despite the attempt in the novel to transfer the alienation from himself to society. The short story reveals that the novel was a not entirely effective bit of one-

upmanship, as it exposes the uncertainty that still underlies the pose of certainty Shaw had given his novel's hero.

2. In revising this novel, mostly in 1892 but also in preparing it for his *Standard Edition*, Shaw emphasized his point about the falseness of social stratification by changing Lord Carbury from a man more conventionally aristocratic to "a true man in a false position." (See Rodenbeck, 41–42.) The Carbury character, besides undergoing a name change, was considerably more developed in revision. After *Immaturity*, this was the most extensively revised of Shaw's novels.

3. Rodenbeck (47) comments that Sholto Douglas is what much nineteenth-century fiction supposed to be a "perfect" gentleman, and thus a character of this type was often the hero. In conventional novels, not only would the perfect gentleman succeed in his romantic endeavors but also his opposite, the "imperfect" gentleman (Marmaduke Lind), would come to a bad end. Shaw thus achieves irony by contrasting the frank, harmless, kind-hearted, good-natured "wickedness" of Marmaduke in living illicitly with Susanna, on the one hand, and the sordid, abominable, empty-minded, and empty-hearted behavior of Douglas in his treatment of Marian on the other. Marmaduke's affair, says Rodenbeck, is presented on a higher moral plane.

4. Briefly, Shaw's "The Quintessence of Ibsenism" (*Major Critical Essays* 48–53) divides people (and individual minds—see my "Shavian Psychology") into three types, "realists," "idealists," and "Philistines," according to how evolved their minds are. Using marriage to define his hierarchy of types, Shaw designates as Philistines the lowest 70 percent, who "comfortably accept marriage as a matter of course, never dreaming of calling it an 'institution,' much less a holy and beautiful one, and being pretty plainly of the opinion that Idealism is a crackbrained fuss about nothing"; as idealists, a more evolved 29 percent who devise "a fancy picture" of marriage as a "beautiful and holy natural institution" out of fear that only by "self-denying conformity to the ideals" will corrupt human nature be held back from "ruinous excesses"; and as the highly evolved realists, the less than 1 percent who perceive and say that marriage "is a failure for many of us. It is insufferable that two human beings, having entered into relations which only warm affection can render tolerable, should be forced to maintain them after they have ceased to exist, or in spite of the fact that they have never arisen." Further, because the idealists, who are politically influential out of all proportion to their numbers, legislate the lives of others by insisting upon the reality of their ideals, they are inclined to either coerce, ostracize, or prosecute to the death anyone who challenges their right to do so. The idealist, therefore, although higher on the evolutionary scale than the Philistine, is the fiercest and most fanatical enemy of the realist and will usually try to hunt him down for the noblest of reasons. Thus the potential for being scapegoated in the career of the realist.

5. Following from Shaw's attack on "rationalism" in *The Quintessence of Ibsenism*, Rodenbeck (45–46) discerns that Conolly's post-Ibsen, visionary realism was imposed upon his original rationalism in Shaw's later revisions. That is, the Conolly of the original version is somewhat more rationalistic than the Conolly of the final version and somewhat less realistic. I would agree, but I also note that there are clear signs in his early novels that Shaw was already struggling toward an understanding of realism like that found in *The*

Quintessence. The *Our Corner* version of *The Irrational Knot*, for example, contains a passage that shows Shaw distinguishing between "good cynicism" (facing unpleasant truths) and "bad cynicism" (believing the worst of everybody) in a way that will eventually lead to dropping the "cynicism" altogether in his ultimate definition of "realism" as the visionary grasping of truth. See my articles "Shavian Psychology" and "Shaw and Yeats: Two Irishmen Divided by a Common Language" for attempts to unravel the semantic snarls involved in Shaw's and his contemporaries' use of the word "realism."

6. In his revision for the 1905 edition, Shaw also made Conolly somewhat more consciously proletarian. As Rodenbeck says (63), the 1905 version was "more clearcut in its conflicts, more powerful in its statements of contrast, and more scrupulous in its depiction of motive." But there is no change of theme or intent.

7. This quotation does not appear in the *Our Corner* version, but it succinctly states what is implied there.

8. This quotation does not appear in the *Our Corner* version, but its content is clearly implied there.

9. The first sentence of this quotation is in the *Our Corner* version, but the second sentence was added later. Obviously, however, the second follows logically from the first.

10. Ronald Reagan used to end every TV episode of "GE Theater" with this slogan! He was a better actor than we knew.

11. This quotation does not appear in the *Our Corner* version, but it is true to the content. Obviously Shaw's stint as a music critic after writing the novels is what made his pen jump to revise in these passages dealing with music. The chapter in which this quotation appears was considerably rewritten and added to, as Conolly explains himself more fully to Elinor McQuinch.

12. In *Immaturity* (120), Shaw begins an industrial motif that will recur in his other novels. He writes that Smith, walking along the Thames, listened "to that distant rattle and shriek of trains, which had sounded to his father as the death knell of sylvan sentiment, but which was to him as characteristic of the country as the song of a blackbird. To his eye, a landscape was barren without the familiar row of white poles supporting an endless stave of music on which the insulators were the only crotchets, and which, by placing the ear against the pole, might be heard humming thunderously. Even across the Thames, and surrounded by gas works and factories decorated with tubes like colossal bassoons, they were the visible link between the maze of brick and stucco on the Middlesex side and the broad commons of Surrey and the downs of the South Coast."

13. The quotation from p. 241 is in the *Our Corner* version, but the quotation from p. 238 is not. The one is simply a rephrasing of the other.

14. While I don't argue with my original wording here, I have since decided that Ibsen is more satirizing of Nora than I realized. See my article "Nora's Change of Dress." Shaw's commentary on *A Doll's House* strikes me now as the weakest and least perceptive segment of *The Quintessence of Ibsenism.*

15. This quotation does not appear in the *Our Corner* version, which has been substantially revised in this chapter to give Nelly McQuinch a chance to reply directly to Marian's Pollyanna approach, but it is a good paraphrase of the original.

16. This quotation does not appear in the *Our Corner* version, but it well fits.

17. Rodenbeck (49) writes that Marian's "refusal to go back to [Conolly] is . . . less an acceptance of the challenge of ultimate freedom than a submission to the rule of society; she has already . . . been declassed by her adultery."

18. The presocialist *Our Corner* version reads: "Now I aim at the greatest attainable justice, which involves the least endurable liberty."

19. In "Mr. Bernard Shaw's Works of Fiction. Reviewed by Himself," Shaw writes that "long before I got to the writing of the last chapter I could hardly stand [Conolly] myself" (239).

20. See my article "Shaw and the Uncrucifying of Christ."

21. This passage is not in the *Our Corner* version but sounds like the author of *Man and Superman* instead.

22. In "Mr. Bernard Shaw's Works of Fiction. Reviewed by Himself" (239), Shaw writes of his principal characters: "My model man, named Conolly, was a skilled work-man who became rich and famous by inventing an electro-motor. He married a woman whom I took no end of trouble to make as 'nice' as the very nicest woman can be according to conventional ideas. The point of the story was that though Conolly was a model of sound sense, intelligence, reasonableness, good temper, and everything that a thoroughly nice woman could desire and deserve, the most hopeless incompatibility developed itself between them."

Chapter 3. Antithesis: A Monster of the Body (*Love Among the Artists*)

1. As for his emphasis upon moral genius, Shaw's remark about the "moral passion" that occurred to him in his midteens is well known (*Sixteen Self Sketches* 28), but less famous is his assertion that his second novel was "one of those fictions in which the moral-ity is original and not ready-made. Now this quality is the true diagnostic of the first order in literature, and indeed in all the arts, including the art of life" (*The Irrational Knot* xvii).

2. For a further development of this idea, see my article "Shaw and the Passionate Mind" (2–11).

3. As Pearson puts it (57), Jack "was the first of a line of historical characters whose imputed share in Shaw's powers of entertainment makes them a good deal more pleasant than the originals could have been."

4. Bernard Shaw in 1880 met an aging Alsatian opera singer, named Richard Deck, who gave him much the same elocution lessons that Jack gives to Madge. Deck also en-couraged Shaw to bank up his hair for satanic effect (Rattray 39).

5. For a development of this idea, see O'Donnell's "The Conflict of Wills in Shaw's Tragicomedy."

6. For an account of the many scenes and characters that Shaw the playwright drew from the novels, see Weintraub's "The Embryo Playwright in Bernard Shaw's Early Novels."

7. Robert Louis Stevenson, in a letter to William Archer, expressed his Victorian alarm at the adrogyny of Shaw's females thus: "I say, Archer, my God, what women!" (Henderson 128).

Chapter 4. Synthesis (Theory): The Mind and Body of the Superman (*Cashel Byron's Profession*)

1. For a further elucidation of Shaw's attempt to arrive at a more accurate and up-to-date understanding of the brain, see my article "Shaw and Yeats: Two Irishmen Divided by a Common Language."

2. In the preface to *Cashel Byron's Profession* (xi), Shaw admits that he tried to win the favor of publishers by making his novel conform, at least superficially, to what they expected of a novel: "In novel-writing there are two trustworthy dodges for capturing the public. One is to slaughter a child and pathosticate over its deathbed for a whole chapter. The other is to describe either a fight or a murder. There . . . lay the whole schoolboy secret of the book's little vogue. I had the old grievance of the author: people will admire him for the feats that any fool can achieve, and bear malice against him for boring them with better work." But of course, as Meisel explains, Shaw's use of such conventions was subversive as well, part of a tactic of permeation in which Shaw entered a convention only to convert it to the uses of the "realistic" imagination.

3. "There is no autobiographical element in the story," says Woodbridge (15).

4. Besides being an avid boxing fan, Shaw "was for many years a very passable boxer" (Irvine 29). See Green's *Shaw's Champions* and Weintraub's "G.B.S., Pugilist and Playwright."

5. Irvine (30). On the subject of Lydia Carew, see Shaw's remarks in "Mr. Bernard Shaw's Works of Fiction. Reviewed by Himself" (238): "Lydia is superhuman all through. On the high authority of William Morris (privately imparted) she is a 'prig-ess'. Other critics, of a more rationalistic turn, revere her as one of the noblest creatures of modern fiction. I have no doubt that the latter view is defensible; but I must admit that, for a man of Morris's turn, her intellectual perfections are rather too obviously machine-made. If Babbage's calculator is ever finished, I believe it will be found quite possible, by putting an extra wheel or two in, to extend its uses to the manufacture of heroines of the Lydia Carew type. Doubtless the superior mechanical accuracy of Lydia's ratiocinative action is calculated to strike awe into the average superstitious bungler, just as the unfinished machine of Babbage strikes awe into me. . . . *Of course I, too, fall far short of Lydia Carew in the reasonableness of my private conduct.* Let me not deny . . . that a post-mortem examination by a capable critical anatomist . . . will reveal the fact that her inside is full of wheels and springs. At the same time it must be distinctly understood that this is no disparagement to her. There is nothing one gets so tired of in fiction as what is called 'flesh and blood'" (italics added).

6. This passage (29) was significantly improved with the insertion of the three sentences after "I had rather be a bear than a man." The older Shaw saw more clearly how close he himself had come to "moral suicide," and this revision, which emphasizes Shaw's concern *to be himself*, strengthens the view that his creation of "G.B.S." was the projection of a personality that was authentic to his being and not merely some bogus disguise. Much of the revision of this novel was done for the 1889 and 1901 editions.

7. Ned Skene is apparently based upon Ned Donelly, one of the men who taught Shaw

to box. This story is told in most of the biographies (for example, Holroyd 103ff.), but see especially Sally Peters, "The Noble Art: Shaw and Boxing."

8. This sentence (217), added to the *To-Day* version, was implied by the original context.

9. This sentence (228) vastly improves upon the *To-Day* version, which lacks epigrammatic punch.

10. This sentence (229), an addition to the *To-Day* version, sums up what Byron has been thinking throughout this trial.

11. It is sometimes difficult to tell whether Shaw's characterizations are contradictory for the purpose of expressing irony or whether the contradictions arise from Shaw's natural, instinctive artistry's getting the better of his conscious theorizing. To put it another way, because Shaw always put more of himself into his characters than the plan perhaps called for, his characters turn out to be human beings as well as symbols. Just as Conolly is more than rationalist, Owen Jack more than willful genius, so Cashel Byron is not merely the unthinking Greek body he was probably intended to be. He turns out to be a rather thoughtful young man, just as Lydia is far more physically active than the stereotypical intellectual she was probably meant to represent. In all this Shaw is headed toward the richer character complex of his plays, which employ the character types from *The Quintessence of Ibsenism* as psychological principles engaged in inner conflict as well.

12. About this bloody affair, described in vivid detail, Shaw once wrote, "Out of the savagery of my imagination I wrote the scene; and out of the savagery of your tastes you delight in it" ("Mr. Bernard Shaw's Works of Fiction. Reviewed by Himself" 236).

13. In his "The Conflict of Wills in Shaw's Tragicomedy," O'Donnell writes, "Ultimately, the worst thing which can happen to an individual in the strife at the psychological center of Shavian drama . . . is to be 'intimidated' or 'discouraged' by another human will. It is in this way that one experiences the humiliation of becoming merely an object in another's world, merely a means to another's personal ends. . . . This discouragement obviously involves an overpowering fear, a sense of total inability to grasp the purposes of the other, and a disintegration of the will. In a world in which humanity consists of an ability to participate as an equal in psychological strife, it is the basic evil."

14. In a letter to me Dan H. Laurence pointed out that Alice Goff, like Gertrude Lindsay of the next novel, was based on Shaw's exasperating girl friend Alice Lockett. See chap. 5, n. 7, following.

15. This sentence (171) is part of an insertion that considerably revised the *To-Day* version, making Alice more aware than she was originally.

Chapter 5. Synthesis (Practice): Mr. Shaw's Profession (*An Unsocial Socialist*)

1. Consider Robert Smith's statement: "I would not give a half-penny for the faith of a votary who would not cut off the whole human race if it differed from him" (*Immaturity* 269). This is an eruption of the familiar Shavian overstatement, no doubt, but a tad disquieting nonetheless. Perhaps it's meant as nothing more than an amusing bit of characterizing bravado.

2. Irvine (31). Of relevance here is the commentary of Bissell in "The Novels of Ber-

nard Shaw" (50–51): "His novels are about the wealthy and the aristocratic; they show an almost morbid consciousness of economic distinctions; and yet he has no consistent point of view toward the society he depicts. He seems to waver between an inclination to idealize a class to which, he is convinced, he rightfully belongs, and a feeling of resentment that wealth and social prestige should so often be accompanied by a cultural development immeasurably inferior to his own. . . . What Shaw needed, then, both to clarify his own personal problems and to give strength and direction to the works of his imagination was a plausible and consistent critical attitude toward the economic structure of society. . . . Much of the value of socialism consists for him in the solution it offers for his personal problems. Now that he has a coherent theory, he finds that he can adjust himself with ease to the present economic structure of society while, at the same time, he looks forward to the ultimate communist Utopia of absolute equality. . . . Shaw's romantic imagination and his power of comic invention, far from being stifled by his immersion in the dismal science, have been gloriously released. . . . Shaw found in Das Kapital . . . a new and exhilarating explanation of the mystery of experience, and a wealth of fascinating ideas that provided both the inspiration and the materials for literary expression. In the vision of a communist Utopia, Shaw found an ideal that would satisfy his romantic yearnings. In the socialist demonstration of the glaring incongruities underlying the economic structure of society, he found just the material he needed for the exercise of his comic genius. Henceforth he could be a social critic and a moralist without fear of falling into dullness and didacticism; for he now saw that the final truth of a matter reveals itself only to the artist-philosopher who combines a passionate imagination with an exquisite levity of mind."

3. Shaw's original title was *The Heartless Man*. Trefusis explains why in his letter to Shaw (254–55): "In noveldom woman still sets the moral standard, and to her the males, who are in full revolt against the acceptance of the infatuation of a pair of lovers as the highest manifestation of the social instinct, and against the restriction of the affections within the narrow circle of blood relationship, and of the political sympathies within frontiers, are to her what she calls heartless brutes. . . . That, indeed, is exactly what I am, judged by the fictitious and feminine standard of morality. Hence some critics have been able plausibly to pretend to take the book as a satire on Socialism."

4. Of this fictional ruling-class recruit in general, Ryan writes: "All . . . are at some level variants of the wise fool or the holy fool, inspired eccentrics and prophetic misfits living as internal exiles in their own society, and thus ideally situated to be used by the author to subvert the ruling-class world from within by insistently exposing what it takes to be normal and desirable as outrageous and intolerable" ("Citizens of Centuries to Come" 8).

5. The character of Chichester Erskine appears to be based upon that of Pakenham Beatty, Shaw's boxing partner (see *Collected Letters* 1:137–38). See Holroyd (103) for the latest biographical rendering of this relationship.

6. In his introduction to *An Unfinished Novel* (12), Weintraub describes Trefusis as a combination of Sidney Webb, Bernard Shaw, and Annie Oakley. Sypher ("Fabian Anti-Novel") reads Trefusis's use of art objects for target practice as illustrative of a deconstructive agenda. In *The Quintessence of Ibsenism* Shaw spoke of the New Drama as involving "a terrible art of sharp-shooting at the audience."

7. The character of Gertrude Lindsay seems directly based on that of Alice Lockett, a young nurse-in-training Shaw had romanced but found exasperating. He wrote chiding letters to her (*Collected Letters* 1:65–67) that distinguished between her two selves—the natural Alice who desired to be a New Woman and the conventional Miss Lockett stuck in mid-Victorian habits—which parallel the distinction he makes in the novel between the natural Gertrude and the conventional Miss Lindsay. See Dan H. Laurence's *The Wicked Failure and the Ill-Used Saint* and my account of that in "Shaw as Dramatic Icon: A Bibliography of Impersonations" (138–39).

8. Unless the "your" is impersonal, there is one brief reference in this novel (221) to the fact that Sidney Trefusis too has written some novels. Agatha says to Trefusis: "This is one of your clever novels. I wish the characters would not talk so much."

9. In *Days with Bernard Shaw* (262), Winsten reports Shaw as saying, "It is better to die a gentleman than a martyr." See my article "Shaw and the Uncrucifying of Christ" for an elucidation.

10. In *Sixteen Self Sketches* (124), Shaw wrote about himself in the third person: "Shaw is an incorrigible and continuous actor, using his skill as deliberately in his social life as in his professional work in the production of his own plays. He does not deny this. 'G.B.S.' he says 'is not a real person: he is a legend created by myself: a pose, a reputation. The real Shaw is not a bit like him.' Now this is exactly what all his acquaintances say of the Rodin bust, that it is not a bit like him. But Shaw maintains that it is the only portrait that tells the truth about him." Shaw must have enjoyed writing this passage, as it allowed him to play three or four contradicting roles at once, but the reader is left with the inference that the supposedly fraudulent G.B.S. "is the only portrait that tells the truth about him."

11. See my article "Shaw and Yeats: Two Irishmen Divided by a Common Language."

Conclusion. The Romance of the Real, Or, The Adventures of the Irishman in His Search for God

1. That Shaw's drama *is* ritualistic is not widely acknowledged. In "Shaw and the Uncrucifying of Christ," I propose that Shaw's plays were as much dramatizing of "the ritual of a lost faith" as were those of Yeats, who was much more explicit about it.

2. In the preface to *Immaturity* (xliv), Shaw writes: "When I had to come out of the realm of imagination into that of actuality I was still uncomfortable. I was outside society, outside politics, outside sport, outside the Church. If the term had been invented then I should have been called The Complete Outsider. But the epithet would have been appropriate only within the limits of British barbarism. The moment music, painting, literature, or science came into question the positions were reversed: it was I who was the Insider. I had the intellectual habit."

Bibliography

In updating this bibliography, I am particularly indebted to Stanley Weintraub's *Bernard Shaw: A Guide to Research* (Pennsylvania State University Press, 1992), Dan H. Laurence's two-volume *Bernard Shaw: A Bibliography* (Clarendon Press, 1983), John R. Pfeiffer's "Continuing Checklist of Shaviana" in the *Shaw* annual (Pennsylvania State University Press, 1980–94), Charles A. Carpenter's annual bibliographies in the *Shaw Review* and *Modern Drama*, Maurice Holmes's *Some Bibliographical Notes on the Novels of George Bernard Shaw* (London: Dulau & Co. Ltd., 1928), and Wearing, Adams, and Haberman's three-volume, annotated secondary bibliography, *G. B. Shaw* (Northern Illinois University Press, 1986). The last contains another seventy items or so on the novels that I did not list here because they are redundant, inconsequential, or irrelevant to this study.

Works by Shaw

An Unfinished Novel, edited by Stanley Weintraub. New York: Dodd, Mead, 1958.

An Unsocial Socialist, Introductions by R. F. Dietrich and Barbara Bellow Watson. New York: W. W. Norton & Co., 1972.

An Unsocial Socialist, edited by Michael Holroyd, with Introduction. New York: Penguin Books–Virago Press, 1991.

An Unsocial Socialist, edited by Dan H. Laurence. In *Selected Non-Dramatic Writings of Bernard Shaw.* Boston: Houghton Mifflin Co., 1965.

An Unsocial Socialist. See *Standard Edition.*

"The Author to the Reader." *Our Corner* (November 1887). Also appears as Preface to 1900 and 1914 editions of *Love Among the Artists.*

Cashel Byron's Profession, edited by Harry T. Moore, with Preface; Introduction by Stanley Weintraub. Carbondale: Southern Illinois University Press, 1968.

Cashel Byron's Profession. See *Standard Edition.*

Collected Letters, 1874–1897, edited by Dan H. Laurence. New York: Dodd, Mead, 1965.

Common Sense About the War. London: Statesman Publishing Co., 1915.

Complete Plays with Prefaces 6 vols. New York: Dodd, Mead, 1963.

Ellen Terry and Bernard Shaw: A Correspondence, edited by Christopher St. John. New York: Theater Arts Books, 1932.

Fabian Essays in Socialism, edited by Bernard Shaw. New York: Doubleday & Co., Inc., 1963.

Florence Farr, Bernard Shaw, W. B. Yeats, Letters, edited by Clifford Bax. London: Home & Van Thal Ltd., 1946.

Immaturity. See *Standard Edition.*

The Irrational Knot. See *Standard Edition.*

Love Among the Artists. New York: Viking Press, 1962.

Love Among the Artists. See *Standard Edition.*

The Matter with Ireland, edited by Dan H. Laurence and David H. Greene. New York: Hill and Wang, 1962.

"The Miraculous Revenge." In *Bernard Shaw: Tales.* New York: Capricorn Books, 1932, 1959.

"Mr. Bernard Shaw's Works of Fiction. Reviewed by Himself." *Novel Review* 33 (February 1892), 236–43. Appears in *Selected Non-Dramatic Writings of Bernard Shaw,* edited by Dan H. Laurence, 309–14. Boston: Houghton Mifflin, 1965.

My Dear Dorothea, edited by Stephen Winsten. New York: Vanguard Press, 1963.

Our Theatres in the Nineties, vol. 1. London: Constable, 1932.

"Passion Play." In *The Bodley Head Bernard Shaw: Collected Plays with Their Prefaces,* vol. 7. London: The Bodley Head, 1974.

Platform and Pulpit, edited by Dan H. Laurence. New York: Hill and Wang, 1961.

"The Quintessence of Ibsenism." In *Major Critical Essays.* See *Standard Edition.*

Sixteen Self Sketches. See *Standard Edition,* 1949.

Standard Edition of the Works of Bernard Shaw. London: Constable & Co, Ltd., 1931–32.

"The St. James's Hall Mystery," edited by Jerald E. Bringle. *Bulletin of Research in the Humanities* (Autumn 1978), 270–96.

Secondary Sources

Abbott, Anthony S. *Shaw and Christianity.* New York: Seabury Press, 1965.

Adams, Elsie. "The Portrait of the Artist in Bernard Shaw's Novels." *English Literature in Transition* 10 (1967), 130–49.

Barzun, Jacques. *The Energies of Art.* New York: Vintage Books, 1962.

Bentley, Eric. *Bernard Shaw, 1856–1950.* Rev. ed. New York: New Directions Paperback, 1957.

Berst, Charles A. "*The Irrational Knot:* The Art of Shaw as a Young Ibsenite." *Journal of English and Germanic Philology* 85, no. 2 (April 1986), 222–48.

———. "Shaw and Religion." *Shaw: The Annual of Bernard Shaw Studies* 1 (1981).

Bissell, Claude T. "The Novels of Bernard Shaw." *University of Toronto Quarterly* 17 (1947–48), 50–51.

Black, Martha Fodaski. *Shaw and Joyce: "The Last Word in Stolentelling."* Gainesville: University Press of Florida, 1995.

Borges, Jorge Luis. *Other Inquisitions, 1937–1952.* New York: Washington Square Press, 1960.

Chappelow, Allan, ed. *Shaw the Villager and Human Being.* New York: Macmillan Co., 1962.

Cherry, D. R. "Shaw's Novels." *Dalhousie Review* 42 (Winter 1962–63), 459–71.

Chesterton, G. K. *George Bernard Shaw.* New York: Hill & Wang, 1958.

Collis, John S. *Shaw.* New York: Alfred A. Knopf, Inc., 1924.

Crawford, Fred D. "Shaw's Collaboration in *The Salt of the Earth.*" *Shaw: The Annual of Bernard Shaw Studies* 9 (1989), 39–44.

Decker, David. "The Temptation of Saint George: A Critical Study of the 1880's Novels of Bernard Shaw." Ph.D. dissertation, University of Washington, 1988. DAI 50 (September 1989), 689-A.

Dietrich, Richard F. *British Drama, 1890–1950: A Critical History.* Boston: Twayne Publishers, 1989.

———. "Deconstruction as Devil's Advocacy: A Shavian Alternative." *Modern Drama* (September 1986), 431–51. Also found in Elsie B. Adams, *Critical Essays on George Bernard Shaw,* 177–96. New York: G.K. Hall & Co., 1991.

———. "Nora's Change of Dress." *Theatre Annual* (December 1981), 20–39.

———. "Shavian Psychology." *Shaw: The Annual of Bernard Shaw Studies* 4 (1984), 149–71.

———. "Shaw and the Passionate Mind." *Shaw Review* (May 1961), 2–11.

———. "Shaw and the Uncrucifying of Christ." *Shaw: The Annual of Bernard Shaw Studies* 8 (1988), 13–38.

———. "Shaw and Yeats: Two Irishmen Divided by a Common Language." *Shaw: The Annual of Bernard Shaw Studies* 15 (1995), 65–83.

Glicksberg, Charles I. "Shaw the Novelist." *Prairie Schooner* 25 (1951), 1–9.

Goode, John. "Margaret Harkness and the Socialist Novel." In *The Socialist Novel in Britain: Towards the Recovery of a Tradition,* edited by H. Gustav Klaus. New York: St. Martin's Press, 1982.

Goodman, Phyllis M. "Beethoven as the Prototype of Owen Jack." *Shaw Review* 7 (January 1965), 12–24.

Gordon, John D. "Novels in Manuscript: An Exhibition from the Berg Collection." *Bulletin of the New York Public Library* 69 (May–June 1965), 317, 396.

Green, Benny. *Shaw's Champions: G.B.S. & Prizefighting from Cashel Byron to Gene Tunney.* London: Elm Tree Books, 1978.

Grene, Nicholas. "The Maturing of *Immaturity:* Shaw's First Novel." *Irish University Review* (Autumn 1990), 225–38.

Henderson, Archibald. "Bernard Shaw's Novels: And Why They Failed." *Dalhousie Review* 34 (Winter 1955) 373–82; rpt., *Shaw Bulletin* 1 (May 1955), 11–18.

———. *George Bernard Shaw: Man of the Century.* New York: Appleton-Century-Crofts, Inc., 1956.

———. "Where Shaw Stands Today." *Bulletin of the Shaw Society of America* 1 (Autumn 1951), 1–6.

Hogan, Robert. "The Novels of Bernard Shaw." *English Literature in Transition, 1880–1920* 8 (1965), 63–114.

Holland, Michael J. "Shaw's Short Fiction: A Path to Drama." *Shaw: The Annual of Bernard Shaw Studies* 9 (1989), 113–30.

Holroyd, Michael. *Bernard Shaw: The Search for Love, 1856–1898.* New York: Random House, 1988.

———. *The Genius of Shaw: A Symposium.* New York: Holt, Rinehart and Winston, 1979.

Huneker, James. "Bernard Shaw and Women." *Harper's Bazaar* 39 (June 1905), 535–38.

Irvine, William. *The Universe of G.B.S.* New York: McGraw-Hill, 1949. Appeared first as "Bernard Shaw's Early Novels." *Trollopian* 2 (June 1947), 27–42.

Karl, Frederick R. *The Contemporary English Novel.* New York: Farrar, Straus, and Cudahy, 1962.

Laurence, Dan H. *G.B.S. in Love.* Originally called *The Wicked Failure and the Ill-Used Saint.* For a summary see R. F. Dietrich's "Shaw as Dramatic Icon: A Bibliography of Impersonations." *Shaw: The Annual of Bernard Shaw Studies* 12 (1992), 138–39.

Lowenstein, F. E. *The History of a Famous Novel.* London: privately printed, 1946.

MacLochlainn, Alf. "Shaw's Mice." *New Edinburgh Review* (March 1975), 10–11.

Meisel, Martin. *Shaw and the Nineteenth Century Theater.* Princeton, N.J.: Princeton University Press, 1963.

Morgan, Charles. *The House of Macmillan, 1843–1943.* London: Macmillan, 1943.

Nethercot, Arthur H. *Men and Supermen: The Shavian Portrait Gallery.* Cambridge: Harvard University Press, 1954.

Norris, Christopher. *Deconstruction: Theory and Practice.* London: Methuen, 1982.

O'Donnell, Norbert F. "The Conflict of Wills in Shaw's Tragicomedy." *Modern Drama* 4 (February 1962), 413–25.

Ohmann, Richard M. *Shaw: The Style and the Man.* Middletown, Conn.: Wesleyan University Press, 1962.

Pearson, Hesketh. *George Bernard Shaw: His Life and Personality.* New York: Atheneum, 1963.

Peters, Sally. "The Noble Art: Shaw and Boxing." *Rackham Journal of the Arts and Humanities* (1991–92), 2–4.

Rao, E. Nageswara. *Shaw the Novelist: A Critical Study of Shaw's Narrative Fiction.* Masulipatam, India: Triveni Publishers, 1959.

Rattray, R. F. *Bernard Shaw: A Chronicle.* New York: Roy Publishers, 1951.

Rider, Dan. *Adventures with Bernard Shaw.* London: Morley & Mitchell, 1929.

Robertson, John Mackinnon. "Cashel Byron's Profession." *Our Corner* 7 (May 1, 1886), 301–5. London: Freethought Publishing Co.

Rodenbeck, John von Behren. "Alliance and Misalliance: A Critical Study of Bernard Shaw's Novels." Ph.D dissertation, University of Virginia, 1964.

———. "Bernard Shaw's Revolt Against Rationalism." *Victorian Studies* 15 (June 1972), 409–37.

———. "*The Irrational Knot,* Shaw and the Uses of Ibsen." *Shaw Review* 12 (May 1969), 66–76.

Rosset, B. C. *Shaw of Dublin: The Formative Years.* University Park: Pennsylvania State University Press, 1964.

Ryan, Kiernan. "Citizens of Centuries to Come: The Ruling-Class Rebel in Socialist Fiction." In *The Rise of Socialist Fiction 1880–1914,* edited by H. Gustav Klaus. New York: St. Martin's Press, 1987.

Saroyan, William. *Here Comes—There Goes—You Know Who.* New York: Pocket Books, Inc., 1963.

Seabrook, Alexander. "Social Criticism in the Novels of Bernard Shaw." Ph.D. dissertation, 1951.

Sen Gupta, S. C. *The Art of Bernard Shaw.* London: Oxford University Press, 1936.

Smith, Warren S. "The Bishop, the Dancer, and Bernard Shaw." *Shaw Review* 3 (January 1969), 2–10.

Stanbrook, the Benedictines of. *In a Great Tradition.* London: Murray, 1956.

Stevenson, R. L. *Letters of Robert Louis Stevenson.* Edited by Sidney Colvin. Rev. ed. Vol. 3. New York: Charles Scribner's Sons, 1896.

Sypher, Eileen. "Fabian Anti-Novel: Shaw's *An Unsocial Socialist.*" *Literature and History* (Autumn 1985), 241–53.

Tahir, Laura. "The Development of a Point of View in Young George Bernard Shaw." Ph.D dissertation, Rutgers University, 1989. DAI 50 (May 1990), 5350-B.

Vincent, Judith. "George Bernard Shaw, Novelist: The Right Man in the Wrong Place?" Ph.D dissertation, University of East Anglia, Norwich, England, 1981.

Weintraub, Stanley. "Bernard Shaw, Charles Lever, and *Immaturity.*" *Shaw Bulletin* 2 (January 1957), 11–15.

———. "Bernard Shaw: Novelist." Ph.D dissertation, Pennsylvania State University, 1956.

———. "The Embryo Playwright in Bernard Shaw's Early Novels." *University of Texas Studies in Literature and Language* 1 (1959), 327–55.

———. "G.B.S., Pugilist and Playwright." In *The Unexpected Shaw,* 37–45. New York: Frederick Ungar Pub. Co., 1982.

———. "Ibsen's *Doll's House* Metaphor Foreshadowed in Victorian Fiction." *Nineteenth Century Fiction* 13 (June 1958), 67–69.

———. "The Novelist in Spite of Himself." In *The Unexpected Shaw,* 24–36. New York: Frederick Ungar Pub. Co., 1982. A slightly revised version of the author's introduction to *An Unfinished Novel.*

———. "A Respectful Distance: James Joyce and His Dublin Townsman Bernard Shaw." *Journal of Modern Literature* 13, no. 1 (March 1986), 61–75.

West, Alick. *George Bernard Shaw: "A Good Man Fallen Among Fabians."* New York: International Publishers, 1950.

"What They Said About Shaw: Some of the Early Reviews of His Books and Plays." *Saturday Review of Literature* 27 (July 22, 1944), 16–17.

Winsten, Stephen. *Days with Bernard Shaw.* New York: Vanguard Press, Inc., 1949.

Woodbridge, Homer. *George Bernard Shaw: Creative Artist.* Carbondale: Southern Illinois University Press, 1963.

Index